TEXAS GOLF

TEXAS GOLF

The Comprehensive Guide to Golf Courses,
Clubs, & Resorts in the Lone Star State

Frank B. Hermes

TAYLOR PUBLISHING COMPANY
Dallas, Texas

Cover photograph was taken at Bear Creek
Golf Club, Dallas, Texas.

Cover Photo: Ken Wagman

Book Design: Bonnie Baumann

Library of Congress Cataloging in Publication Data

Hermes, Frank B.
  Texas golf.

  1. Golf courses—Texas—Directories.   2. Country
clubs—Texas—Directories.   I. Title.
GV962.H47   1987   796.352'06'8764   87–1894
ISBN 0-87833-562-5

Printed in the United States of America

0 9 8 7 6 5 4 3 2 1

In memory of my father,
John Hermes

and dedicated to
my mother, Hazel,
wife, Barbara,
and children, Keli and Marc

ACKNOWLEDGMENTS

A special thanks to Debbie Bauer, my research assistant, and to each of the persons consulted during our information gathering. Each page of this book reflects someone's time and help. The friendliness of the people at the state's golf courses reinforces my opinion about the hospitality and warmth of Texans in general. Play a few rounds at their courses and discover this for yourself.

Contents

Foreword

Golf courses in Texas offer something for every player, whether you are a top-flight professional or just a beginner. Whether you travel east, west, north, or south, you'll never tire of the changing landscape and golf course characteristics of the various private country clubs, resorts, and public courses.

There are over 680 courses, open to either public or private play. Texas boasts three of *Golf Digest's* top 75 public golf courses—Bear Creek East (Dallas-Fort Worth), Bear Creek Masters (Houston) and Grapevine Municipal. In addition, Champions Golf Club in Houston ranks in the top 100 private courses, according to *Golf Digest,* and Horseshoe Bay has been called one of the top 6 inland golf resorts by Dick Wilson in his book *America's Greatest Golfing Resorts.*

Prospects are good for the continued growth of the game in Texas. Over 20 new courses are scheduled to open in 1987 and at least that many are under construction or on the drawing board for the not too distant future. Many existing courses are planning or carrying out expansion and renovation.

The purpose of this guide is to demonstrate the variety of golf opportunities in Texas: where the courses are and how to play them. All is with the intention of encouraging in-state and out-of-state golfers to take advantage of the many opportunities of play in Texas.

How to Use the Texas Golf Directory

CONCEPT

The Directory is a quick and easy guide to golf courses in Texas, where they are located and what it takes for the traveling golfer to play them.

For the purposes of organizing the Directory, the state has been divided into six regions (see accompanying map, page 3) as described by Tom Pollard in an article written for the Comptroller of Public Accounts printed in the March 1983 issue of *Fiscal Notes*. Texas' great size, according to the article, lends itself to being divided into economic regions. Pollard suggests this division because the natural and cultural characteristics, influenced by the presence or absence of natural resources, determines each particular region's development.

We suggest the following three easy steps for use of the Directory:

STEP 1:

If you are going to a specific city or town: Simply refer to the Cities Index on page 173. Once you've located the city, all clubs within that city will be listed beneath.

STEP 2:

If you are going to a specific region (see map, page 3): Counties are listed alphabetically under each region with golf courses listed alphabetically, under the headings "public" or "private" golf courses, under each county. Specific cities within each region are listed directly following the regional map.

STEP 3:

If you are going to a large major area within one of the six regions: Special locator maps give you a perspective for the location of the golf courses within that area. For example, if you are in northwest Houston, you can check for the golf courses in that area and, then, look for the detailed description of its location, the course, and requirements for play.

We have attempted to provide you with all course information, including location from the center of town, par, length and rating from the championship tees, course designer/architect for those who may seek out and enjoy playing courses of a particular designer and days of the week open.

For public and resort courses, we have listed cost of play—green fees and carts—and whether credit cards are accepted. We have also listed requirements for tee times.

For private and military clubs, we have listed each's guest policy from the most restrictive—"you must *play* with a member" to the least restrictive—"will reciprocate with members of other private country clubs provided your pro phones in advance or you bring your membership credentials."

Because personnel and fee information are ever changing, it is advisable to phone ahead to check availability before attempting to play a particular course.

Six Areas for Regional Consideration

Source: Comptroller
of Public Accounts

The Gulf Coast

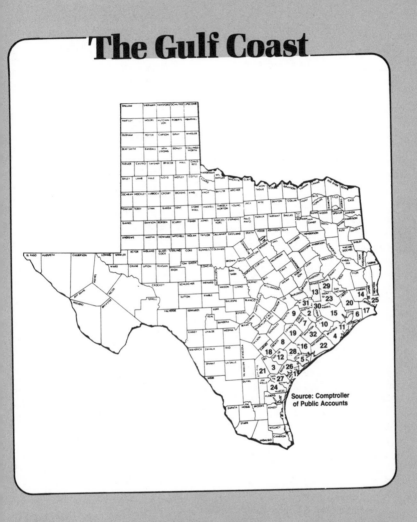

Source: Comptroller
of Public Accounts

The biggest concentration of golf courses—145—falls into the region with the most people.

There are forty public courses, 18 semi-private, 82 private and five resorts within the Gulf Coast area.

In addition, three new courses will open in 1987.

GULF COAST CITIES

Approach shot to the difficult #17 at the TPC in the Woodlands

═══════ ARANSAS ═══════ 1

Rockport

LIVE OAK COUNTRY CLUB
A private club with one 9-hole course
Location: 7 miles W. of Post Office on
HWY 881
Golf Data: Pro Shop Phone: (512)
729-8551; Club Manager: Mike Wells;
Par: 72; (two sets of tees); Yardage: 6061;
Rating: 68.4; Closed Monday.
Guest Policy: You must be a guest of a
member or a member of another private
country club.

ROCKPORT COUNTRY CLUB
A private club with one 18-hole course
Location: Off HWY 35 at 101 Champions Drive
Golf Data: Pro Shop Phone: (512)
729-4182; Club Pro: Jack Blundell; Par:
71; Yardage: 6455; Rating: 71.6; Course
Architect: Bill Cooke; Closed Monday.
Guest Policy: You must be a current
member of a U.S.G.A.-sponsored club or
guest of a member.

*NOTE: Golf Packages available through
the country club. Call 800-242-3159 (in
Texas), or outside Texas: (512) 729-5940.*

═══════ AUSTIN ═══════ 2

Bellville

BELLVILLE GOLF & RECREATION CLUB
**A semi-private club with one 9-hole
course**
Location: 2 miles N. on HWY 36
Golf Data: Pro Shop Phone: (409)
865-9058; Course Manager: John
Mumme; Par: 72 (two sets of tees); Yard-
age: 6057; Rating: 69.1; Open 7 days.
Green Fees: $5 weekdays, $10 weekends
and holidays; Carts: $5 per 9 holes.
Tee Time Procedure: 1st come, 1st
served.

San Felipe

STEPHEN F. AUSTIN GOLF CLUB
**A semi-private club with one 18-hole
course**

Location: Off I-10, adjacent to Stephen F. Austin State Park, on Park Road

Golf Data: Pro Shop Phone: (409) 885-2811; Club Pro: Billy Browne; Par: 70; Yardage: 5918; Rating: 68.4; Open 7 days.

Green Fees: $7 weekdays, $14 weekends and holidays; Carts: $14 for 18 holes.

Tee Time Procedure: Weekends: Friday in person or by phone; Weekdays: 1st come, 1st served.

——————— BEE ——————— 3

Beeville

JOHN C. BEASLEY MUNICIPAL GOLF COURSE

A public club with one 9-hole course

Location: Take 59N to Loop 351, right ½ mile

Golf Data: Pro Shop Phone: (512) 358-4295; Club Pro: Oliver Gonzales; Par: 36; Yardage: 3292; Rating: 71.2 (if 18 holes played); Closed Tuesday.

Green Fees: $4 weekdays, $5 weekends and holidays; Carts: $7 for 9, $12 for 18 holes.

Tee Time Procedure: Call in advance (though not necessary).

BEE LAKE GOLF LINKS

A private club with one 9-hole course

Location: At ANS Chase Field

Golf Data: Pro Shop Phone: (512) 354-5100; Club Pro: D. I. Ingram; Par: 29; Yardage: 3000; Open 7 days.

Guest Policy: Member of military must accompany guest, however, there is open play for tournaments. Call for specifics.

BEEVILLE COUNTRY CLUB

A private club with one 9-hole course

Location: 3 miles N. on Bus. HWY 181

Golf Data: Pro Shop Phone: (512) 358-1216; Club Pro: Steve Patton; Par: 36; Yardage: 3139; Rating: 69.5 (when 18 holes played); Closed Monday.

Guest Policy: You must be a member of another private country club or a guest of a member.

——————— BRAZORIA ——————— 4

Alvin

ALVIN GOLF & COUNTRY CLUB

A semi-private club with one 9-hole course

Location: On County Road 539, ½ mile off HWY 6

Golf Data: Pro Shop Phone: (713) 331-4541; Club Pro: Rex Casey; Par: 70 (two sets of tees); Yardage: 6100; Closed until noon Monday.

Green Fees: $7 weekdays, $9 weekends and holidays; Carts: $10 weekdays, $12 weekends and holidays.

Tee Time Procedure: 1st come, 1st served.

HILLCREST GOLF COURSE

A public club with one 9-hole course

Location: HWY 35 By-Pass, turn right on Fairway Drive, ½ mile

Golf Data: Pro Shop Phone: (713) 331-3505; Club Pro: Charles Wilson; Par: 33; Yardage: 2540; Open 7 days.

Green Fees: $5 weekdays, $7.35 weekends and holidays; Carts: $5 per 9 holes.

Tee Time Procedure: 1st come, 1st served.

Freeport

FREEPORT COMMUNITY GOLF COURSE

A public club with one 18-hole course

Location: Take HWY 288, left at HWY 36, right at Old HWY 36 to Slaughter Road

Golf Data: Pro Shop Phone: (409) 233-8311; Club Manager: Nick Nichols; Par: 71; Yardage: 6693; Rating: 71.7; Course Architects: Sanders Brothers Corp.; Open 7 days.

Green Fees: Resident: $5.30 weekdays, $7.90 weekends and holidays; Carts: $12 for 18 holes; Non-Resident: $7 weekdays, $9 weekends and holidays; Carts: $15 for 18 holes.

Tee Time Procedure: 1st come, 1st served.

Lake Jackson

RIVERSIDE COUNTRY CLUB

A private club with one 18-hole course

Location: 5 miles W. on HWY 332

Golf Data: Pro Shop Phone: (409) 798-9141; Club Pro: Larry Monte; Par: 72; Yardage: 6699; Rating: 71.3; Closed Monday.

Guest Policy: You must be a guest of a member or a member of another private country club.

Old Ocean

OLD OCEAN RECREATION ASSOCIATION
A private club with one 9-hole course

Location: 1 mile S. on HWY 35, turn left at Phillips Petroleum Plant

Golf Data: Pro Shop Phone: (409) 647-9902; Club Pro: Bob Earles; Par: 72 (two sets of tees); Yardage: 6190; Rating: 69.0; Closed Monday.

Guest Policy: You must be a guest of a member.

Pearland

COUNTRY PLACE AT US HOMES
A private club with one 18-hole course

Location: 7 miles S. of HWY 288, on Loop 610 (see #45 on Harris County locator map)

Golf Data: Pro Shop Phone: (713) 436-1533; Director of Golf: Steve Cox; Par: 71; Yardage: 6166; Rating: 69.7; Closed Monday.

Guest Policy: You must play with a member or be a member of another private country club.

GOLFCREST COUNTRY CLUB
A private club with one 18-hole course

Location: On Country Club Drive, off HWY 518 (see #46 on Harris County locator map)

Golf Data: Pro Shop Phone: (713) 485-4323; Club Pro: Gary Hardin; Par: 72; Yardage: 7037; Rating: 73.3; Course Architect: Joe Finger; Closed Monday.

Guest Policy: You must be a guest of a member (on weekends, you must play with member) or be a member of another private country club. Phone for specifics.

Rosharon

BRAZORIA BEND GOLF COURSE
A semi-private club with one 9-hole course

Location: HWY 288 to County Line Road, W. 1½ miles

Golf Data: Pro Shop: (713) 431-2954; Club Pro: Larry Bushee; Par: 36; Yardage: 3104; Course Architect: Frank Cope; Open 7 days.

Green Fees: $6 weekdays, $8 weekends and holidays; Carts: $12.48 for 18 holes.

Tee Time Procedure: 1st come, 1st served.

West Columbia

COLUMBIA LAKES COUNTRY CLUB
A resort club with one 18-hole course

Location: From HWY 288, take HWY 35W

Golf Data: Pro Shop Phone: (409) 345-5455; Club Pro: Gene Amman; Par: 72; Yardage: 6967; Rating: 71.0; Course Architect: Tom Fazio; Closed Monday.

Guest Policy: You must play with a member, be a member of another private country club, or a guest of the resort.

NOTE: For resort and golf package information, phone (800) 231-1030 or (409) 345-5151, or write to Columbia Lakes, 188 Freeman Blvd., West Columbia, TX 77486.

═══ CALHOUN ═══ 5

Port Lavaca

HATCHBEND COUNTRY CLUB
A private club with one 9-hole course

Location: HWY 35, S. of HWY 87

Golf Data: Pro Shop Phone: (512) 552-3037; Club Manager: Bob Mahaffey; Par: 72 (two sets of tees); Yardage: 6093; Rating: 71.3; Closed Monday.

Guest Policy: Anyone can play.

Green Fees: $10 weekdays, $15 weekends and holidays; Carts: $5.25 + tax per person for 18 holes.

Tee Time Procedure: 1st come, 1st served.

═══ CHAMBERS ═══ 6

Anahuac

CHAMBERS COUNTY GOLF COURSE
A public club with one 18-hole course

Location: Intersection of I-10 and HWY 61

Golf Data: Pro Shop Phone: (409) 267-3236; Club Pro: Robby Sharpless; Par: 72; Yardage: 6750; Rating: 69.43; Course Architect: Leon Howard; Open 7 days.

Green Fees: $4.50 weekdays, $6 weekends and holidays; Carts: $6.25 per 9 holes.

Tee Time Procedure: 1st come, 1st served (use ball rack system).

——— COLORADO ——— 7

Columbus

COLUMBUS GOLF CLUB
A public club with one 9-hole course
Location: 1617 Walnut Street
Golf Data: Pro Shop Phone: (409) 732-5575; Club Pro: Richard Laughlin; Par: 35; Yardage: 2767; Open 7 days.
Green Fees: $4.50 weekdays, $9 weekends and holidays; Carts: $6 per 9 holes.
Tee Time Procedure: 1st come, 1st served.

Eagle Lake

EAGLE LAKE RECREATION CENTER
A public club with one 9-hole course
Location: Take either S. McCarty Avenue or HWY 90A to Golf Course Road
Golf Data: Clubhouse Phone: (409) 234-7156; Par: 35; Yardage: 2371; Rating: 68.0 (if 18 holes played); Open 7 days.
Green Fees: $5 weekdays, $8 weekends and holidays; Carts: $10 for 18 holes. Honor system.
Tee Time Procedure: 1st come, 1st served.

New Ulm

THE FALLS
A private club with one 18-hole course
Location: HWY 109S to Piper Lake Road, left at sign
Golf Data: Pro Shop Phone: (409) 992-3177; Club Pro: Tom Cavicchi; Par: 71; Yardage: 6718; Rating: 71.4; Course Architects: Jay Riviere & Dave Marr; Open 7 days.
Guest Policy: You must be a guest of a member. Club will reciprocate with other private country clubs on space available basis.

Weimar

WEIMAR GOLF COURSE
A public club with one 9-hole course
Location: Take Old HWY 90E ½ mile, in Hill Memorial Park
Golf Data: Pro Shop Phone: (409) 725-8624; Club Pros: Johnnie Miksch & Gary Braum; Par: 36; Yardage: 3107; Closed Monday.
Green Fees: $6 weekdays, $10 weekends and holidays; Carts: $5.10 per 9 holes.
Tee Time Procedure: 1st come, 1st served.

——— DeWITT ——— 8

Cuero

CUERO MUNICIPAL GOLF COURSE
A public club with one 9-hole course
Location: In Cuero Municipal Park
Golf Data: Pro Shop Phone: (512) 275-9049; Club Pro: Stanley Koenig; Par: 36; Yardage: 3072; Rating: 69.0 (if 18 holes played); Closed Monday.
Green Fees: $4 weekdays, $5 weekends and holidays; Carts: $12 for 18 holes.
Tee Time Procedure: 1st come, 1st served.

Yorktown

YORKTOWN COUNTRY CLUB
A semi-private club with one 9-hole course
Location: Take HWY 119S 2 miles, turn left at storage tanks (on right), go ¼ mile
Golf Data: Pro Shop Phone: (512) 564-9191; Club Pro: Warner Borth; Par: 70 (two sets of tees); Yardage: 5020; Open 7 days.
Green Fees: $5 anytime; Carts: $5 per 9 holes.
Tee Time Procedure: 1st come, 1st served.

——— FAYETTE ——— 9

LaGrange

FRISCH AUF VALLEY COUNTRY CLUB
A private club with one 9-hole course
Location: Off HWY 71 on Country Club Road

Golf Data: Pro Shop Phone: (409) 968-6113; Club Pro: Dennis Cornelison; Par: 36; Yardage: 3244; Rating: 72.0 (if 18 holes played); Closed Monday.

Guest Policy: You must be a guest of a member or a member of another private country club.

══════ FORT BEND ══════ 10

Fulshear

WESTON LAKES COUNTRY CLUB
A private club with one 18-hole course
Location: From I-10, take HWY 6S to Westheimer (FM 1093), W. 15 miles
Golf Data: Pro Shop Phone: (713) 346-1228; Club Pro: Perry French; Par: 72; Yardage: 7083; Rating: 74.0; Course Architect: Hale Irwin; Closed Monday.
Guest Policy: You must play with a member. Will reciprocate with U.S.G.A.-member clubs if outside 75-mile radius. Phone pro in advance.

Houston

HOUSTON GOLF ACADEMY
A public club with one 9-hole Par 3 course
Location: 1½ miles S. of Westheimer on HWY 6 (see #10 on Harris County locator map)
Golf Data: Pro Shop Phone: (713) 493-3276; Club Pro: Rodney Boling; Par: 27; Yardage: 1556; Open 7 days.
Green Fees: $5.50 for 9, $7.50 for all day weekdays, $10 for 18 holes on weekends; Carts: $7.50 for 9, $10 for 18 holes.
Tee Time Procedure: 1st come, 1st served.

Katy

THE CLUB AT FALCON POINT
A private club with one 18-hole course
Location: From I-10, take Exit 742, turn S. at Katy-Fort Bend Road (see #34 on Harris County locator map)
Golf Data: Pro Shop Phone: (713) 392-7888; Club Pro: William J. Lewis; Par: 72; Yardage: 6771; Rating: 73.6; Course Architects: Bruce Devlin & Bob Von Hagge; Closed Monday.

Guest Policy: You must be a guest of a member or a member of another private country club.

Missouri City

QUAIL VALLEY
A private club with two 18-hole courses, one executive course and a Par 3 course
Location: SW FRWY to HWY 1092, S. to Eldorado Blvd., go left (see #39 on Harris County locator map)
Golf Data: Pro Shop Phone: (713) 437-8277; Club Pro: Bill Hill; *La Quinta* Par: 72; Yardage: 6816; Rating: 73.0; *El Dorado* Par: 70; Yardage: 6680; Rating: 71.6; *Executive* Par: 32; Yardage: 2145; Course Architects: Jack Miller (27 holes) & Jay Riviere (27 holes); Closed Monday.
Guest Policy: You must play with a member or be a member of another private country club. Pro is authorized to extend an invitation. Phone in advance.

WILLOWISP COUNTRY CLUB
A private club with one 18-hole course
Location: US 90A SW to Fondren Road, go left (see #40 on Harris County locator map)
Golf Data: Pro Shop Phone: (713) 437-8210; Club Pro: Randy Lewis; Par: 71; Yardage: 6359; Rating: 68.4; Closed Monday.
Guest Policy: You must play with a member or be a member of another private country club. Phone pro for specifics.

Richmond

FORT BEND COUNTRY CLUB
A private club with one 18-hole course
Location: Take HWY 59S, exit at Thompson HWY (FM 762), turn right 1 mile
Golf Data: Pro Shop Phone: (713) 342-3756; Club Pro: Leon Roberts; Par: 71; Yardage: 6520; Rating: 69.0; Closed Monday.
Guest Policy: You must be a guest of a member (play with member on weekends) or a member of another private country club.

PECAN GROVE PLANTATION COUNTRY CLUB
A private club with one 18-hole course

Location: Take HWY 59S, exit HWY 90, turn left to Richmond, right at FM 359 1 mile

Golf Data: Pro Shop Phone: (713) 342-9649; Club Pro: Matt Jones; Par: 72; Yardage: 6956; Rating: 72.5; Course Architects: Carlton Gibson & Bruce Belin; Closed Monday.

Guest Policy: You must be a guest of a member or a member of another private country club (outside 30 mile radius).

Simonton

VALLEY LODGE GOLF CLUB

A private club with one 9-hole course

Location: HWY 1093 (Westheimer) W. to Wrangler Road, right to club

Golf Data: Pro Shop Phone: (713) 346-1426; Club Manager: Ron Lindsey; Par: 72 (two sets of tees); Yardage: 5694; Rating: 66.5; Closed Monday.

Guest Policy: Will reciprocate with U.S.G.A.-affiliated clubs; also accept daily fee play by invitation. Phone club manager for specifics.

Green Fees: $12 anytime; Carts: $14 for 18 holes.

Tee Time Procedure: 1st come, 1st served.

Stafford

RIVERBEND COUNTRY CLUB

A private club with one 18-hole course

Location: HWY 59S, exit Airport-Kirkwood, take Kirkwood (turns into Dulles) 3 miles (see #49 on Harris County locator map)

Golf Data: Pro Shop Phone: (713) 491-2552; Club Pro: Art Hodde; Par: 72; Yardage: 6768; Rating: 71.8; Course Architect: Press Maxwell; Closed Monday.

Guest Policy: You must be accompanied by a member or be a guest of a member. Pro is authorized to extend invitation.

Sugar Land

SUGAR CREEK COUNTRY CLUB

A private club with 27 holes

Location: HWY 59S, exit Sugarland left, through gate, right on Country Club Drive (see #50 on Harris County locator map)

Golf Data: Pro Shop Phone: (713) 494-9135; Club Pro: Jack Montgomery;

Robert 9 Par: 36; Yardage: 3277; *Trent* 9 Par: 36; Yardage: 3419; *Jones* 9 Par: 36; Yardage: 3411; Ratings: *Robert/Trent:* 70; *Robert/Jones:* 71; *Trent/Jones:* 71; Course Architect: Robert Trent Jones; Closed Monday.

Guest Policy: You must be a guest of a member (play with member on weekends) or a member of another private country club. Phone for specifics.

Sweetwater

SWEETWATER COUNTRY CLUB

A private club with 27 holes

Location: HWY 59S, exit Sweetwater Blvd., left ½ mile (see #51 on Harris County locator map)

Golf Data: Pro Shop Phone: (713) 980-4653; Director of Golf: David Clay; *Palm* 9 Par: 36; Yardage: 3565; *Bayou* 9 Par: 36; Yardage: 3588; *Pecan* 9 Par: 36; Yardage: 3566; Ratings: *Palm/Pecan:* 73.7; *Bayou/Pecan:* 73.7 (Pecan is always back 9); Course Architect: Roger Packard; Closed Monday.

NOTE: *Official home of the Ladies Professional Golf Association tour and LPGA Hall of Fame.*

Guest Policy: You must be a guest of a member or a member of another private country club. Have your pro call in advance.

_____ GALVESTON ___ 11

Dickinson

CHAPPARRAL RECREATION ASSOCIATION

A private club with one 9-hole course

Location: I-45S, exit Holland Road W., turn right at Avenue J

Golf Data: Pro Shop Phone: (409) 925-7800 or (713) 337-2411; Club Manager: Jerry Rohacek; Par: 36; Yardage: 3170; Rating: 67.2 (if 18 holes played); Open 7 days.

Guest Policy: You must be a guest of a member.

DICKINSON COUNTRY CLUB

A private club with one 9-hole course

Location: I-45, exit FM 517, go E. 4 miles

Golf Data: Pro Shop Phone: (713) 337-3031; Club Pro: Bob Tillison: Par: 72

(two sets of tees); Yardage: 6566; Rating: 67.6; Closed Monday.

Guest Policy: You must be a guest of a member or a member of another private country club. Phone in advance.

Friendswood

FRIENDSWOOD COUNTRY CLUB
A semi-private club with one 18-hole course

Location: On FM 528, 7 miles W. of I-45 (see #29 on Harris County locator map)

Golf Data: Pro Shop Phone: (713) 331-4396; Club Pro: Charles Henley; Par: 72; Yardage: 6857; Rating: 72.5; Course Architect: Jay Riviere; Open 7 days.

Green Fees: $10.50 weekdays, $16 weekends and holidays; Carts: $13 for 18 holes.

Tee Time Procedure: Weekends: Wednesday morning in person or by phone; Weekdays: 1st come, 1st served (but call in advance in case of tournament conflict).

Galveston

GALVESTON COUNTRY CLUB
A private club with one 18-hole course

Location: Take Seawall W. to 12 Mile Road, N. to Stewart

Golf Data: Pro Shop Phone: (409) 737-2776; Club Pro: Scooter Montgomery; Par: 72; Yardage: 6451; Rating: 69.7; Closed Monday.

Guest Policy: You must be a guest of a member or a member of another private country club.

THE PIRATES GOLF COURSE
A public club with one 18-hole course

Location: 1700 Sydnor Street

Golf Data: Pro Shop Phone: (409) 744-2366; Club Pro: James Wright; Par: 73; Yardage: 6575; Rating: 70.85; Course Architect: John Plummely; Open 7 days.

Green Fees: $6.31; weekdays, $7.36 weekends and holidays; Carts: $11.56 for 18 holes.

Tee Time Procedure: 1st come, 1st served.

LaMarque

LAKEVIEW COUNTRY CLUB
A private club with one 18-hole course

Location: 1219 Palm

Golf Data: Pro Shop Phone: (409) 935-6811; Club Manager: Alan Hern; Par: 72; Yardage: 6725; Open 7 days.

Guest Policy: You must play with a member or be a member of another private country club.

Texas City

BAYOU GOLF CLUB
A public club with one 18-hole course

Location: W. on Palmer, right on HWY 46, left at 25th Avenue

Golf Data: Pro Shop Phone: (409) 948-8362; Club Pro: Claude Harmon, Jr.; Par: 72; Yardage: 6835; Rating: 72.1; Course Architect: Joe Finger; Open 7 days.

Green Fees: $5 weekdays, $6 weekends and holidays; Carts: $11.56 for 18 holes.

Tee Time Procedure: Weekends: Thursday after 7 a.m. by phone or in person; Weekdays: 1st come, 1st served.

══════ GOLIAD ══════ 12

Goliad

GOLIAD COUNTY GOLF COURSE
A public club with one 9-hole course

Location: Take HWY 59S, left at Highway Department, right at Fannin Street

Golf Data: Pro Shop Phone: (512) 645-8478; Club Manager: Claudette Billo; Par: 36; Yardage: 3144; Rating: 69.7 (if 18 holes played); Open 7 days.

Green Fees: $5 weekdays, $6 weekends and holidays; Carts: $10 + tax for 18 holes ($6 + tax for 9).

Tee Time Procedure: 1st come, 1st served.

══════ GRIMES ══════ 13

Navasota

BLUE BONNETT COUNTRY CLUB
A public club with one 18-hole course

Location: Take HWY 105E 11 miles to FM 2445, left 4 miles

Golf Data: Pro Shop Phone: (409) 894-2207; Club Manager: Roger Johnson; Par: 72; Yardage: 6707; Rating: 71.8; Course Architect: Jay Riviere; Open 7 days.

Green Fees: $8 weekdays, $15 weekends and holidays; Carts: $16 for 18 holes ($13 for single rider); AX, Visa and MC accepted.

Tee Time Procedure: Weekends: Wednesday morning by phone or in person (2 days in advance for holidays); Weekdays: 1st come, 1st served.

NAVASOTA MUNICIPAL GOLF COURSE
A public club with one 9-hole course
Location: 1½ miles W. on HWY 105
Golf Data: Pro Shop Phone: (409) 825-7284; Club Manager: Marvin Cates; Par: 71 (two sets of tees); Yardage: 6000; Open 7 days.
Green Fees: $4 weekdays, $5 weekends and holidays; Carts: $8.50 + tax for 18 holes.
Tee Time Procedure: 1st come, 1st served.

⎯⎯⎯ HARDIN ⎯⎯ 14

Silsbee

SILSBEE COUNTRY CLUB
A private club with one 9-hole course
Location: Take HWY 418N 5 miles, right at Country Club Drive
Golf Data: Pro Shop Phone: (409) 385-4372; Club Pro: Ricky Jay; Par: 36; Yardage: 3200; Rating: 71 (if 18 holes played); Closed Monday.
Guest Policy: You must be a guest of a member or a member of another private country club.

Village Mills

WILDWOOD GOLF CLUB
A semi-private club with one 18-hole course
Location: HWY 69N, ½ mile to Wildwood sign, left 3 miles
Golf Data: Pro Shop Phone: (409) 834-2940; Club Pro: Mac Spikes; Par: 72; Yardage: 6723; Rating: 71.9; Course Architect: Leon Howard; Open 7 days
Green Fees: $8 weekdays, $10 weekends and holidays; Carts: $14 for 18 holes (Monday special: golf & cart $10).
Tee Time Procedure: Weekends: Thursday morning in person or by phone; Weekdays: 1st come, 1st served.

⎯⎯⎯ HARRIS ⎯⎯ 15

Atascocita

ATASCOCITA COUNTRY CLUB
A private club with three 9-hole courses
Location: Take HWY 59N, right at FM 1960 7½ miles to Pinehurst Trails (see #23 on locator map)
Golf Data: Pro Shop Phone: (713) 852-8115; Club Pro: Bill Dowling; *Pinehurst* 9 Par: 35; Yardage: 3292; *Point* 9 Par: 36; Yardage: 3435; *Shores* 9 Par: 35; Yardage: 3305; Ratings: *Pinehurst/Point:* 71.5; *Pinehurst/Shores:* 70.9; *Point/Shores:* 71.5; Closed Tuesday.
Guest Policy: You must be a guest of a member or a member of another private country club. Phone pro for specifics.

Baytown

GOOSE CREEK COUNTRY CLUB
A private club with one 18-hole course
Location: I-10, take Baytown exit to Baker Road, left 1 mile, turn right at Country Club View (see #24 on locator map)
Golf Data: Pro Shop Phone: (713) 424-5565; Club Pro: Glen Von Bieberstein; Par: 72; Yardage: 6700; Rating: 70.0; Closed Monday.
Guest Policy: You must be a guest of a member or a member of another private country club who reciprocates. Phone first and bring your credentials.

Channelview

CHANNELVIEW GOLF COURSE
A semi-private club with one 18-hole course
Location: I-10 to Sheldon Road, N. 5 miles (see #25 on locator map)
Golf Data: Pro Shop Phone: (713) 452-2183; Club Manager: Paul Luna; Par: 72; Yardage: 6240; Rating: 68.5; Open 7 days.
Green Fees: $5 weekdays, $7 weekends and holidays; Carts: $11 for 18 holes ($8 for single riders weekdays only).
Tee Time Procedure: 1st come, 1st served.

Clear Lake

CLEAR LAKE GOLF CLUB
A private club with one 18-hole course

Location: 1202 Reseda (see #26 on locator map)
Golf Data: Pro Shop Phone: (713) 488-0252; Club Pro: John Maca; Par: 72; Yardage: 6757; Rating: 70.5; Closed Monday.
Guest Policy: You must be a guest of a member or a member of another private country club. Phone for specifics.

Crosby

INDIAN SHORES GOLF & TENNIS CLUB
A semi-private club with one 9-hole course
Location: 2141 White Feather Trail (see #27 on locator map)
Golf Data: Pro Shop Phone: (713) 324-2592; Club Pro: Leonard Jacobsen; Par: 72; Yardage: 6610; Rating: 68.9; Closed Monday.
Green Fees: $4 weekdays, $7 weekends and holidays; Carts: $5.50 + tax per 9 holes; AX, Visa and MC accepted.
Tee Time Procedure: 1st come, 1st served.

NEWPORT ON LAKE HOUSTON
A private club with one 18-hole course
Location: 16401 Golf Club Drive (see #28 on locator map)
Golf Data: Pro Shop Phone: (713) 328-2541; Club Pro: Richard Imboden; Par: 72; Yardage: 6601; Rating: 70.0; Closed Monday.
Guest Policy: You must be a guest of a member who must call at least 24 hours in advance or a member of another private country club. Phone pro for an invitation.

Hockley

TENNWOOD GOLF CLUB
A private club with 27 holes
Location: HWY 290W
Golf Data: Pro Shop Phone: (713) 757-4000; Club Manager: Barry Harrison; *East* 9 Par: 36; Yardage: 3446; Rating: 36.1; *North* 9 Par: 35; Yardage: 3059; Rating: 34.2; *West* 9 Par: 36; Yardage: 3125; Rating: 34.7; Closed Monday.
Guest Policy: You must play with member. Course owned by Tenneco.

Houston

Public Golf Courses

BEAR CREEK GOLF WORLD
A public club with three 18-hole courses
Location: I-10 to HWY 6N, 3½ miles to Clay Road (see #1 on locator map)
Golf Data: Pro Shop Phone: (713) 859-8188; Club Pro: Robert Olson; *Masters* Par: 72; Yardage: 7048; Rating: 74.2; *Presidents* Par: 72; Yardage: 6562; Rating: 69.1; Course Architect: Jay Riviere (both courses); *Executive* Par: 66; Yardage: 5340; Rating: 64.29; Open 7 days.
NOTE: *Site of the All-American Intercollegiate Invitational Golf Tournament. Masters course ranked in Top 50 Public Courses by* Golf Digest *and Hole #18 rated in top 100 golf holes by* Golf Magazine.
Green Fees: Masters: $20 anytime; Presidents: $14; Executive: $12; Carts: $16 for 18 holes ($13 for single rider weekdays only); AX, Visa and MC accepted.
Tee Time Procedure: Weekends: Nonmembers call Friday; Weekdays: Call week in advance.

BROCK PARK GOLF COURSE
A public club with one 18-hole course
Location: 3201 John Ralston Road (see #3 on locator map)
Golf Data: Pro Shop Phone: (713) 458-1350; Club Pro: Jody Hawkins; Par: 72; Yardage: 6487; Rating: 70.7; Open 7 days.
Green Fees: $5.50 weekdays, $7.50 weekends and holidays; Carts: $12.80 for 18 holes.
Tee Time Procedure: Weekends-Holidays: Call 1 day in advance after 6:35 a.m.; Weekdays: 1st come, 1st served.

GLENBROOK GOLF COURSE
A public club with one 18-hole course
Location: 8205 N. Bayou (see #5 on locator map)
Golf Data: Pro Shop Phone: (713) 644-4081; Club Pro: Gene Hill; Par: 67; Yardage: 5517; Open 7 days.
NOTE: *Course constantly changing due to work on flood plain.*
Green Fees: $5.50 weekdays, $7.50 weekends and holidays; Carts: $7 for 18 holes.

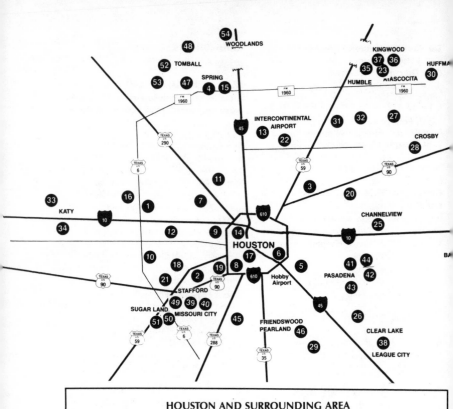

HOUSTON AND SURROUNDING AREA

HOUSTON
1. Bear Creek Golf World
2. Braeburn C. C.
3. Brock Park G. C.
4. Champions G. C.
5. Glenbrook G. C.
6. Gus Wortham Park G. C.
7. Hearthstone C. C.
8. Herman Park G. C.
9. Houston C. C.
10. Houston Golf Academy
11. Inwood Forest C. C.
12. Lakeside C. C.
13. Lochinvar C. C.
14. Memorial Park G. C.
15. Northgate C. C.
16. Pine Forest C. C.
17. River Oaks C. C.
18. Sharpstown Park G. C.
19. South Main G. C.
20. Texaco C. C.
21. Westwood C. C.
22. World Houston G. C.

ATASCOCITA
23. Atascocita C. C.

BAYTOWN
24. Goose Creek C. C.

CHANNELVIEW
25. Channelview G. C.

CLEAR LAKE
26. Clear Lake C. C.

CROSBY
27. Indian Shores Golf & Tennis
28. Newport on Lake Houston

FRIENDSWOOD
29. Friendswood C. C.

HUFFMAN
30. Lake Houston Golf Club

HUMBLE
31. El Dorado C. C.
32. Walden on Lake Houston

KATY
33. Green Meadows G. C.
34. The Club at Falcon Point

KINGWOOD
35. Burkedale C. C.
36. Deerwood C. C.
37. Kingwood C. C.

LEAGUE CITY
38. South Shore Harbour C. C.

MISSOURI CITY
39. Quail Valley
40. Willowisp C. C.

PASADENA
41. Baywood C. C.
42. Chemlake G. C.
43. Pasadena Municipal G. C.
44. San Jacinto College G. C.

PEARLAND
45. Country Place at U.S. Homes
46. Golfcrest C. C.

SPRING
47. Raveneaux C. C.
48. Willow Creek G. C.

STAFFORD
49. River Bend C. C.

SUGARLAND
50. Sugar Creek C. C.

SWEETWATER
51. Sweetwater C. C.

TOMBALL
52. Tomball C. C.
53. Treeline G. C.

WOODLANDS
54. Woodlands Inn & C. C.

Tee Time Procedure: Weekends-Holidays: Call 1 day in advance after 7 a.m.; Weekdays: 1st come, 1st served.

GUS WORTHAM PARK GOLF COURSE
A public club with one 18-hole course
Location: I-45 S, exit Wayside, left ¾ mile (see #6 on locator map)
Golf Data: Pro Shop Phone: (713) 921-3227; Club Pro: Paul Reed; Par: 71; Yardage: 6414; Rating: 69.5; Open 7 days.
Green Fees: $5.50 weekdays, $7.50 weekends and holidays; Carts: $13 for 18 holes.
Tee Time Procedure: Weekends-Holidays: Call 1 day in advance after 6:30 a.m.; Weekdays: 1st come, 1st served.

HERMAN PARK GOLF COURSE
A public club with one 18-hole course
Location: 6000 block of Fannin Street in Herman Park (see #8 on locator map)
Golf Data: Pro Shop Phone: (713) 529-9788; Club Pro: Elroy Marti; Par: 71; Yardage: 6265; Rating: 70.0; Open 7 days.
Green Fees: $5.50 weekdays, $7.50 weekends and holidays; Carts: $10 for 18 holes.
Tee Time Procedure: Weekends-Holidays: Call 1 day in advance after 7 a.m.; Weekdays: 1st come, 1st served.

MELROSE GOLF COURSE
A public club with one 18-hole Par 3 course
Location: I-45 exit Camino Road, E. 2 miles
Golf Data: Pro Shop Phone: (713) 847-0875; Club Manager: Kirk Currie; Par: 54; Yardage: 1515; Open 7 days.
Green Fees: $2.50/9 and $4/18 weekdays; $3/9 and $5/18 weekends and holidays.
Tee Time Procedure: 1st come, 1st served.

MEMORIAL PARK GOLF COURSE
A public club with one 18-hole course
Location: 6001 Memorial Park Loop Road (see #14 on locator map)
Golf Data: Pro Shop Phone: (713) 862-4033; Club Pro: J. B. Hutcens; Par: 72; Yardage: 7333; Rating: 73.0; Open 7 days.

Green Fees: $5.50 weekdays, $7.50 weekends and holidays; Carts: $11 for 18 holes.
Tee Time Procedure: Weekends-Holidays: Must be present at 6:30 a.m. 1 day in advance; Weekdays: 1st come, 1st served.

SHARPSTOWN PARK GOLF COURSE
A public club with one 18-hole course
Location: 8200 Beltline Blvd. (see #18 on locator map)
Golf Data: Pro Shop Phone: (713) 988-2099; Club Pro: Nat Johnson; Par: 70; Yardage: 6655; Rating: 70.0; Open 7 days.
Green Fees: $5.50 weekdays, $7.50 weekends and holidays; Carts: $12 for 18 holes ($8.50 for single riders); Visa and MC accepted.
Tee Time Procedure: Weekends-Holidays: Call 1 day in advance after 7 a.m.; Weekdays: 1st come, 1st served.

SOUTH MAIN GOLF CLUB
A public club with one 9-hole Par 3 course
Location: Corner of Willow Bend & S. Main Street near I-610 (see #19 on locator map)
Golf Data: Pro Shop Phone: (713) 665-9626; Club Pro: Ruben Lopez; Par: 27; Yardage: 1190; Open 7 days.
Green Fees: $3 weekdays, $4.80 weekends and holidays; Carts: $2.50 per 9 holes.
Tee Time Procedure: 1st come, 1st served.

WORLD HOUSTON GOLF COURSE
A public club with one 18-hole course
Location: 4000 Green Road near Intercontinental Airport (see #22 on locator map)
Golf Data: Pro Shop Phone: (713) 449-8384; Club Pro: Trey Stiles; Par: 72; Yardage: 6617; Rating: 71.2; Open 7 days.
Green Fees: $8.50, weekdays, $13 weekends and holidays; Carts: $15 for 18 holes.
Tee Time Procedure: Call 1 week in advance anytime.
NOTE: A number of hotels near Houston Intercontinental Airport are in close proximity to course. Phone pro shop for list.

Private Golf Courses

BRAEBURN COUNTRY CLUB
A private club with one 18-hole course
Location: 8101 Bissonnet (see #2 on locator map)
Golf Data: Pro Shop Phone: (713) 774-8788; Club Pro: Jack Sellman; Par: 72; Yardage: 6700; Rating: 70.0; Closed Monday.
Guest Policy: You must be a guest of a member.

CHAMPIONS GOLF CLUB
A private club with two 18-hole courses
Location: 13722 Champions Blvd. (see #4 on locator map)
Golf Data: Pro Shop Phone: (713)-444-6262; Club Pro: Jimmy Burke; *Cypress Creek* Par: 71; Yardage: 7121; Rating: 72.0; Course Architect: Ralph Plummer; *Jack Rabbit* Par: 72; Yardage: 7166; Rating: 72; Course Architects: George & Tom Fazio; Closed Monday.
NOTE: Rated as one of Top 100 golf courses by Golf Digest magazine. Site of 1969 U.S.G.A. Open.
Guest Policy: You must be a member of another private country club. Phone for specifics and bring credentials.

HEARTHSTONE COUNTRY CLUB
A private club with one 18-hole course
Location: 7615 Ameswood (see #7 on locator map)
Golf Data: Pro Shop Phone: (713) 463-2204; Club Pro: Carter Ham; Par: 71; Yardage: 6527; Rating: 70.5; Closed Monday.
NOTE: Third 9 under construction.
Guest Policy: You must play with a member or be a member of another private country club. Pro is authorized to extend an invitation.

HOUSTON COUNTRY CLUB
A private club with one 18-hole course
Location: 1 Potomac (see #9 on locator map)
Golf Data: Pro Shop Phone: (713) 465-8381; Club Pro: Charlie Epps; Par: 72; Yardage: 7056; Rating: 73.0; Closed Monday.
Guest Policy: You must be a guest of a member.

INWOOD FOREST COUNTRY CLUB
A private club with 27 holes
Location: 7600 Antonione Drive (see #11 on locator map)
Golf Data: Pro Shop Phone: (713) 448-0239; Club Pro: Mike Baker; Par: 72; Yardage: 6728; Rating: 72.0; 3rd 9 Par: 36; Yardage: 3210; Course Architect: Jay Riviere; Closed Monday.
Guest Policy: You must be a guest of a member or a member of another U.S.G.A.-member private country club. Pro can extend an invitation.

LAKESIDE COUNTRY CLUB
A private club with one 18-hole course
Location: 100 Wilcrest (see #12 on locator map)
Golf Data: Pro Shop Phone: (713) 497-2228; Club Pro: Jerry Smith; Par: 72; Yardage: 6490; Rating: 70.7; Closed Monday.
Guest Policy: You must play with a member. Members of other recognized private country clubs are welcome, but still must play with a member.

LOCHINVAR COUNTRY CLUB
A private club with one 18-hole course
Location: 2000 Farrell Road (see #13 on locator map)
Golf Data: Pro Shop Phone: (713) 821-0220; Club Pro: Terry Kendrick; Par: 72; Yardage: 6950; Rating: 72.0; Course Architect: Jack Nicklaus; Closed Monday.
Guest Policy: You must be a guest of a member. Saturday morning, you must be accompanied by a member. All charges must be made by member.

NORTHGATE COUNTRY CLUB
A private club with one 18-hole course
Location: 17110 Northgate Forest Drive (see #15 on locator map)
Golf Data: Pro Shop Phone: (713) 444-5302; Club Pro: Vic Carder; Par: 70; Yardage: 6484; Rating: 71.1; Course Architects: Bruce Devlin & Bob Von Hagge; Closed Monday.
Guest Policy: You must be a guest of a member or a member of another private country club. Phone for specifics.

PINE FOREST COUNTRY CLUB
A private club with 27 holes
Location: 18003 Clay Road (see #16 on locator map)

Golf Data: Pro Shop Phone: (713) 463-1234; Club Pro: John B. Weaver; *White* 9 Par: 36; Yardage: 3364; Rating: 36.3; *Green* 9 Par: 36; Yardage: 3471; Rating: 36.9; *Gold* 9 Par: 36; Yardage: 3342; Rating: 36.2; Course Architect: Jay Riviere; Closed Monday.

Guest Policy: A member must play with a guest unless the guest is a member of a U.S.G.A.-recognized club located outside a 75-mile radius of Houston. Pro can extend course privileges.

RIVER OAKS COUNTRY CLUB
A private club with one 18-hole course
Location: 1600 River Oaks Blvd. (see #17 on locator map)
Golf Data: Pro Shop Phone: (713) 529-2605; Club Pro: Dick Harmon; Par: 72; Yardage: 6868; Rating: 72.6; Closed Monday.
Guest Policy: You must play with a member.

TEXACO COUNTRY CLUB
A private club with one 18-hole course
Location: On Texaco Road (see #20 on locator map)
Golf Data: Pro Shop Phone: (713) 453-7501; Club Pro: Steve Haskins; Par: 72; Yardage: 6300; Rating: 69.6; Open 7 days.
Guest Policy: You must be a guest of a member (play with a member on weekends) or a member of another private country club. Phone in advance.

WESTWOOD COUNTRY CLUB
A private club with one 18-hole course
Location: 8888 Country Creek Drive (see #21 on locator map)
Golf Data: Pro Shop Phone: (713) 774-3011; Club Pro: David Findlay; Par: 72; Yardage: 7005; Rating: 73.4; Course Architect: Joe Finger; Closed Monday.
Guest Policy: You must be a guest of a member or a member of another private country club. Phone pro for an invitation.

Huffman
LAKE HOUSTON GOLF CLUB
A public club with one 18-hole course
Location: From Houston, take HWY 59N, right at 1960 E., left (N.) at FM 2100, right at Afton Way (see #30 on locator map)

Golf Data: Pro Shop Phone: (713) 324-1841; Club Pro: Jack Forester; Par: 72; Yardage: 6844; Rating: 72.6; Course Architect: Jay Riviere; Open 7 days.
Green Fees: $10.50 weekdays, $16.50 weekends and holidays; Carts: $16.50 for 18 holes; AX, Visa and MC accepted.
Tee Time Procedure: Call 7 days in advance (NOTE: American Golf Club members may phone 8 days in advance).

Humble
EL DORADO COUNTRY CLUB
A private club with one 18-hole course
Location: 7900 North Belt (see #31 on locator map)
Golf Data: Pro Shop Phone: (713) 458-1010; Club Pro: Terry Tyler; Par: 72; Yardage: 7118; Rating: 73.8; Course Architect: Jay Riviere; Closed Monday.
Guest Policy: You must be a guest of a member or a member of another private country club. Phone for specifics.

WALDEN ON LAKE HOUSTON GOLF & COUNTRY CLUB
A private club with one 18-hole course
Location: HWY 59N, FM 1960 right 7 miles (see #32 on locator map)
Golf Data: Pro Shop Phone: (713) 852-3551; Club Pro: J. D. Murchison; Par: 72; Yardage: 6781; Rating: 72.5; Course Architects: Bruce Devlin & Bob Von Hagge; Closed Monday.
Guest Policy: You must be a guest of a member. On weekends, you must play with a member.

Katy
GREEN MEADOWS GOLF CLUB
A semi-private club with one 18-hole course
Location: I-10 W, exit Katy-Fort Bend Road, take HWY 90A W, turn right at Avenue D, 1 mile to Franz Road, left (see #33 on locator map)
Golf Data: Pro Shop Phone: (713) 391-3670; Club Pro: Mike McRoberts; Par: 70; Yardage: 5850; Rating: 65.4; Open 7 days.
Green Fees: $9.50 weekdays, $12.65 weekends and holidays; Carts: $14.80 for 18 holes.
Tee Time Procedure: Weekends-Holidays: Friday at 8 a.m. in person or by phone; Weekdays: 1st come, 1st served.

Kingwood

BURKEDALE COUNTRY CLUB
A private club with one 18-hole course
Location: 805 Hamblen Blvd. (see #35 on locator map)
Golf Data: Pro Shop Phone: (713) 358-3101; Club Pro: Scott Curiel; Par: 71; Yardage: 6660; Rating: 72.3; Course Architect: John Plumbley; Open 7 days.
Guest Policy: You must be a guest of a member or a member of another private country club.

DEERWOOD COUNTRY CLUB
A private club with one 18-hole course
Location: 1717 Forest Garden (see #36 on locator map)
Golf Data: Pro Shop Phone: (713) 360-1065; Club Pro: Carl Baker; Par: 72; Yardage: 7108; Rating: 74.4; Course Architect: Joe Finger; Closed Monday.
Guest Policy: You must play with a member.

KINGWOOD COUNTRY CLUB
A private club with 3 18-hole courses
Location: 1700 Lake Kingwood Trail (see #37 on locator map)
Golf Data: Pro Shop Phone: (713) 358-2171; Club Pro: Richard Killian; *Island* Par: 72; Yardage: 7309; Rating: 74.0; Course Architect: Joe Finger; *Lake* Par: 72; Yardage: 7089; Rating: 71.0; Course Architect: Bruce Littrell; *Marsh* Par: 72; Yardage: 6840; Rating: 71.0; Closed Monday.
NOTE: 6th hole of Island course selected as best designed hole by Golf Course Architects. 18th hole featured as one of the toughest holes in the world by Golf Digest *magazine.*
Guest Policy: You must be a guest of a member or a member of a C.C.A., U.S.G.A. or A.C.I.-program course. Phone for specifics.

League City

SOUTH SHORE HARBOUR COUNTRY CLUB
A private club with one 18-hole course
Location: 4300 South Shore (see #38 on locator map)
Golf Data: Pro Shop Phone: (713) 334-0525; Club Pro: Greg Scott; Par: 71; Yardage: 6907; Rating: 71.5; Course Architects: Jay Riviere & Dave Marr; Closed Monday.
Guest Policy: You must play with a member or be a member of a C.C.A.-managed course outside a 75-mile radius.

Pasadena

Public Golf Courses

PASADENA MUNICIPAL GOLF COURSE
A public club with one 18-hole course
Location: 1000 Duffer Lane (see #43 on locator map)
Golf Data: Pro Shop Phone: (713) 481-0834; Club Pro: Wayne Batten; Par: 71; Yardage: 6800; Rating: 71.4; Open 7 days.
Green Fees: $5.80 weekdays, $8.50 weekends and holidays; Carts: $12.75 for 18 holes.
Tee Time Procedure: Weekends-Holidays: Wednesday at 7:30 a.m. in person or by phone; Weekdays: 1st come, 1st served.

SAN JACINTO COLLEGE GOLF COURSE
A public club with one 9-hole course
Location: 8060 Spencer HWY (see #44 on locator map)
Golf Data: Pro Shop Phone: (713) 476-1880; Par: 36; Yardage: 2440; Open 7 days.
Green Fees: $2 weekdays, $4 weekends and holidays; No carts available.
Tee Time Procedure: 1st come, 1st served.

Private Golf Courses

BAYWOOD COUNTRY CLUB
A private club with one 18-hole course
Location: 5500 Genoa-Red Bluff Road (see #41 on locator map)
Golf Data: Pro Shop Phone: (713) 487-0050; Club Pro: Johnny Dill; Par: 72; Yardage: 6621; Rating: 72.0; Closed Monday.
Guest Policy: You must be accompanied by a member or out-of-town guests must be members of another private country club.

CHEMLAKE GOLF COURSE
A private club with one 9-hole course
Location: 9502 Bayport Blvd. (see #42 on locator map)
Golf Data: Celanese Phone: (713) 474-6200; Par: 36; Yardage: 3400; Rating:

70.7 (if 18 holes played); Open 7 days.
Guest Policy: You must be a guest of a member. Will reciprocate with members of other Celanese Company clubs only.

Spring

RAVENEAUX COUNTRY CLUB
A private club with two 18-hole courses
Location: 9415 Cypress Wood Drive (see #47 on locator map)
Golf Data: Pro Shop Phone: (713) 370-6370; Club Pro: Bob Prange; *Old Course* Par: 71; Yardage: 6701; Rating: 71.6; *New Course* Par: 71; Yardage: 6601; Rating: 70.9; Course Architects: Bruce Devlin & Bob Von Hagge (both courses); Closed Monday.
Guest Policy: Guest must be accompanied by member. Club will reciprocate with other private country clubs. Have pro phone ahead to make arrangements.

WILLOW CREEK GOLF CLUB
A private club with one 18-hole course
Location: In North Hampton subdivision (see #48 on locator map)
Golf Data: Pro Shop Phone: (713) 376-4061; Club Pro: Brett Baske; Par: 72; Yardage: 6920; Rating: 73.0; Course Architects: Bruce Devlin & Bob Von Hagge; Closed Monday.
Guest Policy: You must play with a member or be sponsored by a member. Reciprocates with other private country clubs outside a 50-mile radius.

Tomball

TOMBALL COUNTRY CLUB
A private club with one 9-hole course
Location: 22303 Waldenway (see #52 on locator map)
Golf Data: Pro Shop Phone: (713) 351-5102; Club Pro: Bobby Martin; Par: 70 (two sets of tees); Yardage: 6201; Rating: 68.5; Open 7 days.
Guest Policy: Out-of-town country club members are welcome.

TREELINE GOLF CLUB
A public club with one 18-hole course
Location: 17505 N. Eldredge PKWY (see #53 on locator map)
Golf Data: Pro Shop Phone: (713) 376-1542; Club Pro: Skip Cisneros; Par: 68; Yardage: 5380; Rating: 66.1; Open 7 days.

Green Fees: $7.35 weekdays, $10.50 weekends and holidays; Carts: $14.70 for 18 holes.
Tee Time Procedure: Weekends-Holidays: 1 week in advance, in person or by phone; Weekdays: 1st come, 1st served.

———— JACKSON ———— 16

Edna

EDNA COUNTRY CLUB
A semi-private club with one 9-hole course
Location: W. on HWY 59, left at Apollo Drive, right at Country Club Drive
Golf Data: Pro Shop Phone: (512) 782-3010; Club Manager: Gradis Graven; Par: 36; Yardage: 3232; Closed Monday.
Guest Policy: Out-of-towners may pay guest fees.
Green Fees: $6 weekdays, $8 weekends and holidays; Carts: $6 per 9 holes.
Tee Time Procedure: 1st come, 1st served.

Ganado

MUSTANG CREEK COUNTRY CLUB
A semi-private club with one 9-hole course
Location: Take HWY 59W, turn right at Mustang Creek Country Club Road
Golf Data: Pro Shop Phone: (512) 771-9390; Club Pro: Harlan Tegeler; Par: 36; Yardage: 3425; Open 7 days.
Guest Policy: Out-of-towners may pay green fees.
Green Fees: $8 anytime; Carts: $6 per 9 holes.
Tee Time Procedure: 1st come, 1st served.

———— JEFFERSON ———— 17

Beaumont

Public Golf Courses

BAYOU DIN GOLF CLUB
A public club with one 18-hole course
Location: From I-10, take HWY 69S, exit Fannette, right 3 miles, left at LaBelle, 3 miles

Golf Data: Pro Shop Phone: (409) 796-1327; Club Pro: Ed Campbell; Par: 71; Yardage: 6285; Rating: 68.0; Open 7 days.

Green Fees: $5.50 weekdays, $6.50 weekends and holidays; Carts: $6 per person for 18 holes (or $8.50 for single rider); Visa & MC accepted.

Tee Time Procedure: 1st come, 1st served.

HENRY HOMBERG MUNICIPAL GOLF CLUB
A public club with one 18-hole course

Location: I-10 W, exit Walden, go S.

Golf Data: Pro Shop Phone: (409) 842-3220; Club Pro: Ronald Pfleider; Par: 72; Yardage: 6800; Rating: 71.0; Open 7 days.

Green Fees: $5 weekdays, $6 weekends and holidays; Carts: $12 for 18 holes.

Tee Time Procedure: 1st come, 1st served (use club system).

Private Golf Courses

BEAUMONT COUNTRY CLUB
A private club with one 18-hole course

Location: Hwy 69N, exit Lucas, turn E., left at Pine Street

Golf Data: Pro Shop Phone: (409) 892-9804; Club Pro: Paul Mowery, Jr.; Par: 72; Yardage: 6426; Rating: 68.9; Closed Monday.

Guest Policy: Must be a member of another private country club outside a 60-mile radius. Fees must be charged to home club.

WILLOW CREEK COUNTRY CLUB
A private club with one 18-hole course

Location: I-10, exit FM 364, N. 2½ miles

Golf Data: Pro Shop Phone: (409) 892-9097; Club Pro: John Kenneth Barlow; Par: 71; Yardage: 6603; Rating: 71.0; Course Architect: Johnny B. Barlow; Closed Monday.

Guest Policy: You must be a guest of a member or a member of another private country club outside a 50-mile radius.

Groves

PORT GROVES GOLF CLUB
A semi-private club with one 9-hole course

Location: Take Lincoln to Monroe, then left

Golf Data: Pro Shop Phone: (409) 962-0406; Club Pro: Jim Hurley; Par: 70 (two sets of tees); Yardage: 5835; Open 7 days.

Green Fees: $2.10 per 9 holes; Carts: $2.50 per person per 9 holes.

Tee Time Procedure: 1st come, 1st served.

Port Arthur

BABE DIDRIKSON ZAHARIAS MUNICIPAL GOLF COURSE
A public club with one 18-hole course

Location: Intersection of 75th Street and 9th Avenue

Golf Data: Pro Shop Phone: (409) 722-8286; Club Pro: Johnnie B. Barlow; Par: 72; Yardage: 6957; Course Architects: Leon & Charles Howard; Open 7 days.

Green Fees: $4 weekdays, $5 weekends and holidays; Carts: $10.56 for 18 holes.

Tee Time Procedure: 1st come, 1st served (use ball rack system).

PORT ARTHUR COUNTRY CLUB
A private club with one 18-hole course

Location: HWY 73W to Country Club Road, then right

Golf Data: Pro Shop Phone: (409) 796-1311; Club Pro: Jim Estes; Par: 71; Yardage: 6746; Rating: 72.4; Closed Monday.

Guest Policy: You must be a member of another private country club and present current membership card. Call pro in advance for specifics.

Sour Lake

PINEWOOD COUNTRY CLUB
A private club with one 18-hole course

Location: 7 miles W. of Beaumont on HWY 105

Golf Data: Pro Shop Phone: (409) 753-2521; Club Pro: Brian Lietzke; Par: 72; Yardage: 6727; Rating: 71.8; Course Architect: Henry Ransom; Closed Monday.

Guest Policy: You must be a member of another U.S.G.A.-member club and/or bonafide country club or PGA, or a guest of a member. You may charge back to your club outside 50-mile radius. Phone for tee times & bring credentials.

KARNES —— 18

Kenedy

KARNES COUNTY COUNTRY CLUB
A semi-private club with one 9-hole course
Location: 1 mile S. on HWY 181
Golf Data: Pro Shop Phone: (512) 583-3200; Club Pro: Bob Dietz; Par: 72 (two sets of tees); Yardage: 6235; Closed Monday.
Green Fees: $6 weekdays, $9 weekends and holidays; Carts: $15 for 18 holes ($7.50 for single rider).
Tee Time Procedure: 1st come, 1st served.

LAVACA —— 19

Halletsville

HALLETSVILLE GOLF ASSOCIATION
A public club with one 9-hole course
Location: In Halletsville Park
Golf Data: Pro Shop Phone: (512) 798-7190; Club Manager: Rick Barrow; Par: 36; Yardage: 3025; Rating: 68.0 (if 18 holes played); Open 7 days.
Green Fees: $4.25 weekdays, $5.25 weekends and holidays; Carts: $14 for 18 holes.
Tee Time Procedure: 1st come, 1st served.

Yoakum

YOAKUM GOLF CLUB
A public club with one 9-hole course
Location: HWY 77E, right at Airport Road to City Park
Golf Data: Pro Shop Phone: (512) 293-5682; Club Pro: Tom Chilek; Par: 72 (two sets of tees); Yardage: 6117; Rating: 69.0; Closed Monday until noon.
Green Fees: $5 weekdays, $7 weekends and holidays; Carts: $10.50 for 18 holes.
Tee Time Procedure: 1st come, 1st served.

LIBERTY —— 20

Cleveland

KIRBYWOOD GOLF CLUB
A semi-private club with one 9-hole course
Location: Off HWY 321 in Kirbywood subdivision
Golf Data: Pro Shop Phone: (713) 592-0606; Club Manager: Leo Lakovich; Par: 36; Yardage: 2812; Rating: 69.7 (if 18 holes played); Closed Monday.
Green Fees: $7 weekdays, $10 weekends and holidays; Carts: $14 for 18 holes ($10.50 if single rider).
Tee Time Procedure: 1st come, 1st served.

Liberty

MAGNOLIA RIDGE COUNTRY CLUB
A private club with one 9-hole course
Location: 1 mile E. of HWY 90 on Old Beaumont Road
Golf Data: Pro Shop Phone: ((409) 336-3551; Club Pro: Mike Jerome; Par: 72 (two sets of tees); Yardage: 6438; Rating: 71.9; Course Architect: John Plummer; Closed Monday.
Guest Policy: You must be a guest of a member or a member of another private country club.

LIVE OAK —— 21

Three Rivers

LIVE OAK RECREATION ASSOCIATION
A private club with one 9-hole course
Location: 4 miles S. on HWY 281
Golf Data: No Phone; Par: 36; Yardage: 3100; Open 7 days.
Guest Policy: Non-county residents may pay green fees and play.
Green Fees: $3 anytime; Carts: $10 for 18 holes.
Tee Time Procedure: 1st come, 1st served.

MATAGORDA —— 22

Bay City

BAYCEL GOLF CLUB
A private club with one 9-hole course
Location: HWY 60S, take FM 2668 right, 1st left beyond Celanese Corp. plant
Golf Data: Celanese Phone: (409) 245-4871 ext 4075; Club Manager: Ron Cowart; Par: 71 (two sets of tees); Yardage: 5960; Rating: 68.5; Open 7 days.

Guest Policy: You must be a guest of a member. Will reciprocate with other Celanese clubs only.

BAY CITY COUNTRY CLUB
A private club with one 9-hole course
Location: 3 miles W. on HWY 35
Golf Data: Pro Shop Phone: (409) 245-3990; Club Pro: Kenneth Etie; Par: 36; Yardage: 3111; Rating: 71.0 (if 18 holes played); Closed Monday.
Guest Policy: You must be a guest of a member or a member of another private country club. Phone in advance.

Palacios

PALACIOS COUNTRY CLUB
A public club with one 9-hole course
Location: 2 miles S. on HWY 35
Golf Data: Pro Shop Phone: (512) 972-2666; Club Pro: Darrell Tedder; Par: 36; Yardage: 3088; Open 7 days.
Green Fees: $7 all day weekdays, $8 all day weekends and holidays; Carts: $5 per 9 holes.
Tee Time Procedure: 1st come, 1st served.

═══ MONTGOMERY ═══ 23

Conroe

Public Golf Courses

CONROE GOLF CENTER
A public club with one 9-hole Par 3 course
Location: 12000 I-45 S
Golf Data: Pro Shop Phone: (409) 273-4002; Club Pro: Rick Lewis; Par: 27; Yardage: 1123; Course Architects: Rick Lewis & Scott Wolfe; Open 7 days.
Green Fees: $5 for 9, $7 for 18 holes anytime.
Tee Time Procedure: 1st come, 1st served.

Private Golf Courses

APRIL SOUND COUNTRY CLUB & RESORT
A resort club with two 18-hole courses and a 9-hole executive course
Location: I-45, exit HWY 105, 9 miles W.
Golf Data: Pro Shop Phone: (409) 588-1700; Club Pro: Bill Westerlund;

White 9 Par: 35; Yardage: 2928; *Blue* 9 Par: 35; Yardage: 3221; Blue/White Rating: 69.5; *Red* 9 Par: 32; Yardage: 2336; Open 7 days (closed Tuesday November-March).
Guest Policy: You must be a guest of a member, be a member of a C.C.A.-member club or another U.S.G.A.-member country club, or a guest of the resort.
NOTE: *For resort or golf package information, phone (409) 588-1101, or write to April Sound CC, P.O. Box 253, Conroe, TX 77305.*
Green Fees: $15 weekdays, $20 weekends and holidays; Carts: $16 for 18 holes.
Tee Time Procedure: Call 1 week in advance Monday thru Sunday.

CONROE COUNTRY CLUB
A private club with one 9-hole course
Location: On Loop 336SW
Golf Data: Pro Shop Phone: (409) 756-5251; Club Chairman: Sam Kellum; Par: 72 (two sets of tees); Yardage: 6492; Rating: 70.0; Closed Monday.
Guest Policy: You must be a guest of a member or a member of another private country club. Phone in advance.

PANORAMA COUNTRY CLUB
A private club with 3 9-hole courses
Location: 23 Greenbriar Road
Golf Data: Pro Shop Phone: (409) 756-5815; Club Pro: Ron Clark; *Winged Foot* 9 Par: 36; Yardage: 3456; Rating: 36.7; *Thunderbird* 9 Par: 36; Yardage: 3315; Rating: 35.3; *Rolling Hills* 9 Par: 36; Yardage: 3451; Rating: 37.3; Course Architects: Jay Riviere (Winged Foot & Thunderbird) & Joe Finger (Rolling Hills); Closed Monday.
Guest Policy: You must be a guest of a member or a member of another private country club. Phone in advance to make arrangements.

RIVER PLANTATION GOLF & COUNTRY CLUB
A private club with three 9-hole courses
Location: 1 Country Club Drive
Golf Data: Pro Shop Phone: (409) 273-2611; Club Pro: Gary Sowinski; *Augusta* 9 Par: 36; Yardage: 3410; Rating: 36.8; *Biloxi* 9 Par: 36; Yardage: 3396;

Rating: 36.3; *Charleston* 9 Par: 35; Yardage: 3070; Rating: 35.1; Closed Monday.
Guest Policy: You must be a member of a reciprocating club. Pro may extend an invitation.

WEDGEWOOD COUNTRY CLUB
A private club with one 18-hole course
Location: Take Loop 336W to Longmeier, right 2½ miles
Golf Data: Pro Shop Phone: (409) 539-7349; Owner: Tom Negri; Par: 72; Yardage: 7069; Course Architects: Bill Rogers & Ron Prichard; Closed Monday.
Guest Policy: You must be a guest of a member.

Montgomery

CLUB DEL LAGO
A resort club with one 18-hole course
Location: 500 LaCosta Drive near Lake Conroe
Golf Data: Pro Shop Phone: (409) 582-6100; Director of Golf: Don Massengale; Par: 71; Yardage: 6825; Rating: 70.9; Course Architects: Jay Riviere & Dave Marr; Open 7 days.
Guest Policy: All play is welcome at this time.
NOTE: *For resort and golf package information, phone (800) 558-1317 (in Texas, (800) 833-3078) or (409) 582-6100, or write to Del Lago, ATT. Reservations, 600 Del Lago Blvd., Montgomery, TX 77356.*
Green Fees: $16 weekdays, $22 weekends and holidays; Carts: $16 for 18 holes ($12 for a single rider).
Tee Time Procedure: Call anytime if you plan to stay at resort; all others may call 1 week in advance.

WALDEN ON LAKE CONROE
A resort club with one 18-hole course
Location: 13101 Walden Drive at Lake Conroe
Golf Data: Pro Shop Phone: (409) 582-6441 or (713) 353-9737; Club Pro: Ron Colville; Par: 72; Yardage: 6765; Rating: 74.2; Open 7 days.
Guest Policy: You must play with a member on weekends or be a guest at the resort. Guests of members may play weekdays on a space available basis.
NOTE: *For resort conference, and golf package information, phone (409) 582-6441 or write to Walden on Lake*

Conroe, ATT. Reservations, Montgomery, TX 77356.
Green Fees: $21 weekdays, $27 weekends and holidays; Carts: $18 for 18 holes.

Willis

TEXAS NATIONAL COUNTRY CLUB
A public club with one 18-hole course
Location: 2 miles E. on FM 2432
Golf Data: Pro Shop Phone: (409) 539-2752 or (713) 353-2972; Club Pro: Bob Payne; Par: 72; Yardage: 6700; Rating: 72.6; Course Architect: Jack Miller; Open 7 days.
NOTE: *Home of Texas Golf Hall of Fame. Also, site of Houston Amateur Golf Association.*
Green Fees: $12 weekdays, $17 weekends and holidays; Carts: $15 for 18 holes.
Tee Time Procedure: Weekends-Holidays: Call anytime in advance; Weekdays: 1st come, 1st served.

Woodlands

WOODLANDS INN & COUNTRY CLUB
A semi-private resort club with three 18-hole courses
Location: I-45, exit Woodlands PKWY, go W. (see #54 on Harris County locator map)
North & West Golf Data: Pro Shop Phone: (713) 367-1100; Director of Golf: Kent Wood; *North* Par: 72; Yardage: 6881; Rating: 72.2; *West* Par: 72; Yardage: 6969; Rating: 72.6; Course Architects: Joe Lee (original 18) and Bruce Devlin & Bob Von Hagge (2nd 9s on North and West); Open 7 days.
Guest Policy: North courses is reserved for members, their guests and resort guests; the West course is strictly for members and their guests.
NOTE: *For resort and golf package information, phone (713) 756-7198 or write to Woodlands Inn & CC, ATT. Reservations, 2301 Midland, Woodlands, TX 77380.*
Green Fees: $20 weekdays, $25 weekends and holidays; Carts: $16 for 18 holes.
Tee Time Procedure: Call immediately after making resort reservations.

TPC Golf Data: Pro Shop Phone: (713) 367-7285; Director of Golf: Duke Butler; Par: 72; Yardage: 7045; Rating: 74.4; Course Architects: Bruce Devlin & Bob Von Hagge; Open 7 days.
NOTE: Site of Houston Open. Part of PGA-sponsored Tournament Players Club network.
Guest Policy: Daily fee course.
Green Fees: April-May: $50 anytime; March-June, September-November: $39 weekdays, $45 weekends and holidays; January-February, July-August, December: $29 weekdays, $36 weekends and holidays. All rates include carts.
Tee Time Procedure: Call up to two weeks in advance anytime.

———— NUECES ———— 24

Bishop

CHEMCEL GOLF CLUB
A private club with one 9-hole course
Golf Data: Celanese Phone: (512) 584-3511; Par: 72 (two sets of tees); Yardage: 6095; Open 7 days.
Guest Policy: You must play with a member. Will reciprocate with other Celanese Corp. clubs only.

Corpus Christi

Public Golf Courses

GABE LOZANO SENIOR GOLF CENTER
A public club with 27 holes
Location: 4401 Old Brownsville Road (see #2 on locator map)
Golf Data: Pro Shop Phone: (512) 883-3696; Club Pro: Bruce Haddad; 18-hole Par: 72; Yardage: 7115; Rating: 72.5; Executive 9 Par: 30; Yardage: 1947; Open 7 days.
Green Fees: $5.50 weekdays (Short 9: $2.50), $6.50 weekends and holidays (Short 9: $3); Carts: $10 for 18 holes ($6 for 9); Visa & MC accepted.
Tee Time Procedure: Weekends-Holidays: Wednesday at 8 a.m. by phone or in person; Weekdays: 1 day in advance.

OSO BEACH MUNICIPAL GOLF COURSE
A public club with one 18-hole course

Location: Off Ocean Drive at 5600 Alameda Drive (see #5 on locator map)
Golf Data: Pro Shop Phone: (512) 991-5351; Club Pro: Jimmie Taylor; Par: 70; Yardage: 6179; Rating: 67.4; Open 7 days.
Green Fees: $5.50 weekdays, $6.50 weekends and holidays; Carts: $10 for 18 holes. ($6 for 9).
Tee Time Procedure: Weekends-Holidays: 3 days in advance after 8 a.m. by phone or in person; Weekdays: Call 1 day in advance.

Private Golf Courses

CORPUS CHRISTI COUNTRY CLUB
A private club with one 18-hole course
Location: S. of Padre Island Drive at 6300 Everhart (see #1 on locator map)
Golf Data: Pro Shop Phone: (512) 991-7870; Club Pro: Tom Burke, Jr.; Par: 72; Yardage: 6574; Rating: 70.9; Course Architect: Robert Trent Jones; Open 7 days.
Guest Policy: You must be a member of another bonafide private country club. Phone for specifics.

KINGS CROSSING
A private club with one 18-hole course
Location: Intersection of S. Staples & Yorktown (see #3 on locator map)
Golf Data: Kings Crossing Phone: (512) 991-2582; Director of Golf: Charles Cowan; Par: 71; Yardage: 7010; Course Architect: Bill Coore.
Guest Policy: Will reciprocate with all U.S.G.A. clubs outside 75-mile radius.

N.A.S. GULF WINDS GOLF COURSE
A private club with one 18-hole course
Location: At the Naval Air Station (see #4 on locator map)
Golf Data: Pro Shop Phone: (512) 939-3250; Club Pro: Rudy Barranko; Par: 70; Yardage: 6337; Rating: 70.0; Open 7 days.
Guest Policy: You must be a member of the military or their guests.

PADRE ISLES COUNTRY CLUB
A private club with one 18-hole course
Location: North Padre Island at #1 Commodore Drive (see #6 on locator map)

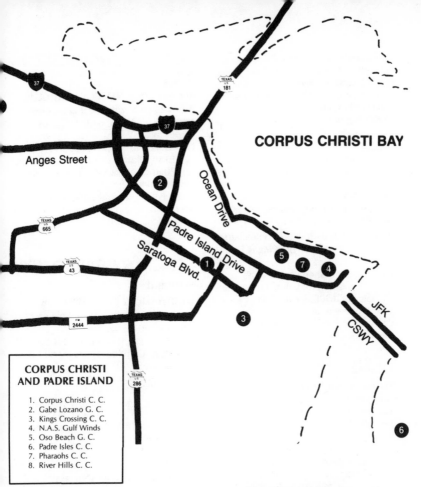

CORPUS CHRISTI BAY

Anges Street

Ocean Drive

Padre Island Drive

Saratoga Blvd.

JFK CSWY

**CORPUS CHRISTI
AND PADRE ISLAND**

1. Corpus Christi C. C.
2. Gabe Lozano G. C.
3. Kings Crossing C. C.
4. N.A.S. Gulf Winds
5. Oso Beach G. C.
6. Padre Isles C. C.
7. Pharaohs C. C.
8. River Hills C. C.

Golf Data: Pro Shop Phone: (512) 949-8006; Club Pro: Charles Eskridge; Par: 72; Yardage: 6650; Rating: 71.7; Course Architect: Bruce Littrell; Closed Monday.

Guest Policy: You must be a member of another U.S.G.A.-member private country club.

NOTE: Guest cards are also issued by area hotels and condominiums. For a list, phone (512) 882-5603 or write to the Corpus Christi Convention & Tourist Bureau, Box 2664, Corpus Christi, TX 78403.

Green Fees: $12 weekdays, $15 weekends and holidays; Carts: $15 for 18 holes.

Tee Time Procedure: Call 1 week in advance.

PHARAOHS COUNTRY CLUB
A private club with one 18-hole course
Location: S. off Padre Island Drive where Nile Crosses at 7111 Pharaoh (see #7 on locator map)

Golf Data: Pro Shop Phone: (512) 991-2477; Club Pro: David Scott; Par: 70; Yardage: 6409; Rating: 70.0; Closed Monday.

Guest Policy: You must be a guest of a member or a member of another private country club.

RIVER HILLS COUNTRY CLUB
A private club with one 18-hole course
Location: 1½ miles W. of HWY 77 at Robstown intersection (see #8 on locator map)

Golf Data: Pro Shop Phone: (512) 387-3563; Club Pro: Tom Inman; Par: 70;

Yardage: 6167; Rating: 67.2; Closed
Monday.

Guest Policy: You must be a guest of a
member or a member of another private
country club. Phone in advance for
specifics.

════ ORANGE ════ 25

Lawrence

**DUPONT EMPLOYEES RECREATION
ASSOCIATION**
A private club with one 18-hole course
Location: Intersection of Irving & FM
1006
Golf Data: Pro Shop Phone: (409)
886-1779; Club Pro: Jimmy Fetters; Par:
71; Yardage: 6300; Rating: 69.0; Closed
until Monday noon.
Guest Policy: You must play with a
member.

Orange

SUNSET GROVE COUNTRY CLUB
A private club with one 18-hole course
Location: 16th Street to Sunset Drive,
turn left
Golf Data: Pro Shop Phone: (409)
883-9454; Club Pro: Lonney Drucker;
Par: 71; Yardage: 6319; Rating: 69.0;
Closed Monday.
Guest Policy: You must play with a
member or be a member of another
private country club. Phone for specifics.

Vidor

RIVERWOOD GOLF COURSE
A semi-private club with one 18-hole
course
Location: 5 miles S. on HWY 105
Golf Data: Pro Shop Phone: (409)
768-1710; Club Manager: Howard Barlow; Par: 71; Yardage: 6771; Open 7
days.
Green Fees: $5.21 weekdays, $6.25
weekends and holidays; Carts: $10.41 for
18 holes.
Tee Time Procedure: Weekends-Holidays:
Call Wednesday after 6 p.m.; Weekdays:
1st come, 1st served.

════ REFUGIO ════ 26

Refugio

REFUGIO COUNTY COUNTRY CLUB
A private club with one 9-hole course
Location: 4 miles S. on HWY 77 to
Woodsboro HWY
Golf Data: Pro Shop Phone: (512)
526-9188; Club Manager: Anna Goforth;
Par: 70 (two sets of tees); Yardage: 5888;
Closed Monday.
Guest Policy: You must play with a
member or be a member of another
private country club.

════ SAN PATRICIO ════ 27

Portland

NORTH SHORE COUNTRY CLUB
A private club with one 18-hole course
Location: 801 Broadway
Golf Data: Pro Shop Phone: (512)
643-1546; Club Pro: James Black; Par:
72; Yardage: 6785; Rating: 71.7; Course
Architects: Bruce Devlin & Bob Von
Hagge; Closed Monday.
Guest Policy: You must play with a
member or be a member of a U.S.G.A. or
C.C.A. club. Only C.C.A. members may
charge back to club.

Sinton

SAN PATRICIO GOLF COURSE
A public club with one 18-hole course
Location: 2½ miles N. on HWY 181
Golf Data: Pro Shop Phone: (512)
364-9013; Club Manager: Bill Evans; Par:
72; Yardage: 6433; Rating: 69.5; Open 7
days.
Green Fees: $4 weekdays, $5 weekends
and holidays; Carts: $13.50 for 18 holes.
Tee Time Procedure: 1st come, 1st
served.

════ VICTORIA ════ 28

Victoria

COLONY CREEK COUNTRY CLUB
A private club with one 18-hole course
Location: HWY 59 to John Stockbauer
Road, take to 301 Colony Creek Drive

Golf Data: Pro Shop Phone: (512) 576-0018; Club Pro: Jim Brisbin; Par: 71; Yardage: 6400; Rating: 69.9; Course Architect: Dick Watson; Course open 7 days (clubhouse closed Tuesday).
Guest Policy: Members of out-of-town private country clubs call in advance.

RIVERSIDE GOLF CLUB
A public club with one 18-hole course
Location: In Riverside Municipal Park
Golf Data: Pro Shop Phone: (512) 573-4521; Club Pro: William F. Shelton; Par: 72; Yardage: 6599; Rating: 71.0; Closed Monday.
Green Fees: $7 weekdays, $9 weekends and holidays; Carts: $9.50 for 18 holes.
Tee Time Procedure: 1st come, 1st served.

VICTORIA COUNTRY CLUB
A private club with one 18-hole course
Location: 14 Spring Creek Road
NOTE: For next two years only one 9 holes will be open at time as course is being redesigned by the firm of Dye/ Shirley of Houston. Clay Edwards is the head professional. Phone for specifics (512) 575-6161.

━━━━━ WALKER ━━━━━ 29

Huntsville
COUNTRY CAMPUS PUBLIC COURSE
A public club with one 9-hole course
Location: 11 miles N. on HWY 19
Golf Data: Pro Shop Phone: (409) 291-6599; Club Manager: Paul Bilsing; Par: 74 (two sets of tees); Yardage: 6280; Rating: 69.5; Open 7 days.
Green Fees: $3.25 weekdays, $4.25 weekends and holidays; Carts: $10 for 18 holes.
Tee Time Procedure: Weekends-Holidays: Call Friday (or 1 day in advance); Weekdays: 1st come, 1st served.

ELKINS LAKE COUNTRY CLUB
A private club with one 18-hole course
Location: I-45 S, 2 miles, exit 75
Golf Data: Pro Shop Phone: (409) 295-4312; Club Pro: Ray Sarno; Par: 72; Yardage: 6640; Rating: 72.7; Course Architect: Ralph Plummer; Closed Monday.

Guest Policy: You must be a guest of a member. Pro may extend invitation.

━━━━━ WALLER ━━━━━ 30

Hempstead
HEMPSTEAD GOLF CLUB
A public club with one 9-hole course
Location: 1 mile W. on HWY 290
Golf Data: Pro Shop Phone: (409) 826-3212; Club Manager: Rick Blume; Par: 72 (two sets of tees); Yardage: 6595; Rating: 72.8; Open 7 days (closed Monday during winter).
Green Fees: $4 weekdays, $6 weekends and holidays; Carts: $12 for 18 holes ($8 if single rider).
Tee Time Procedure: 1st come, 1st served.

Waller
WALLER COUNTRY CLUB ESTATES
A semi-private club with one 9-hole course
Location: HWY 290W, HWY 362 left, go 4½ miles and follow signs
Golf Data: Pro Shop Phone: (409) 372-3672; Club Pro: Fred Weisner; Par: 70 (two sets of tees); Yardage: 6188; Closed Monday.
Green Fees: $6.25 weekdays, $9.50 weekends and holidays; Carts: $10.50 for 18 holes ($7.85 for single rider).
Tee Time Procedure: 1st come, 1st served.

━━━━━ WASHINGTON ━━━━━ 31

Brenham
BRENHAM COUNTRY CLUB
A private club with one 9-hole course
Location: 3 miles E. on HWY 105
Golf Data: Pro Shop Phone: (409) 836-1733; Club Pro: James Gillespie; Par: 36; Yardage: 3100; Rating: 68.2 (if 18 holes played); Closed Monday.
Guest Policy: Accepts daily green fee play, but one must call in advance.
Green Fees: $8 weekdays, $12 weekends and holidays; Carts: $7.50 + tax per 9 holes.

Tee Time Procedure: Weekends-Holidays: 1st come, 1st served before 10 a.m. (members' tee times start at 10); Weekdays: 1st come, 1st served.

——— WHARTON ——— 32

El Campo

EL CAMPO COUNTRY CLUB
A private club with one 9-hole course
Location: On Sandy Corner Road
Golf Data: Pro Shop Phone: (409) 543-6592; Club Pro: Gary Bueltel; Par: 71 (two sets of tees); Yardage: 6095; Rating: 68.5; Closed Monday.

Guest Policy: You are welcome as an out-of-town country club member. Phone pro for specifics.

Newgulf

NEWGULF ATHLETIC CLUB
A private club with one 9-hole course

Location: E. on HWY 1301
Golf Data: Pro Shop Phone: (409) 657-4639; Club Pro: Harry Norrell; Par: 72; Yardage: 6164; Rating: 69.0; Open 7 days.

Guest Policy: You must be a member of another private country club or a guest of a member.

Wharton

WHARTON COUNTRY CLUB
A private club with one 9-hole course
Location: On Country Club Drive
Golf Data: Pro Shop Phone: (409) 532-5940; Greens Supervisor: Bob Baker; Par: 71 (two sets of tees); Yardage: 6034; Rating: 71.0; Closed Monday.

Guest Policy: You are welcome as an out-of-town country club member or as a guest of a member.

1. Three U.S. Open golf tournaments have been held in Texas, none since 1969. Name the site and winner of one of the three.

Make Yourself a Better Putter

by Rives McBee
PGA Golf Professional

Have you ever asked yourself, after seeing PGA tour professionals on television make all those 5-, 10-, and 15-foot putts with such ease, how they do that with such consistency?

Well, if you have, join the club. It is amazing to see the ease with which these golfers make all those putts, but it shouldn't be a surprise to anyone who knows the inside details of the professional tour.

No, there is no secret drink or magic potion involved.

The answer is that these stars of the game are playing daily on the best conditioned golf courses in the world and the greens on which they earn their livings are pretty much the same from day to day.

The PGA tour has certain specifications which are maintained throughout the year and host facilities of tour events are required to adhere to these specifications to the letter. Naturally, conditions such as the weather do have a way of causing some of these to be impossible to comply with, but the key ingredient is the way the greens are maintained and prepared.

Steve Barley, director of golf course maintenance at Las Colinas Sports Club, host site of the Byron Nelson Classic, says that "most of the year we cut our greens at $3/16$th of an inch. In the summer months we raise our mowers to a quarter of an inch. And during the Nelson Classic and a couple of weeks before the tournament we lower the mowers to $1/8$th of an inch.

"This provides the players with smoother surfaces to play on and therefore they make more putts due to the consistency, which is what they are used to playing. The greens also firm up so that footprints and cleat marks don't show as much as they would normally."

John Anderson, director of golf course maintenance for the Bear Creek Golf Club at DFW Airport, also follows the same guidelines that Barley uses, but he never cuts the greens below the $3/16$th of an inch level due to the amount of play that Bear Creek has.

Since it is a resort open to the public the play is heavier than at most tour sites. Anderson is quick to add, however, "even though we are open to the public we try to put as much effort into making the course as enjoyable as a country club. We try to maintain it in the same way so that we can make golfers happy and they'll want to return.

"We recently switched from bermuda to bent grass greens on both our courses so that we could give the golfers a better putting surface. Naturally, bermuda grass is stronger and can take more play, but the quality facilities in this area try to maintain good bent grass greens and we felt we could eliminate the two transition periods by going to bent grass."

The transition periods Anderson refers to are the fall, when most bermuda courses have to overseed their greens with rye or bent grass to help them maintain a green color during the winter (since bermuda grass goes dormant after the first freeze) and the spring, when these grasses have to be taken out of the bermuda greens to allow the bermuda to grow.

Because the average Texas golfer plays several different courses and doesn't have the luxury of controlled putting surfaces, the types of grasses used for the greens within the state are important.

Cut of green can determine speed of putt.

Learning how to read and to putt the greens and the little things to make the task easier will make you a better putter.

For the purposes of putting consideration, Texas can be broken into four distinctive regions. The West Gulf Coastal Plain includes most of east and south Texas; the North Central Plains which covers an area from the Red River near Wichita Falls down through Abilene to Del Rio; the Great Plains encompasses the Panhandle and stretches south to Midland and Odessa, and The Trans Pecos region covers most of West Texas including El Paso.

These regions are important because there is a distinct borderline where particular grasses used for the various putting surfaces will thrive. Any facility east of this borderline should, and probably does, maintain bermuda grass greens. The only exceptions are at the most affluent clubs with large operating budgets, primarily in the Dallas-Fort Worth and Houston areas. The cost is too prohibitive for most small clubs or municipal courses to maintain bent grass greens in this area.

West of the borderline, bent grass is a common grass used for putting surfaces. The nights are cooler and the humidity is lower during the day which are a must for bent grass growth.

What are the characteristics of each type grass? What are their contributions to golf in Texas?

BERMUDA GRASS

There are several types of bermuda grasses in Texas. The most common types are the plain common bermuda and the hybrid (328 bermuda) which is used in the eastern regions of Texas.

Common bermuda is very large bladed and really has no texture to make a smooth surface for putting. Most common bermuda greens are not very large and the only drainage is the natural surface design of the green when it was built.

Most of the smaller clubs in east Texas have common bermuda because of its low-cost maintenance.

Unfortunately, putting on these surfaces can be a nightmare for they are usually grainy, bumpy, and not very true. If the grass is left too long, you can't hit a ball hard enough to get it to the hole and the ball will bounce all over the place on its way to the hole.

One good aspect, however, is you don't have many three putts because the greens aren't very large and you don't hit past the hole very often. It must be stressed, however, long bermuda greens can do a lot of damage to a good putting stroke and it is very difficult to go from fast greens to slow and then back to fast greens.

Rives McBee checks the contour of the green
to determine the break.

Hybrid or 328 bermuda is a much better putting surface. Because of its small grass blades, it can be kept like most bent grass greens. With a good maintenance program, which includes mowing in different directions each time and weekly brushings, hybrid bermuda can be as fast or faster than bent grass greens and putts true.

However, if not properly prepared, hybrid bermuda can become too thick and grainy—a miserable putting surface. You can never hit the ball hard enough and, when you do, the chances of the ball going into the hole are slim at best.

There are not many things a golfer can do in this situation but grin and bear it and do the best he can under the circumstances. However, some people with poor putting strokes like slow, bumpy greens because it puts them on the same level as a good putter.

The best advice for playing slow bermuda greens is to try to figure out which direction the water drains off the green, look for the direction the grain is going, use a heavier putter, and . . . do the best you can.

On a good hybrid bermuda green with good subsurface drainage, it is almost impossible to find the grain. It's best to check the direction of the prevailing wind gusts and to determine which direction is west.

Most bermuda greens will grow in the direction of the prevailing wind and towards the setting sun. This is one of the only ways to read big, flat bermuda greens.

Naturally, if there are undulations, you must follow the "lay of the land" and allow for the contours.

Overseeded bermuda is even harder to putt because in most cases the grass is new and will grow in all directions. It is also slower than normal. In this case, don't read any break into short putts. Stroke them firmly into the center of the hole.

BENT GRASS

Bent grass greens are the finest putting surfaces in the world. The ball rolls truer and smoother without the normal hop you get from bermuda grass. Bent grass greens are usually fast putting surfaces and a light putter generally works best. A golfer with a good putting touch can become a magician on smooth, slightly undulating greens and can make others scratch their heads in disbelief.

But, beware. In some cases, where the maintenance program is not up to par, bent grass greens can be a horror show if allowed to become too wet and spongy. Footprints can be seen all over and cleat marks look like mountains to putt over to get to the hole.

Even on well maintained bent grass some spike marks do show up. This is a case of a careless golfer not having respect for his fellow golfer's problem of having to putt over "his" mistake. When you leave the green, tap down your spike marks with your putter and leave the green in the same condition you found it—or even better if the case may arise.

Reading bent grass greens is the same as reading bermuda grass. You need to figure out the drainage of the green (where water rolls off the green), the prevailing wind, and the direction of the setting sun.

In mountainous regions, it is to your advantage to know the dominant mountain nearest the course because putts will break "away" from that mountain even though it looks like it will break toward it.

Another factor is whether a green is wet or dry. If it is wet, it will be slower, if dry, faster.

In the spring when the grass is growing the green will be slightly slower than during the summer and winter. Also, grass grows during the day and will be slightly slower at the end of the day, unless they have had a lot of traffic, in which case they will be faster and bumpier.

In putting at the end of the day short putts are tougher because of the amount of footwear around the cup. Towards the end of the day the cup may actually be raised slightly and cause putts to fall off to the right or left of the hole. Hit these putts with authority. Naturally, no one stepped on the cup, but they did step within a foot of the hole to retrieve their ball.

Another tip to better bent grass green putting is to watch for the direction the maintenance crew mowed the greens the day you play. The light colored grass means the mower was going away from you. The putt should roll better and be a little faster than normal. If the grass has a darker color, the mower was coming towards you. Your putt will be a little slower because the grain is in your direction. If you can see both colors in several rows as you look toward the cup, you will putt across the direction the mowers cut that morning. The speed of your putt will vary all the way to the hole.

One factor affecting the putting on both bent grass and bermuda greens is the wind condition. In Texas, and on bent grass particularly, the wind can actually play a part in your putting game. On very windy days you must have a strong constitution because putts can actually be blown out of the hole or even off the green!

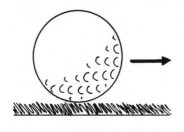

Ball putted into the grain will have a tendency to bounce and take away some of the roll. Ball must be hit harder to get the ball to the hole.

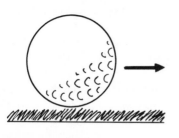

Ball putted down grain or with the grain will have a tendency to roll a little faster than normal. Ball must be stroked with this in mind and allowances made for the grain.

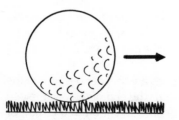

Ball putted cross grain will have a tendency to break more in the direction the grain is growing. If the natural contour calls for the ball to break to the left and the grain is also going to the left, a little more break should be read into the putt.

The key is to use the wind to your advantage. Downwind, the ball will roll faster; into the wind, the ball needs to be hit harder; and with a cross wind, more break should be allowed for the wind and the direction it is blowing. The wind can actually make a naturally breaking putt go straight.

Texas has produced some of the finest golfers in the world over the years and their training on some of the best golf courses anywhere has helped and will continue to help prepare them for the challenges faced. To become great golfers they had to learn to putt well under very difficult conditions. Texas offered, and offers, that variety.

Choose a putter that suits your individual taste and stick with it as long as possible. Don't be changing putters or putting strokes all the time. It will only make your putting game worse.

The best advice anyone can give a weekend golfer is to *use the practice green*. Learn to read putts. Learn how the grain will affect your putting stroke. Learn how the wind will affect your putting stroke. Learn what affect water has on your putting stroke.

And practice . . . practice . . . practice!

(Rives McBee is a teaching pro in the Dallas area, who has played the PGA Tour for five years and has served as head professional at Las Colinas C.C. and Las Colinas Sports Club. In 1966, after qualifying for the U.S. Open, he tied the tournament and course record, a 64 at Olympia Club in San Francisco. He also won the 1973 National Club Pro Championship at Pinehurst, NC.)

   2. Where is the Texas Golf Hall of Fame located?

Don't Panic in the Wind!

by Art Hodde
PGA Golf Professional

Wind is probably a golfer's worst enemy. And as a result most people are afraid to play in the wind.

In Texas, a golfer *has* to learn to play in windy conditions.

You must alter your strategy and not let the wind distract you. A golfer must remember that in windy conditions scores, not only for yourself but for others, will be two to three shots higher. As a result, you should not panic but rather play within yourself.

The two most important things to remember are choose the right club and don't overswing. Other adjustments must be made according to the direction the wind is blowing.

To check wind direction toss some grass in the air, look at tree tops, observe other people's shots, and if you can see the pin, check the direction the flag is blowing. If there is water nearby, the lake will look choppy downwind and calm upwind.

Most golfers underplay the wind—dramatically. They adjust by one club when they should be thinking three or four clubs. U.S. Golf Association research shows that wind can drastically affect the flight of the ball, cutting down distance by as much as 30 percent into the wind and increasing distance by over 20 percent with the wind. For example, if you normally hit your tee shot 249 yards it might only travel 190 yards into a 20 mph wind.

Into the wind the ball will fly higher and roll less. Extra roll can be considerable with the wind at your back, even with a short iron.

Balance and set-up are important in hitting wind shots. Your weight should be balanced between the ball and the heel of the foot and you may want to widen your stance slightly when hitting into the wind or into a crosswind. Swing normally. Don't let the wind rush you into a quick swing.

Wind can also affect putting. It's important to remain still during your putting stroke. A wider stance helps.

Learn the affects of wind and play within yourself.

Normal set-up under normal wind conditions.

Ball positioned normal instance but teed tilted back to accelerate lift with the wind.

Ball positioned back in stance and teed forward to encourage low trajectory into the wind.

HEADWIND

When playing into a headwind it is a cinch you are going to lose yardage. Don't make the mistake of trying to swing harder to compensate. Take from one to four clubs more, depending upon the strength of the wind, and make a three-quarter swing to maintain your balance.

Play the ball slightly back—an inch or two—in your normal stance. Also, place more weight on your left side at address and keep it there throughout the swing to encourage a low trajectory. You should also square your clubface to the target.

Tee your ball slightly forward on your tee shots to encourage striking the ball with a descending blow which will help keep the trajectory low.

Remember, on a pitch shot the ball will stop quickly as the wind adds backspin to the shot. Use a less lofted club to encourage run and to make sure the ball gets to the hole.

On putts into the wind you should strike the ball harder.

DOWNWIND

When playing with the wind, the ball will travel farther. Take one or two clubs less depending upon the strength of the wind and take a three-quarter swing to help maintain your balance.

The tendency here is to try for that "really long ball" and overswing. Take your normal stance and make a normal swing. *Play within yourself.*

On your tee shot, place your ball on the tee pointed slightly to the rear which will encourage hitting the ball on the upswing, getting more loft.

Remember that on a pitch shot, the wind will take the spin off the ball and it will run more than a normal pitch. Use a more lofted club and concentrate on hitting down at impact to impart greater spin.

You may not have to hit your putts as hard with the wind at your back.

CROSSWIND

A crosswind is likely to affect your shots in two ways—loss of distance and accuracy. It's wise to use more club than you normally would and allow for drift.

In other words, if the wind is blowing from left to right, aim somewhat to the left of target depending on strength of wind; if the wind is from right to left, aim somewhat to the right to compensate.

Also, if you tend to slice or fade, a left to right wind will accentuate the movement, and if the wind is right to left, you won't slice as much.

You will have to aim further left of target or as not as far left depending upon your situation. The reverse is true for a right to left wind.

It is also important to note from which side of the fairway you are approaching the target. If the wind is left to right and you are on the right side of the fairway, you'll be hitting into a quartering wind and need more club to reach the target. If you are on the left side, the wind will tend to favor your shot and you'll need less club. The reverse is true for a right to left wind.

Remember on pitch shots, the direction of the wind may impart spin so that when the ball hits the green it may jump left or right depending on direction of the wind. You may have to aim further right or left to compensate accordingly.

A crosswind may affect your putting, increasing or decreasing the amount of break on a putt depending on the wind direction. For example, a wind from the left with a left breaking putt may increase the break and must be allowed for.

Learn how to play in all conditions and play within yourself to make golf a more enjoyable game.

(Art Hodde is head professional at Riverbend C. C. in Stafford and a member of the Texas Golf Hall of Fame. He has served as President, Secretary and Treasurer of the Southern Texas PGA.)

3. This female golf legend from Beaumont has been called the greatest woman athlete of all time. Who is she?

The Metroplex

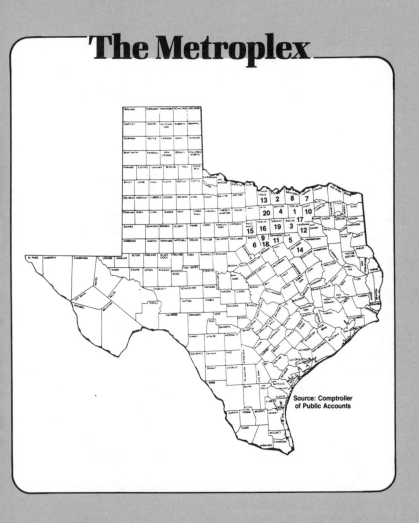

Source: Comptroller
of Public Accounts

More golf courses are under construction within the Metroplex than any other region.

Ten new courses are scheduled to open in 1987 and over 10 more are on the drawing board.

They will be added to 116 golf courses now open for play. Thirty-eight are public, 18 semi-private, 65 private and there is one resort.

THE METROPLEX CITIES

4. Where did the present day Senior PGA Golf Tour get its start?

No. 17 at Bear Creek West

═══════ COLLIN ═══════ 1

Anna

HURRICANE CREEK COUNTRY CLUB
A private club with one 18-hole course
Location: I-75, exit 48W, right on Service
Road 1¾ miles
Golf Data: Pro Shop Phone: (214)
924-3247; Club Pro: Don Bonner; Par:
72; Yardage: 7054; Rating: 73.8; Course
Architect: Leon Howard; Closed Monday.
Guest Policy: You must be sponsored by
a member. Phone pro for specifics.

Frisco

STONEBRIAR COUNTRY CLUB
A private club with one 18-hole course
Location: At intersection of Loop 121
and Carpenter Road
NOTE: *18 holes designed by Finger, Dye
& Shirley is scheduled to open in the Fall
1987 or Spring 1988.*

McKinney

EL DORADO COUNTRY CLUB
A private club with one 18-hole course
Location: Exit 39, going North on HWY
75

Golf Data: Pro Shop Phone: (214)
542-2666; Club Pro: Harold Haren; Par:
72; Yardage: 6559; Rating: 70.7; Course
Architect: Gary Roger Baird; Closed
Monday.
Guest Policy: You must play with a
member. That member does not have to
be present, but guest fees vary if not with
member. Golf professional may extend
invitation. Phone golf shop first.

McKINNEY COUNTRY CLUB
A private club with one 9-hole course
Location: 1 mile E. of HWY 5 on FM
1378
Golf Data: Pro Shop Phone: (214)
524-7731; Club Pro: Jerry Estes; Par: 72
(two sets of tees); Yardage: 6068; Rating:
69.3; Closed Monday.
Guest Policy: You must play as a guest of
a member or be a member of another
U.S.G.A. club.

McKINNEY MUNICIPAL GOLF COURSE
A public club with one 9-hole course
Location: HWY 380 to HWY 5N 1½
miles
Golf Data: Pro Shop Phone: (214)
542-4523; Club Manager: W. C. Spenser;
Par: 36; Yardage: 3395; Open 7 days.

Green Fees: $5.50 weekdays, $6.50 weekends and holidays; Carts: $6.80 for 9 holes.

Tee Time Procedures: 1st come, 1st served.

STONEBRIDGE RANCH

A private club with two 18-hole courses

Location: N. of El Dorado PKWY and S. of HWY 380, between Preston Road and N. Central EXPY

NOTE: Two 18-hole courses, one designed by Art Hills and the other by Pete Dye, are scheduled to open in 1988.

Plano

Public Golf Courses

CHASE OAKS GOLF COURSE

A public club with 27 holes

Location: I-75 N, exit 32, take S. Access Road to entrance (see #38 on Dallas locator map)

Golf Data: Pro Shop Phone: (214) 422-0044; Director of Golf: Gary Dee; *Blackjack* 18 Par: 72; Yardage: 6811; Rating: 73.3; *Sawtooth* (duals 9s) Par: 72; Yardage: 6449; Rating: 71.2; Course Architects: Bruce Devlin & Bob Von Hagge; Open 7 days.

NOTE: 3rd 9 has completely separate tee boxes hitting to the same green to create 18 holes.

Green Fees: Blackjack: $25 weekdays, $35 weekends and holidays; Sawtooth: $20 weekdays, $25 weekends and holidays; Carts: $20 for 18 holes; AX, Visa & MC accepted.

Tee Time Procedure: 3 days in advance at noon by phone or in person.

PLANO MUNICIPAL GOLF COURSE

A public club with one 18-hole course

Location: I-75, exit 15th Street E., right to 14th Street, left (see #41 on Dallas locator map)

Golf Data: Pro Shop Phone: (214) 423-5444; Club Pro: Rich Richeson; Par: 72; Yardage: 6789; Rating: 71.8; Course Architects: Don January & Dick Jennings; Open 7 days.

Green Fees: $8 weekdays, $10 weekends and holidays; Carts: $13.80 for 18 holes. Special senior and junior rates weekdays.

Tee Time Procedure: Weekends: Plano residents 6:45 a.m. Thursday in person (or lottery at 6:30 p.m.), non-Plano residents 7:30 a.m. Friday by phone; (Holidays: Call 2 days in advance); Weekdays: 1st come, 1st served.

DALLAS AND SURROUNDING AREA

DALLAS

1. Cedar Crest G. C.
2. Grover C. Keeton G. C.
3. L. B. Houston G. C.
4. Stevens Park G. C.
5. Tenison Park G. C.
6. Bent Tree C. C.
7. Brookhaven C. C.
8. Brook Hollow C. C.
9. Dallas Athletic Club
10. Dallas C. C.
11. EDS G. C.
12. Lakewood C. C.
13. The Northwood Club
14. Oak Cliff C. C.
15. Preston Trail C. C.
16. Prestonwood C. C.
17. Royal Oaks C. C.
18. Sleepy Hollow C. C.

COPPELL

19. River Chase C. C.

CARROLLTON

20. Columbian C. C.
21. Country Place G. C.
22. Indian Creek G. C.

DALLAS/FORT WORTH AIRPORT

23. Bear Creek G. C.

DeSOTO

24. Thorntree C. C.

GARLAND

25. Eastern Hills C. C.
26. Firewheel Golf Park
27. Oakridge C. C.

GRAND PRAIRIE

28. Grand Prairie Municipal G. C.
29. Sunset G. C.
30. Woodcrest C. C.

GRAPEVINE

31. Grapevine Municipal G. C.

IRVING

32. Hackberry Creek C. C.
33. Las Colinas C. C.
34. Las Colinas Sports Club

LEWISVILLE

35. Oak Ridge Park G. C.

MESQUITE

36. Falcon's Lair C. C.
37. Mesquite Municipal G. C.

PLANO

38. Chase Oaks G. C.
39. Gleneagles C. C.
40. Los Rios C. C.
41. Plano Municipal G. C.

RICHARDSON

42. Canyon Creek C. C.
43. Sherrill Park G. C.

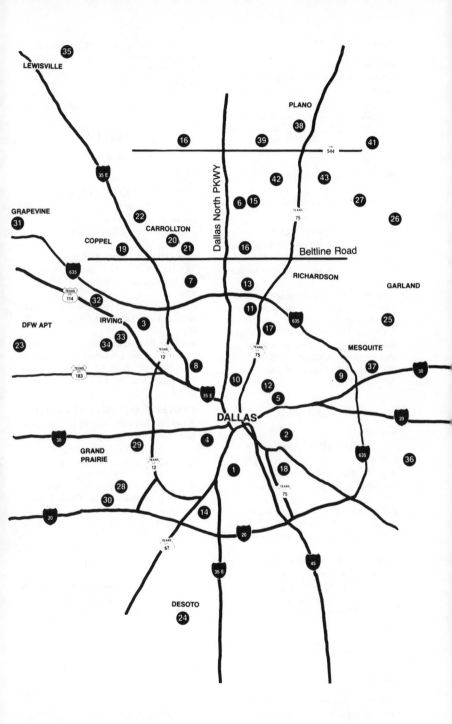

LEWISVILLE

PLANO

Dallas North PKWY

GRAPEVINE

CARROLLTON

COPPEL

Beltline Road

RICHARDSON

GARLAND

DFW APT

IRVING

MESQUITE

DALLAS

GRAND
PRAIRIE

DESOTO

47

Private Country Clubs

GLENEAGLES COUNTRY CLUB
A private club with two 18-hole courses
Location: I-75, exit FM 544 W (see #39 on Dallas locator map)
Golf Data: Pro Shop Phone: (214) 867-8888; Club Pro: Will Brewer; *Kings* Par: 71; Yardage: 6707; Rating: 72.5; *Queens* Par: 71; Yardage: 6886; Rating: 73.2; Course Architects: Bruce Devlin & Bob Von Hagge (both courses); Closed Monday.
Guest Policy: You must play with a member.

LOS RIOS COUNTRY CLUB
A private club with one 18-hole course
Location: I-75, exit Plano PKWY E., right on FM 544 (see #40 on Dallas locator map)
Golf Data: Pro Shop Phone: (214) 424-8913; Club Pro: Carl Crawley; Par: 71; Yardage: 6531; Rating: 70.7; Course Architect: Don January; Closed Monday.
Guest Policy: You must be a guest of a member or a member of a C.C.A.-managed club. Phone for specifics.

─────── COOKE ─────── 2

Gainesville

GAINESVILLE MUNICIPAL GOLF COURSE
A public club with one 18-hole course
Location: I-35, exit HWY 82W, 3 miles to Weber Drive
Golf Data: Pro Shop Phone: (817) 665-2161; Club Manager: Butch Links; Par: 71; Yardage: 6315; Rating: 68.5; Open 7 days.
Green Fees: $4 weekdays, $6 weekends and holidays; Carts: $10.50 for 18 holes.
Tee Time Procedures: Weekends: Phone Thursday morning; Holidays: two days in advance; Weekdays: 1st come, 1st served.

Lake Kiowa

LAKE KIOWA GOLF COURSE
A private club with one 18-hole course
Location: 8½ miles E. of Gainesville on FM 902
Golf Data: Pro Shop Phone: (817) 668-7394; Club Pro: Brown McCrory;

Par: 72; Yardage: 6636; Rating: 71.4; Closed Monday.
Guest Policy: You must play with a member.

─────── DALLAS ─────── 3

Public Golf Courses

Dallas

CEDAR CREST GOLF COURSE
A public club with one 18-hole course
Location: I-35 S, exit Illinois, left to Sutherland, left 3 blocks (see #1 on locator map)
Golf Data: Pro Shop Phone: (214) 943-1004; Club Pro: Leonard Jones: Par: 71; Yardage: 6550; Rating: 71; Open 7 days.
Green Fees: $8.50 weekdays, $10 weekends and holidays; Carts: $13.50 for 18 holes.
Tee Time Procedures: Weekends: Dallas residents 6 a.m. Thursdays in person, non-Dallas residents 12 noon by phone; Weekdays-Holidays: Call 2 days in advance.

GROVER C. KEETON GOLF COURSE
A public club with one 18-hole course
Location: I-30 E, exit Jim Miller Road, right 2.2 miles (see #2 on locator map)
Golf Data: Pro Shop Phone: (214) 388-4831; Club Pro: Kim J. Brown; Par: 72; Yardage: 6511; Rating: 70.2; Course Architect: David Bennett; Open 7 days.
NOTE: In 1983, American Society of Golf Course Architects ranked in top 25 new courses in the last 5 years.
Green Fees: $8.50 weekdays, $10 weekends and holidays; Carts: $14.33 for 18 holes.
Tee Time Procedures: Weekends: Dallas residents 6 a.m. Thursday in person, non-Dallas residents 12 noon by phone; Weekdays-Holidays: Call 2 days in advance.

L. B. HOUSTON GOLF COURSE
A public club with one 18-hole course
Location: From I-35, exit Royal Lane W., left at Luna Road (see #3 on locator map)
Golf Data: Pro Shop Phone: (214) 869-1778; Club Pro: Mickey Carey; Par:

72; Yardage: 6705; Rating: 71.8; Open 7 days.

Green Fees: $8.50 weekdays, $10 weekends and holidays; Carts: $14.33 for 18 holes.

Tee Time Procedures: Weekends: Dallas residents 6 a.m. Thursday in person, non-Dallas residents 12 noon by phone; Weekdays-Holidays: Call 2 days in advance.

STEVENS PARK GOLF COURSE
A public club with one 18-hole course
Location: I-30 W, exit Sylvan, left and follow signs (see #4 on locator map)
Golf Data: Pro Shop Phone: (214) 670-7506; Club Pro: Jimmy Powell; Par: 71; Yardage: 6305; Rating: 68.5; Open 7 days.

Green Fees: $8.50 weekdays, $10 weekends and holidays; Carts: $14.33 for 18 holes.

Tee Time Procedures: Weekends: Dallas residents 6 a.m. Thursday in person, non-Dallas residents at 12 noon by phone; Weekdays-Holidays: Call 2 days in advance.

TENISON PARK GOLF COURSE
A public club with two 18-hole courses
Location: I-30 E, exit Dolphin, left at Samuel (see #5 on locator map)
Golf Data: Pro Shop Phone: (214) 823-5350; Club Pro: Bob Smith; *East* Par: 72; Yardage: 6762; Rating: 71.5; *West* Par: 71; Yardage: 6862; Rating: 71.2; Open 7 days.

Green Fees: $8.50 weekdays, $10 weekends and holidays; Carts: $14.33 for 18 holes.

Tee Time Procedures: Weekends: Dallas residents 5 a.m. Thursday in person, non-Dallas residents 12 noon by phone; Weekdays-Holidays: Call 2 days in advance.

Garland
FIREWHEEL GOLF PARK
A public club with one 18-hole course
Location: I-75 N, exit Campbell Road E., follow signs (see #25 on locator map)
Golf Data: Pro Shop Phone: (214) 494-7136; Club Pro: Jerry Andrews; Par: 72; Yardage: 7061; Rating: 73.0; Course Architect: Dick Phelps; Closed Tuesday.

NOTE: Second 18 holes scheduled to open in late summer 1987.
Green Fees: $12 weekdays, $18 weekends and holidays; Carts: $15 for 18 holes.

Tee Time Procedure: Thursday at 8 a.m. for following week (until next Thursday).

Grand Prairie
GRAND PRAIRIE MUNICIPAL GOLF COURSE
A public club with 27 holes
Location: I-20 W, exit 1382, right 1 mile (see #27 on locator map)
Golf Data: Pro Shop Phone: (214) 264-1100; Club Pro: Jan Smith; *Red* 9 Par: 36; Yardage: 3209; *White* 9 Par: 35; Yardage: 3026; *Blue* 9 Par: 36; Yardage: 3267; Open 7 days.

Green Fees: $8 weekdays, $9 weekends and holidays; Carts: $11.60 for 18 holes.

Tee Time Procedures: Weekends: Thursday, 7 a.m. in person, after 8 a.m. by phone (Holidays: Call 2 days in advance); Weekdays: 1st come, 1st served.

SUNSET GOLF COURSE
A public club with one 9-hole course
Location: I-30 W, exit Loop 12S, HWY 80 W (see #28 on locator map)
Golf Data: Pro Shop Phone: (214) 337-9303; Club Pros: Kenny & Bob Mims; Par: 36; Yardage: 3205; Rating: 69.9 (if 18 holes played); Open 7 days.

Green Fees: $5.50 weekdays, $6.50 weekends and holidays; Carts: $5.50 per 9 holes.

Tee Time Procedure: 1st come, 1st served.

Mesquite
MESQUITE MUNICIPAL GOLF COURSE
A public club with one 18-hole course
Location: I-30 E, exit Beltline, go under to Service Road, then left (see #37 on locator map)
Golf Data: Pro Shop Phone: (214) 270-7457; Club Pro: David Lipscomb; Par: 71; Yardage: 6925; Rating: 72.9; Course Architects: Jarvis, Putty & Jarvis; Open 7 days.

Green Fees: $5 weekdays, $7 weekends and holidays; Carts: $13.14 for 18 holes.

Tee Time Procedures: Weekends: Thursday at 8 a.m. in person or by phone (Holidays: Call 2 days in advance); Weekdays: 1st come, 1st served.

Richardson

SHERRILL PARK MUNICIPAL GOLF COURSE
A municipal club with two 18-hole courses
Location: I-75, exit Campbell Road E., Jupiter Road N. (see #43 on locator map)
Golf Data: Pro Shop Phone: (214) 234-1416; Club Pro: Ronnie Glanton; *#1* Par: 72; Yardage: 6800; Rating: 72.0; *#2* Par: 70; Yardage: 6083; Rating: 66.0; Course Architect: Leon Howard; Open 7 days.
Green Fees: $5 weekdays, $7 weekends and holidays; Carts: $12.20 for 18 holes.
Tee Time Procedures: Weekends: Richardson residents 12 noon (draw numbers at 11 a.m.) Thursday, non-Richardson residents 8 a.m. Friday in person or by phone (Holidays: same procedure, 2 days in advance); Weekdays: 1st come, 1st served.

Private Country Clubs

Carrollton

COLUMBIAN COUNTRY CLUB
A private club with one 18-hole course
Location: I-35, exit Beltline E., left at Country Club Road (see #20 on locator map)
Golf Data: Pro Shop Phone: (214) 242-6496; Club Pro: Tom Galvin; Par: 71; Yardage: 6747; Rating: 73.0; Course Architects: Ralph Plummer (original 9), Leon Howard (additional 9) & Joe Finger (revised 18); Closed Monday.
Guest Policy: You must be invited by and play with a member.

COUNTRY PLACE GOLF CLUB
A private club with one 9-hole Par 3 course
Location: I-635, exit Marsh Lane N., left at Country Place Drive (see #21 on locator map)
Golf Data: Pro Shop Phone: (214) 245-9304; Golf Pro: Fran Bealmear; Par: 27; Yardage: 1245; Closed Monday.
Guest Policy: You must play with a member. Phone for specifics.

Coppell

RIVER CHASE COUNTRY CLUB
A private club with one 18-hole course
Location: I-35, Sandy Lake exit W., left at MacArthur (see #19 on locator map)
NOTE: 18-hole course designed by George and Jim Fazio is scheduled to open late 1987-early 1988.

Dallas

BENT TREE COUNTRY CLUB
A private club with one 18-hole course
Location: North Dallas Pkwy. N., right on Westgrove (see #6 on locator map)
Golf Data: Pro Shop Phone: (214) 931-3310; Club Pro: David Price; Par: 72; Yardage: 7265; Rating: 74.8; Course Architect: Desmond Muirhead; Closed Monday.
NOTE: Site of Senior Players (PGA) Reunion Pro-Am.
Guest Policy: You must play with a member or be a member of another private country club. Phone for specifics.

BROOKHAVEN COUNTRY CLUB
A private club with three 18-hole courses
Location: I-635, exit Marsh Lane N., left at Brookhaven (see #7 on locator map)
Golf Data: Pro Shop Phone: (214) 241-2761; Club Pro: Ras Allen; *Masters* (All Men) Par: 72; Yardage: 7058; Rating: 72.8; *Championship* Par: 72; Yardage: 6720; Rating: 71.3; *Presidents* Par: 72; Yardage: 5812; Rating: 65.1; Closed Monday.
NOTE: Site of Texas State Junior Girls Championship.
Guest Policy: You must be a guest of a member or a member of another private country club.

BROOK HOLLOW COUNTRY CLUB
A private club with one 18-hole course
Location: 8301 Harry Hines Blvd. (see #8 on locator map)
Golf Data: Pro Shop Phone: (214) 637-1914; Club Pro: Robert Hoyt; Par: 71; Yardage: 6713; Rating: 71.0; Course Architect: Alfred Tillinghast; Closed Monday.
Guest Policy: Out-of-town guests must be sponsored by member.

DALLAS ATHLETIC CLUB
A private club with two 18-hole courses
Location: I-635, exit LaPrada, right to entrance (see #9 on locator map)
Golf Data: Pro Shop Phone: (214) 279-6515; Club Pro: Dennis Ewing; *Blue* Par: 72; Yardage: 6710; Rating: 73.4; Course Architect: Jack Nicklaus (redesign 1986); *Gold* Par: 70; Yardage: 6553; Rating: 70.8; Course Architect: Ralph Plummer; Closed Monday.
NOTE: Original Blue course site of 1963 PGA Tournament.
Guest Policy: You must play with a member.

DALLAS COUNTRY CLUB
A private club with one 18-hole course
Location: 4110 Beverly (see #10 on locator map)
Golf Data: Pro Shop Phone: (214) 521-3520; Club Pro: Billy Harris; Par: 70; Yardage: 6266; Rating: 69.6; Course Architects: Ralph Plummer & Byron Nelson (Jay Morrish: redesign); Closed Monday.
Guest Policy: You must be a guest of a member.

EDS GOLF COURSE
A private club with one 9-hole course
Location: I-75, exit Forest Lane W. to EDS entrance (see #11 on locator map)
Golf Data: Pro Shop Phone: (214) 661-6065; Club Manager: Mark Robinson; Par: 35; Yardage: 2930; Open 7 days.
NOTE: EDS headquarters and golf course once grounds for Preston Hollow Country Club and site of 1956 Dallas Centennial and Texas International Opens, forerunners to today's Byron Nelson Classic.
Guest Policy: For EDS employees and their guests only.

LAKEWOOD COUNTRY CLUB
A private club with one 18-hole course
Location: 6430 Gaston Avenue (see #12 on locator map)
Golf Data: Pro Shop Phone: (214) 821-7690; Club Pro: Cary Collins; Par: 71; Yardage: 6584; Rating: 71.0; Course Architect: Ralph Plummer; Closed Monday.

Guest Policy: You must play with a member.

THE NORTHWOOD CLUB
A private club with one 18-hole course
Location: 6524 Alpha Lane (see #13 on locator map)
Golf Data: Pro Shop Phone: (214) 934-0544; Club Pro: Bob Elliott; Par: 71; Yardage: 6775; Rating: 72.0; Course Architect: William H. Diddell; Closed Monday.
NOTE: Site of 1952 U.S.G.A. Open.
Guest Policy: You must be accompanied by member.

OAK CLIFF COUNTRY CLUB
A private club with one 18-hole course
Location: I-35, exit HWY 67S to Red Bird Lane, left (see #14 on locator map)
Golf Data: Pro Shop Phone: (214) 333-3595; Club Pro: Mark Eaves; Par: 70; Yardage: 6474; Rating: 70.7; Closed Monday.
Guest Policy: You must be guest of a member or a member of another private country club. Phone for specifics.

PRESTON TRAIL GOLF CLUB
A private club with one 18-hole course
Location: 17201 Preston Trail Drive (see #15 on locator map)
Golf Data: Pro Shop Phone: (214) 248-8448; Club Pro: Bob Goetz; Par: 71; Yardage: 7003; Rating: 72.1; Course Architect: Ralph Plummer; Closed Monday.
Guest Policy: You must play with a member. Men only club (you must be 21 years old).

PRESTONWOOD COUNTRY CLUB
A private club with two 18-hole courses
Location: Creek Course: 15909 Preston Road; Hills Course: Midway N., left at W. Plano PKWY, right at LaCosta (see #16 on locator map)
Golf Data: Creek Pro Shop Phone: (214) 233-6166; Club Pro: Cotton Dunn; Par: 71; Yardage: 6659; Rating: 72.0; Closed Monday; Hills Pro Shop Phone: (214) 307-1508; Par: 72; Yardage: 6843; Rating: 71.5; Course Architect: Dave Bennett; Closed Monday.
Guest Policy: Reciprocal policy requires guest to play with a member. Phone pro for an introduction.

ROYAL OAKS COUNTRY CLUB
A private club with one 18-hole course
Location: 7915 Greenville Avenue (see #17 on locator map)
Golf Data: Pro Shop Phone: (214) 691-0339; Club Pro: Randy Smith; Par: 71; Yardage: 6938; Rating: 74.3; Course Architects: Don January & Billy Martindale (original), Jay Morrish (redesign); Closed Monday.
Guest Policy: You must play with a member.

SLEEPY HOLLOW GOLF & COUNTRY CLUB
A private club with two 18-hole courses
Location: 4747 S Loop 12 (see #18 on locator map)
Golf Data: Pro Shop Phone: (214) 371-3430; Club Pro: Joe Dreisbach; *River* Par: 71; Yardage: 7044; Rating: 73.4; *Lake* Par: 70; Yardage: 6052; Rating: 68.3; Closed Monday.
Guest Policy: You must be a guest of a member or a member of another private country club. Phone for specifics.

DeSoto

THORNTREE COUNTRY CLUB
A private club with one 18-hole course
Location: I-35 S, exit Wintergreen, W. 3½ miles (see #24 on locator map)
Golf Data: Pro Shop Phone: (214) 296-7317; Club Pro: Mark Mai; Par: 72; Yardage: 6915; Rating: 72.3; Course Architects: The Mai Family; Closed Monday.
Guest Policy: You must play with a member or be a member of another private country club. Phone for specifics.

Garland

EASTERN HILLS COUNTRY CLUB
A private club with one 18-hole course
Location: 3000 Country Club Drive (see #25 on locator map)
Golf Data: Pro Shop Phone: (214) 278-3051; Club Pro: Gail Davis; Par: 70; Yardage: 6492; Rating: 71.5; Closed Monday.
Guest Policy: You must be a guest of a member or a member of another private country club. Phone for specifics.

OAKRIDGE COUNTRY CLUB
A private club with one 18-hole course
Location: 2800 Diamond Oaks Drive (see #27 on locator map)
Golf Data: Pro Shop Phone: (214) 530-8004; Club Pro: Mike Nedrow; Par: 71; Yardage: 6603; Rating: 71.7; Course Architect: Jack Kidwell; Closed Monday.
Guest Policy: Out-of-town private country club members are welcome. Be sure to bring credentials.

Grand Prairie

WOODCREST COUNTRY CLUB
A private club with one 18-hole course
Location: I-20 to exit 1832 N to 3502 Country Club Drive (see #30 on locator map)
Golf Data: Pro Shop Phone: (214) 264-2974; Club Pro: Bob Frongillo; Par: 72; Yardage: 6437; Rating: 70.2; Course Architect: Don January; Closed Monday.
Guest Policy: Out-of-town private country club members are welcome. Home professional must call to make arrangements. Be sure to bring credentials.

Irving

HACKBERRY CREEK COUNTRY CLUB
A private club with one 18-hole course
Location: 1901 Royal Lane (see #32 on locator map)
Golf Data: Pro Shop Phone: (214) 869-9364; Club Pro: Greg Scott; Par: 72; Yardage: 7013; Rating: 74.5; Course Architects: Joe Finger & Byron Nelson; Closed Monday.
Guest Policy: You must be a guest of a member and play with member. No person may play as a guest more than one time during any calendar month. Members of C.C.A.-associate club outside a 50-mile radius may play.

LAS COLINAS COUNTRY CLUB
A private club with one 18-hole course
Location: 4900 O'Connor Road (see #33 on locator map)
Golf Data: Pro Shop Phone: (214) 255-7552; Club Pro: Rex Baxter; Par: 71; Yardage: 6809; Rating: 71.5; Course Architect: Joe Finger; Closed Monday.
Guest Policy: You must play with a member.

LAS COLINAS GOLF & SPORTS CLUB
A private club with two 18-hole courses
Location: 4200 N. MacArthur Road (see #34 on locator map)
Golf Data: Pro Shop Phone: (214) 258-7777; Club Pro: Scott Erwin; *TPC* Par: 70; Yardage: 6767; Rating: 73.6; *Cottonwood* Par: 72; Yardage: 6872; Rating: 72.6; Course Architects: Jay Morrish & Ben Crenshaw (both courses); TPC open 7 days, Cottonwood closed Monday.
NOTE: TPC is site of Byron Nelson Classic and a member of the Tournament Players Club network.
Guest Policy: Cottonwood is available for members and their guest play only; TPC is for guests of the Conference Center and Mandalay and guests of members.
NOTE: Golf packages available, phone (800) 268-6282 or write to Four Seasons Fitness Resort and Spa, 4150 N. Mac-Arthur Blvd., Irving, TX. Also guests of the Mandalay Four Seasons Hotel (214) 556-0800 have golf privileges at the TPC.
Green Fees: TPC charges $50 anytime. Carts are $10 per person for 18 holes. AX, Visa and MC accepted.
Tee Time Procedure: Call 48 hours in advance.

TWIN WELLS GOLF COURSE
A public club with one 18-hole course
Location: Loop 12 at Shady Grove Road
NOTE: 18-hole course designed by Ault, Clark & Associates and developed by American Golf Corporation is scheduled to open in the Spring 1988.

Mesquite
FALCON'S LAIR COUNTRY CLUB
A private club with one 18-hole course
Location: I-20 E, exit Lawson Road S. (see #36 on locator map)
NOTE: 18 holes designed by Robert Trent Jones is scheduled to open in late 1987-early 1988.

Richardson
CANYON CREEK COUNTRY CLUB
A private club with one 18-hole course
Location: 625 Lookout Drive (see #42 on locator map)
Golf Data: Pro Shop Phone: (214) 231-3083; Club Pro: Thomas J. Henner;

Par: 70; Yardage: 6695; Rating: 70.7; Course Architect: Press Maxwell; Open 7 days.
Guest Policy: Guest must be accompanied by member. Only reciprocate with other C.C.A. clubs.

Carrollton
INDIAN CREEK GOLF COURSE
A public club with one 18-hole course
Location: Off Frankford on Indian Creek Drive (see #22 on Dallas locator map)
Golf Data: Pro Shop Phone: (214) 323-5083; Club Pro: John Folwell; Par: 72; Yardage: 7218; Rating: 74.7; Course Architect: Dick Phelps; Open 7 days.
NOTE: Second 18 holes, designed by Dick Phelps, will open in the Spring 1988.
Green Fees: $9.50 weekdays, $12.50 weekends and holidays; Carts: $12 for 18 holes.
Tee Time Procedure: Phone 3 days in advance.

Corinth
OAKMONT COUNTRY CLUB
A private club with one 18-hole course
Location: I-35, exit at Shady Shores Road, W.
Golf Data: Pro Shop Phone: (817) 565-1414; Club Pro: Russell Orth; Par: 72; Yardage: 6908; Rating: 72.7; Course Architect: Roger Packard; Closed Monday.
Guest Policy: You must play with a member.

Denton
Public Golf Courses

NORTH TEXAS GOLF LINKS
A public club with one 18-hole course
Location: I-35, exit Avenue D, W. (at Sheraton Hotel)
Golf Data: Pro Shop Phone: (817) 387-5180; Director of Golf: Jerry Greiner; Par: 70; Yardage: 6395; Rating: 70.4; Open 7 days.
Green Fees: $7 weekdays, $9 weekends and holidays; Carts: $8 for 9, $14 for 18 holes. Accept all major credit cards.

Tee Time Procedure: Weekends: Phone Thursday after 7:30 a.m.; Weekdays: 1st come, 1st served.

TEXAS WOMEN'S UNIVERSITY GOLF COURSE
A public club with one 18-hole course
Location: E. side of TWU campus
Golf Data: Pro Shop Phone: (817) 898-3163; Club Pro: John Hamlett; Par: 70; Yardage: 5600; Rating: 66.9; Open 7 days.
Green Fees: $7 weekdays, $8 weekends and holidays; Carts: $6 + tax for 9, $11 + tax for 18 holes.
Tee Time Procedures: 1st come, 1st served (use ball rack).

Private Country Clubs

DENTON COUNTRY CLUB
A private club with one 18-hole course
Location: On Country Club Drive, 5 miles S. of city
Golf Data: Pro Shop Phone: (817) 387-2812; Club Pro: Russell Pulley; Par: 71; Yardage: 6425; Rating: 69.8; Closed Monday.
Guest Policy: You must be a guest of a member or a member of another private country club (phone in advance).

Lewisville

OAK RIDGE PARK GOLF CLUB
A public club with one 18-hole course
Location: 6 Park Place II at Lake Lewisville Park (see #35 on locator map)
Golf Data: Pro Shop Phone: (214) 436-5332; Club Pro: Bob Veal; Par: 73; Yardage: 6749; Rating: 69.3; Course Architects: The Veal Family; Open 7 days.
Green Fees: $6.50 weekdays, $7.50 weekends and holidays; Carts: $12.50 for 18 holes.
Tee Time Procedure: Weekends-Holidays: Call 1 week in advance; Weekdays: 1st come, 1st served.

——————— ELLIS ——————— 5

Ennis

LAKESIDE COUNTRY CLUB
A private club with one 9-hole course
Location: Next to Lake Clark on Country Club Drive

Golf Data: Pro Shop Phone: (214) 875-3641; Club Manager: Karl Krammer; Par: 71 (two sets of tees); Yardage: 6033; Closed Monday.
Guest Policy: You must play with a member or be a member of another private country club.

Red Oak

RED OAK VALLEY GOLF CLUB
A semi-private club with one 18-hole course
Location: I-35, take 408 exit E., turn N. on Service Road
Golf Data: Pro Shop Phone: (214) 576-3249; Club Manager: Steve Thiemann; Par: 72; Yardage: 5911; Rating: 67.0; Course Architect: Red Womack; Open 7 days.
Green Fees: $6 weekdays, $8 weekends and holidays; Carts: $12 + tax for 18 holes.
Tee Time Procedure: 1st come, 1st served.

Waxahachie

WAXAHACHIE COUNTRY CLUB
A private club with one 18-hole course
Location: 1400 W. Main
Golf Data: Pro Shop Phone: (214) 937-3521; Club Pro: Loy Terry; Par: 70; Yardage: 6130; Rating: 67.7; Closed Monday.
Guest Policy: You must be a guest of a member or a member of another private country club. On weekends, you must play with a member.

——————— ERATH ——————— 6

Stephensville

LEGENDS COUNTRY CLUB
A semi-private club with one 18-hole course
Location: Take Washington to Harbin, right to Loop, right, then right at River North Blvd., left at dead end and right at Ben Hogan Drive
Golf Data: Pro Shop Phone: (817) 968-2200; Club Manager: Liz Albrecht; Par: 71; Yardage: 6304; Rating: 65.0; Open 7 days.

Green Fees: $7.50 weekdays, $10 weekends and holidays; Carts: $6.50 for 9, $12.50 for 18 holes.
Tee Time Procedure: Call anytime.

TEJAS GOLF COURSE
A public club with one 9-hole course
Location: HWY 281 to 1089 Tejas Lane
Golf Data: Pro Shop Phone: (817) 965-3904; Club Manager: Bill DeLoach; Par: 35; Yardage: 3245; Open 7 days.
Green Fees: $5.50 weekdays, $7 weekends and holidays; Carts: $4.80 per 9 holes.
Tee Time Procedure: 1st come, 1st served.

———— FANNIN ———— 7

Bonham
BONHAM COUNTRY CLUB
A private club with one 9-hole course
Location: 500 W. Russell
Golf Data: Pro Shop Phone: (214) 583-8815; Club Pro: Mike Beezley; Par: 71 (two sets of tees); Yardage: 5755; Rating: 68.0; Open 7 days.
Guest Policy: You must be a guest of a member or a member of another private country club.

———— GRAYSON ———— 8

Denison
DENISON ROD & GUN COUNTRY CLUB
A private club with one 18-hole course
Location: On FM 84
Golf Data: Pro Shop Phone: (214) 465-4488; Club Manager: Badgett Stedman; Par: 71; Yardage: 6134; Rating: 68.8; Closed Monday.
Guest Policy: You must be a guest of a member or a member of another private country club outside a 50-mile radius.

GRAYSON COUNTY GOLF COURSE
A public club with one 18-hole course
Location: At Grayson County Airport
Golf Data: Pro Shop Phone: (214) 786-9719; Club Pro: Mike Hurley; Par: 72; Yardage: 6497; Course Architects: Grayson College; Open 7 days.

Green Fees: $6 weekdays, $9 weekends and holidays; Carts: $12.50 for 18 holes.
Tee Time Procedure: 1st come, 1st served.

Pottsboro
TANGLEWOOD GOLF CLUB & RESORT
A semi-private club with one 18-hole course
Location: From Sherman, take HWY 120 N. to Lake Texoma
Golf Data: Pro Shop Phone: (214) 786-4140; Club Pro: Dwight Nevil; Par: 72; Yardage: 6997; Rating: 73.0; Course Architect: Ralph Plummer; Open 7 days.
Guest Policy: You must be a guest of a member or be staying at the hotel.
NOTE: Golf Packages available: for information, call (214) 786-2968 or, in Dallas, call (214) 268-0944.
Green Fees: $12.50 weekdays, $17.50 weekends and holidays; Carts: $7.81 per person weekdays, $9 per person weekends for 18 holes.
Tee Time Procedure: Call anytime if planning to stay at hotel.

Sherman
WOODLAWN COUNTRY CLUB
A semi-private club with one 18-hole course
Location: HWY 75N, turn right between cemetery and church, go 1 mile
Golf Data: Pro Shop Phone: (214) 893-3240; Club Pro: Sale Omohundro; Par: 71; Yardage: 6700; Rating: 70.4; Closed Monday.
Green Fees: $10 weekdays, $20 weekends and holidays; Carts: $14.58 for 18 holes.
Tee Time Procedure: 1st come, 1st served.

———— HOOD ———— 9

Granbury
DeCORDOVA BEND COUNTRY CLUB
A private club with one 18-hole course
Location: On Country Club Drive
Golf Data: Pro Shop Phone: (817) 326-2381; Club Pro: Bill Richards; Par: 70; Yardage: 6430; Rating: 70.7; Closed Monday.

Guest Policy: You must play with a member or be a member of another private country club.

GRANBURY RECREATION ASSOCIATION
A semi-private club with one 9-hole course
Location: On FM 430
Golf Data: Pro Shop Phone: (817) 573-9912; Club Manager: Earle Bruce; Par: 36; Yardage: 2990; Rating: 68.15 (if 18 holes played); Open 7 days.
Green Fees: $8 weekdays, $12 weekends and holidays for 18 holes; $5 weekdays, $9 weekend-holidays for 9 holes; Carts: $7.50 for 9; $12.50 for 18 holes.
Tee Time Procedure: 1st come, 1st served.

PECAN PLANTATION COUNTRY CLUB
A private club with one 18-hole course
Location: On Westover Drive
Golf Data: Pro Shop Phone: (817) 573-2641; Director of Golf: Kelly Monroe; Par: 72; Yardage: 6879; Rating: 73.5; Closed Monday.
Guest Policy: You must be a guest of a member. Also reciprocates with DeCordova Bend Country Club.

Tolar
STAR HOLLOW GOLF CLUB
A private club with one 9-hole course
Location: HWY 377, turn right at 2nd blinking light (FM 27), 8 miles
Golf Data: Pro Shop Phone: (817) 835-4398; Club Manager: Jim Mitchell; Par: 35; Yardage: 2895; Closed Tuesday.
Guest Policy: You must be a guest of a member.

———— HUNT ———— 10

Commerce
SAND HILLS GOLF CLUB
A semi-private club with one 9-hole course
Location: HWY 50 S, turn left at Maloy Road, go 1½ miles
Golf Data: Pro Shop Phone: (214) 886-9508; Club Manager: Melba Hartline; Par: 36; Yardage: 3045; Rating 70.0 (if 18 holes played); Closed Monday.

Green Fees: $7.50 weekdays, $10 weekends and holidays; Cart. for 9, $10 for 18 holes.
Tee Time Procedure: 1st come, 1st served.

Greenville
OAK CREEK COUNTRY CLUB
A private club with one 9-hole course
Location: On FM 1570
Golf Data: Pro Shop Phone: (214) 454-6445; Club Pro: Kenny Hartline; Par: 36; Yardage: 3192; Closed Monday.
Guest Policy: You must play with a member or be a member of another private country club. Guests can play only once a month.

WRIGHT PARK GOLF CLUB
A public club with one 9-hole course
Location: 1½ miles S. of I-30 on HWY 69
Golf Data: Pro Shop Phone: (214) 455-3346; Club Pro: Bob Hartline; Par: 35; Yardage: 3250; Rating: 70 (if 18 holes played); Open 7 days.
Green Fees: $5 weekdays, $7.50 weekends and holidays; Carts: $6.50 for 9, $12 for 18 holes.
Tee Time Procedure: 1st come, 1st served.

Quinlan
TAWAKONI GOLF CLUB
A semi-private club with one 18-hole course
Location: 7½ miles E. on FM 35
Golf Data: Pro Shop Phone: (214) 447-2981; Club Pros: John Lively Sr., John Lively Jr. & Billy Lively; Par: 72; Yardage: 6657; Rating: 71.2; Closed Monday.
Green Fees: $7.30 weekdays, $15.60 weekends and holidays; Carts: $12.50 for 18 holes.
Tee Time Procedure: 1st come, 1st served.

Wolfe City
WEBB HILL COUNTRY CLUB
A private club with one 18-hole course
Location: 14 miles N. of Greenville on HWY 34

Golf Data: Pro Shop Phone: (214) 455-4471; Club Pro: Charles Ranley; Par: 72; Yardage: 7000; Open 7 days.

Guest Policy: You must play with a member or be a member of another private country club.

══════ JOHNSON ══════ 11

Cleburne

CLEBURNE MUNICIPAL GOLF COURSE
A public club with one 18-hole course
Location: Take HWY 67 W., S. on Nolan River Road to Country Club Road, turn W.

Golf Data: Pro Shop Phone: (817) 645-9078; Club Pro; Ronnie Humphrey; Par: 71; Yardage: 6326; Rating: 69.0; Open 7 days.

Green Fees: $5.50 weekdays, $7 weekends and holidays; Carts: $6.50 per 9 holes.

Tee Time Procedure: 1st come, 1st served.

RIVERVIEW COUNTRY CLUB
A private club with one 18-hole course
Location: On Nolan River Road, 3 miles S. of HWY 67

Golf Data: Pro Shop Phone: (817) 641-0221; Club Pro: Ron Ward; Par: 72; Yardage: 6605; Rating: 70.7; Closed Monday.

Guest Policy: You must be a guest of a member or a member of another private country club outside Johnson City.

Joshua

MOUNTAIN VALLEY COUNTRY CLUB
A private club with one 18-hole course
Location: HWY 174N, turn right at Short Mart, left at 1st street, right at dead end

Golf Data: Pro Shop Phone: (817) 295-7126; Club Manager: Bill Hill; Par: 71; Yardage: 6390; Rating: 70.4; Closed Monday.

Guest Policy: You must play with a member on weekends.

══════ KAUFMAN ══════ 12

Kemp

CEDAR CREEK COUNTRY CLUB
A private club with one 18-hole course

Location: HWY 175E, 4 miles, turn right at Country Club sign

Golf Data: Pro Shop Phone: (214) 498-6761; Club Pro: Benny Passons; Par: 72; Yardage: 6728; Rating: 70.1; Closed Monday.

Guest Policy: You must play with a member or be a member of another private country club.

COUNTRY GOLD COUNTRY CLUB
A private club with one 18-hole course
Location: Intersection of HWY 274 & HWY 148

Golf Data: Pro Shop Phone: (214) 498-8888; Club Pro: Newell Nugent; Par: 72; Yardage: 6750; Rating: 72.02; Closed Monday during winter.

Guest Policy: You must play with a member or be a member of another private country club (must pay cash, no charge backs).

Terrell

OAK GROVE COUNTRY CLUB
A semi-private club with one 9-hole course
Location: From Moore Street, turn N. on 9th Street, W. at Colquitt for 1 mile

Golf Data: Pro Shop Phone: (214) 563-8553; Club Pro: Charles Bishop; Par: 70; Yardage: 6300; Rating: 69.71; Closed Monday.

Guest Policy: Non-county residents may pay green fees.

Green Fees: $8.42 weekdays, $12.62 weekends and holidays; Carts: $5.79 per 9 holes.

Tee Time Procedure: Weekends-Holidays: Course reserved for members between 12-4 p.m.; 1st come, 1st served any other time.

══════ MONTAGUE ══════ 13

Bowie

TOP OF LAKES
A private club with one 9-hole course
Location: At Amon Carter Lake
Golf Data: Pro Shop Phone: (817) 872-5401; Club Pro: Chuck Bailey; Par: 70 (two sets of tees); Yardage: 5424; Closed Monday.

Guest Policy: You must be a member of another private country club or a guest of a member.

Nocona

NOCONA HILLS COUNTRY CLUB
A semi-private club with one 18-hole course
Location: Take HWY 1956E to HWY 3031, N. 2 miles
Golf Data: Pro Shop Phone: (817) 825-3444; Pro Shop Manager, Pat Childs; Par: 71; Yardage: 6420; Rating: 69.0; Open 7 days.
Green Fees: $5 weekdays, $6.50 weekends and holidays; Carts: $15 for 18 holes.
Tee Time Procedure: 1st come, 1st served.

NOCONA MUNICIPAL GOLF CLUB
A public club with one 18-hole course
Location: W. on HWY 82
Golf Data: Pro Shop Phone: (817) 825-7250; Club Manager: Tom Uselton; Par: 70; Yardage: 4639; Open 7 days.
Green fees: $3.50 weekdays, $5 weekends and holidays; Carts: $6 per 9 holes.
Tee Time Procedure: 1st come, 1st served.

———— NAVARRO ———— 14

Corsicana

CORSICANA COUNTRY CLUB
A private club with one 18-hole course
Location: Take Beeton Street N. to Country Club sign
Golf Data: (214) 874-2441; Club Pro: Mac Brunton; Par: 71; Yardage: 6425; Rating: 70.2; Closed Monday.
Guest Policy: You must play with a member or be a member of certain reciprocating clubs. Phone for specifics.

OAKS GOLF CLUB
A public club with one 9-hole course
Location: Take Old HWY 75N
Golf Data: Pro Shop Phone: (214) 874-9042; Club Manager: William Cherry; Par: 71 (two sets of tees); Yardage: 6100; Open 7 days.

Green Fees: $5.25 weekdays, $7.85 weekends and holidays; Carts: $6.30 per 9 holes.
Tee Time Procedure: 1st come, 1st served.

———— PALO PINTO ———— 15

Mineral Wells

HOLIDAY HILLS COUNTRY CLUB
A semi-private club with one 18-hole course
Location: Take 1st Street S.
Golf Data: Pro Shop Phone: (817) 325-8403; Club Pro: Jack Johnson; Par: 71; Yardage: 5821; Rating: 68.0; Open 7 days.
Green Fees: $9 weekdays, $14 weekends and holidays; Carts: $12 + tax for 18 holes.
Tee Time Procedure: 1st come, 1st served (NOTE: Members play until 10 a.m. Saturday).

Possum Kingdom Lake

THE CLIFFS   779-3926
A private club with one 18-hole course
Location: On State Road 16 between Brady and Graham
NOTE: *18 holes designed by Bruce Devlin & Bob Von Hagge is scheduled to open in 1987.*

———— PARKER ———— 16

Dennis

SUGAR TREE COUNTRY CLUB
A semi-private club with one 18-hole course
Location: ON FM 1543, 10 miles S.W. of Weatherford   817-594-5435
NOTE: *18-hole course designed by Phil Lumsden & Benny Passons to resemble famous golf holes from around the world will open in Summer 1987 as a semi-private club until Phase 1 of the development is completed at which time the club becomes private.*

Weatherford

LIVE OAK COUNTRY CLUB
A public club with one 9-hole course

Location: 1½ miles S. of courthouse on Bethel Road

Golf Data: Pro Shop Phone: (817) 594-7596; Par: 35; Yardage: 3162; Closed Monday.

Green Fees: $6.30 weekdays, $7.35 weekends and holidays for 9 holes; $8.40 weekdays, $10.50 weekends and holidays for 18 holes; Carts: $6.30 per 9 holes.

Tee Time Procedure: 1st come, 1st served.

Willow Park

SQUAW CREEK GOLF CLUB
A semi-private club with one 18-hole course

Location: I-20, exit Ranch House Road, go N. (see #31 on Fort Worth locator map)

Golf Data: Pro Shop Phone: (817) 441-8185; Club Pro: Lynn Vaughan; Par: 71; Yardage: 6717; Rating: 70.0; Course Architect: Ralph Plummer; Closed Monday.

Green Fees: $10 weekdays, $12 weekends and holidays; Carts: $12.60 for 18 holes; Visa, MC accepted.

Tee Time Procedure: Non-Members Weekends-Holidays: two days in advance at 7 a.m. in person or by phone; Weekdays: 1st come, 1st served.

════ ROCKWALL ════ 17

Rockwall

LAKESIDE VILLAGE GOLF COURSE
A private club with one 9-hole Par 3 course

Location: HWY 30, exit Rdge Road, left to Service, left 1 mile

Golf Data: Pro Shop Phone: (214) 722-3051; Club Manager: Gordon McPherson; Par: 27; Yardage: 1171; Open 7 days.

Guest Policy: You must be a guest of a member.

THE SHORES COUNTRY CLUB
A semi-private club with one 18-hole course

Location: HWY 30, exit Ridge Road left, left at stop sign, left at HWY 205 (stop light), follow to entrance

Golf Data: Pro Shop Phone: (214) 722-0301; Club Pro: Steve Wheelis; Par: 72; Yardage: 7183; Rating: 74.2; Course Architect: Ralph Plummer; Closed Monday.

Green Fees: $20 weekdays, $40 weekends and holidays; Carts: $7.36 per person for 18 holes.

Tee Time Procedures: Weekends-Holidays: Two days in advance at 8 a.m. in person or by phone; Weekdays: Call in advance.

════ SOMERVELL ════ 18

None

════ TARRANT ════ 19

Public Golf Courses

Arlington

DITTO GOLF COURSE
A public club with one 18-hole course

Location: 801 Brown Avenue (see #19 on locator map)

Golf Data: Pro Shop Phone: (817) 275-5941; Club Pro: Garry Wolff; Par: 72; Yardage: 6661; Open 7 days.

Green Fees: $8 weekdays, $9 weekends and holidays; Carts: $12 for 18 holes.

Tee Time Procedures: Weekends-Holidays: Wednesday after 5:30 a.m. in person, Thursday after 6:30 a.m. by phone; Weekdays: 1st come, 1st served.

LAKE ARLINGTON GOLF COURSE
A public club with one 18-hole course

Location: 1516 Green Oaks Blvd. (see #20 on locator map)

Golf Data: Pro Shop Phone: (817) 451-6101; Club Pro: Trent Mize; Par: 71; Yardage: 6485; Rating: 70.2; Open 7 days.

Green Fees: $8 weekdays, $9 weekends and holidays; Carts: $12 for 18 holes.

Tee Time Procedure: Weekends-Holidays: Three days in advance at 5:30 a.m. in person, two days in advance by phone; Weekdays: 1st come, 1st served.

MEADOWBROOK GOLF COURSE
A public club with one 9-hole executive course

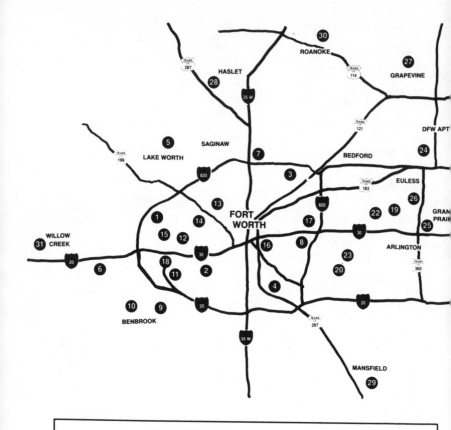

FORT WORTH AND SURROUNDING AREA

FORT WORTH
1. Carswell AFB G. C.
2. Colonial C. C.
3. Diamond Oaks C. C.
4. Glen Garden C. C.
5. Lake Country Golf & C. C.
6. Lost Creek C. C.
7. Marriott's G. C. at Fossil Creek
8. Meadowbrook G. C.
9. Mira Vista C. C.
10. Pecan Valley G. C.
11. Ridglea C. C.
12. Rivercrest C. C.
13. Rockwood Park G. C.
14. Rockwood Par 3
15. Shady Oaks C. C.
16. Sycamore Creek G. C.
17. Woodhaven C. C.
18. Z. Boaz G. C.

ARLINGTON
19. Ditto G. C.
20. Lake Arlington G. C.
21. Meadowbrook G. C.
22. Rolling Hills C. C.
23. Shady Valley G. C.

DALLAS/FORT WORTH AIRPORT
24. Bear Creek G. C.

FORT WORTH
1. Carswell AFB G. C.
2. Colonial C. C.
3. Diamond Oaks C. C.
4. Glen Garden C. C.
5. Lake Country Golf & C. C.
6. Lost Creek C. C.
7. Marriott's G. C. at Fossil Creek
8. Meadowbrook G. C.
9. Mira Vista C. C.
10. Pecan Valley G. C.
11. Ridglea C. C.
12. Rivercrest C. C.
13. Rockwood Park G. C.
14. Rockwood Par 3
15. Shady Oaks C. C.
16. Sycamore Creek G. C.
17. Woodhaven C. C.
18. Z. Boaz G. C.

ARLINGTON
19. Ditto G. C.
20. Lake Arlington G. C.

21. Meadowbrook G. C.
22. Rolling Hills C. C.
23. Shady Valley G. C.

DALLAS/FORT WORTH AIRPORT
24. Bear Creek G. C.

GRAND PRAIRIE
25. Great Southwest G. C.
26. Riverside C. C.

GRAPEVINE
27. Grapevine Municipal G. C.

HASLET
28. Willow Springs G. C.

MANSFIELD
29. Walnut Creek C. C.

ROANOKE
30. Trophy Club C. C.

WILLOW PARK
31. Squaw Creek G. C.

Location: 1300 Dugan Street (see #21 on locator map)

Golf Data: Pro Shop Phone: (817) 275-0221; Club Manager: James Marsh; Par: 33; Yardage: 2069; Open 7 days.

Green Fees: $5.50 weekdays, $6.50 weekends and holidays; No motorized carts.

Tee Time Procedures: 1st come, first served.

Dallas/Fort Worth Airport

HYATT BEAR CREEK

A public club with two 18-hole courses

Location: SW corner of DFW Airport on W. Airfield Drive (see #24 on Fort Worth locator map and #23 on Dallas locator map)

Golf Data: Pro Shop Phone: (214) 453-0140; Director: John Hungerford; Club Pro: Larry Box; *East* Par: 72; Yardage: 6609; Rating: 72.0; *West* Par: 72; Yardage: 6670; Rating: 72.0; Course Architect: Ted Robinson (both courses); Open 7 days.

NOTE: East course rated as one of top 25 public courses in the United States by Golf Digest magazine.

Green Fees: $25 weekdays, $31 weekends and holidays; Carts: $20 for 18 holes; AX, Visa and MC accepted.

NOTE: Golf packages available at Amfac Hotel, phone (214) 453-8400.

Tee Time Procedures: 12 noon three days in advance in person or by phone.

Grapevine

GRAPEVINE MUNICIPAL GOLF COURSE

A public club with one 18-hole course

Location: E. edge of Lake Grapevine (see #27 on Fort Worth locator map and #31 on Dallas locator map)

Golf Data: Pro Shop Phone: (817) 481-0421; Club Pro: James (Jim) Smith; Par: 72; Yardage: 7022; Rating: 73.5; Course Architects: Joe Finger & Byron Nelson; Open 7 days.

NOTE: Ranked in top 75 public courses in United States by Golf Digest magazine. Hole #13 one of top 50 holes for public courses in the country according to Golf Magazine.

Green Fees: $9 weekdays, $11 weekends and holidays; Carts: $13 for 18 holes.

Tee Time Procedure: Three days in advance at 7 a.m. in person and at 1 p.m. by phone.

Fort Worth

MEADOWBROOK GOLF COURSE

A public club with one 18-hole course

Location: 1815 Jensen (see #8 on locator map)

Golf Data: Pro Shop Phone: (817) 457-4616; Club Pro: Charlie Roberts; Par: 71; Yardage: 6416; Rating: 70.3; Open 7 days.

Green Fees: $7 weekdays, $8 weekends and holidays; Carts: $13.65 for 18 holes.

Tee Time Procedures: Weekends-Holidays: Monday at 12 noon in person or by phone; Weekdays: 1st come, 1st served.

PECAN VALLEY GOLF COURSE

A public club with two 18-hole courses

Location: 6800 Lakeside Drive (see #10 on locator map)

Golf Data: Pro Shop Phone: (817) 249-1845; Club Pro: Jim Henderson; *River* Par: 72; Yardage: 6430; Rating: 69.4; *Hills* Par: 72; Yardage: 6529; Rating: 70.5; Open 7 days.

Green Fees: $7 weekdays, $8 weekends and holidays; Carts: $12 for 18 holes.

Tee Time Procedure: Weekends-Holidays: Monday at 12 noon in person or by phone; Weekdays: 1st come, 1st served.

ROCKWOOD PARK MUNICIPAL GOLF COURSE

A public club with three 9-hole courses

Location: 1851 Jacksboro HWY (see #13 on locator map)

Golf Data: Pro Shop Phone: (817) 624-1771; Club Pro: Sam Knight; *Red* Par: 35; Yardage: 3050; *Blue* Par: 36; Yardage: 3689; *White* Par: 36; Yardage 3208; Open 7 days.

Green Fees: $6 weekdays, $8 weekends and holidays; Carts: $13.65 for 18 holes.

Tee Time Procedures: Weekends-Holidays: Monday at 12 noon in person or by phone; Weekdays: 1st come, 1st served.

ROCKWOOD PAR 3 GOLF COURSE

A public club with one 9-hole Par 3 course

Location: I-30 W, exit University, N. to Park 1st left after river (see #14 on locator map)

Golf Data: Pro Shop Phone: (817) 624-8311; Club Manager: A. C. Arrington; Par: 27; yardage: 65–90 yards per hole; Open 7 days.

Green Fees: $2 for 9, $3.50 for 18 holes, $5 for all day; No motorized carts.

Tee Time Procedures: 1st come, 1st served.

SYCAMORE CREEK GOLF COURSE
A public club with one 9-hole executive course
Location: 2324 E. Vickery (see #16 on locator map)

Golf Data: Pro Shop Phone: (817) 535-7241; Acting Head Pro: Charlie Roberts; Par: 30; Yardage: 1852; Open 7 days.

Green Fees: $4 anytime; Carts: $6.32 per 9 holes.

Tee Time Procedures: 1st come, 1st served.

Z. BOAZ GOLF COURSE
A public club with one 18-hole course
Location: 3240 Lackland (see #18 on locator map)

Golf Data: Pro Shop Phone: (817) 738-6287; Club Pro: Chuck Young; Par: 70; Yardage: 5972; Rating: 67.2; Open 7 days.

Green Fees: $7 weekdays, $8 weekends and holidays; Carts: $12 for 18 holes.

Tee Time Procedures: Weekends/ Holidays: Monday at noon in person or by phone; Weekdays: 1st come, 1st served.

Haslet
WILLOW SPRINGS GOLF COURSE
A public club with one 18-hole course
Location: HWY 81-287, exit Willow Springs, take to end. (see #28 on locator map)

Golf Data: Pro Shop Phone: (817) 439-3169; Course Manager: Joe C. Lindsay, Jr.; Par: 72; Yardage: 6250; Rating: 69.4; Open 7 days.

Green Fees: $5 weekdays, $7 weekends and holidays; Carts: $10.50 for 18 holes.

Tee Time Procedure: Saturday anytime for the following weekend in person or by phone; Weekdays: 1st come, 1st served.

Private Golf Courses

Arlington
ROLLING HILLS COUNTRY CLUB
A private club with one 18-hole course
Location: 401 Lamar Blvd. W. (see #22 on locator map)

Golf Data: Pro Shop Phone: (817) 275-5671; Club Pro: George Alexander; Par: 71; Yardage: 6115; Rating: 68.5; Closed Monday.

Guest Policy: You must be a member of another U.S.G.A. club. Weekends and holidays, guests must play with a member. Phone for specifics.

SHADY VALLEY GOLF CLUB
A private club with one 18-hole course
Location: 3621 W. Park Row (see #23 on locator map)

Golf Data: Pro Shop Phone: (817) 275-8771; Club Manager: C. M. Fitzgerald; Par: 70; Yardage: 6742; Rating: 71.7; Course Architect: C. H. Wileman, Jr.; Closed Monday.

Guest Policy: Private country club members are welcome as guests. Please phone in advance.

Fort Worth
CARSWELL AFB GOLF COURSE
A private club with one 18-hole course
Location: 6520 White Settlement (see #1 on locator map)

Golf Data: Pro Shop Phone: (817) 738-8402; Club Manager: Jim Cook; Par: 71; Yardage: 6613; Rating: 71.8; Course Architect: Ben Hogan; Closed Monday.

Guest Policy: You must play with a member or be a member of the Air Force.

COLONIAL COUNTRY CLUB
A private club with one 18-hole course
Location: 3735 Country Club Circle (see #2 on locator map)

Golf Data: Pro Shop Phone: (817) 927-4243; Club Pro: Roland Harper; Par: 70; Yardage: 7096; Rating: 73.0; Course Architect: Perry Maxwell & John Breedemus; Closed Monday.

NOTE: *Home of Colonial National Invitational Golf Tournament. Rated in top 30 America's greatest courses by Golf Digest magazine. Site of 1941 U.S.G.A. Open.*

Site of 1975 Tournament Players Championship (2nd).
Guest Policy: You must play with a member.

DIAMOND OAKS GOLF & COUNTRY CLUB
A private club with one 18-hole course
Location: 5821 Diamond Oaks Drive (see # 3 on locator map)
Golf Data: Pro Shop Phone: (817) 834-6261; Club Pro: Doug Higgins; Par: 70; Yardage: 6723; Rating: 71.4; Course Architect: Chas. Akey; Closed Monday.
Guest Policy: You must be a member of another private club. Have your pro phone in advance.

GLEN GARDEN COUNTRY CLUB
A private club with one 18-hole course
Location: 2916 Glen Garden Drive S. (see #4 on locator map)
Golf Data: Pro Shop Phone: (817) 535-7582; Club Pro: Bill Bradford; Par: 71; Yardage: 6062; Rating: 69.1; Closed Monday.
Guest Policy: You must play with a member.

LAKE COUNTRY GOLF & COUNTRY CLUB
A private club with one 18-hole course
Location: 8505 Spring Street (see #5 on locator map)
Golf Data: Pro Shop Phone: (817) 236-8421; Club Pro: David Hersman; Par: 72; Yardage: 6518; Rating: 71.6; Course Architects: Perry Maxwell (front 9) Billy Martindale & Don January (back 9); Closed Monday.
Guest Policy: You must play with a member. Private country club members are welcome. Phone pro in advance and bring credentials.

LOST CREEK COUNTRY CLUB
A private club with one 18-hole course
Location: I-30W to Link Crest exit, take Service Road E. to Lost Creek Blvd. S. (see #6 on locator map)
Golf Data: Pro Shop Phone: (817) 244-3312; Club Pro: Alan Poynor; Par: 71; Yardage: 6400; Rating: 69.9; Closed Monday.
Guest Policy: You must be a guest of a member or a member of another private country club. Phone for specifics.

MARRIOTT'S GOLF COURSE AT FOSSIL CREEK
A resort club with one 18-hole course
Location: Near intersection of Loop 820 and HWY 35W (see #7 on locator map)
NOTE: *18-hole course designed by Arnold Palmer & Ed Seay scheduled to open in the Spring 1987.*

MIRA VISTA COUNTRY CLUB
A private club with one 18-hole course
Location: I-20, exit Bryan Irvin Road, S. to Belaire Drive (see #9 on locator map)
NOTE: *18-hole course designed by Jay Morrish & Tom Weiskopf scheduled to open in the Summer 1987.*

RIDGLEA COUNTRY CLUB
A private club with two 18-hole courses
Location: 3700 Barney Anderson Drive (see #11 on locator map)
Golf Data: Pro Shop Phone: (817) 732-8111; Club Pro: Keith Davidson; *Men's* Course (Men only) Par: 72; Yardage: 7100; Rating: 73.7; Closed Tuesday; *Family* Course Par: 71; Yardage: 6425; Rating: 70.2; Closed Monday.
Guest Policy: Out-of-county private club members are welcome. Phone pro for specifics.

RIVERCREST COUNTRY CLUB
A private club with one 18-hole course
Location: 1501 Western (see #12 on locator map)
Golf Data: Pro Shop Phone: (817) 738-9221; Club Pro: Steve Cain; Par: 71; Yardage: 6400; Rating: 68.0; Closed Monday.
Guest Policy: You must be a guest of a member.

SHADY OAKS COUNTRY CLUB
A private club with 27 holes
Location: 320 Roaring Springs (see #15 on locator map)
Golf Data: Pro Shop Phone: (817) 429-9801; Club Pro: Mike Wright; Par: 71; Yardage: 6975; Rating: 71.0; Par 3 Par: 27; Yardage: 1228; Closed Monday.
Guest Policy: You must be sponsored by a member.

WOODHAVEN COUNTRY CLUB
A private club with one 18-hole course
Location: 913 Country Club Lane (see #17 on locator map)

Golf Data: Pro Shop Phone: (817) 457-2143; Club Pro: Mike Dugger; Par: 71; Yardage: 6465; Rating: 70.5; Course Architect: Leon Howard; Closed Monday.

Guest Policy: Out-of-town private club members are welcome. Phone pro in advance.

Grand Prairie

GREAT SOUTHWEST GOLF CLUB
A private club with one 18-hole course
Location: 612 Avenue J E. (see #25 on locator map)

Golf Data: Pro Shop Phone: (817) 647-0116; Club Pro: Terry Alsup; Par: 71; Yardage: 6771; Rating: 72.3; Course Architect: Ralph Plummer; Open 7 days.

Guest Policy: Out-of-town private country club members are welcome. Phone pro in advance.

RIVERSIDE CLUB
A private club with one 18-hole course
Location: 3000 Riverside Pkwy (see #26 on locator map)

Golf Data: Pro Shop Phone: (214) 640-7800; Director of Golf: Jay Clements; Par: 72; Yardage: 7025; Rating: 74.4; Course Architect: Roger Packard; Closed Monday.

Guest Policy: Club reciprocates with other private country clubs outside 100-mile radius of Metroplex, if pro phones in advance. You must play with a member.

Mansfield

WALNUT CREEK COUNTRY CLUB
A private club with 27 holes
Location: 1151 Country Club Drive (see #29 on locator map)

Golf Data: Pro Shop Phone: (817) 473-6114 or 477-3191 (metro); Club Pro: Don Prigmorel; *Willows* 9 Par: 36; Yardage: 3102; *Pecan* 9 Par: 35; Yardage: 3334; *Willows/Pecan* Rating: 70.0; Course Architect: Don January & Billy Martindale; *Oaks* 9 Par: 37; Yardage: 3616; Course Architects: Bob Bascher, Stan Wreyford & Don Prigmore; Closed Monday.

Guest Policy: You must be a guest of a member or a member of another private country club. Phone pro for specifics.

Roanoke

TROPHY CLUB COUNTRY CLUB
A private club with 27 holes
Location: 500 Trophy Club Drive (see #30 on locator map)

Golf Data: Pro Shop Phone: (817) 430-0641; Club Pro: Larry Hayes; *Oak* 9 Par: 36; Yardage: 3457; *Creek* 9 Par: 36; Yardage; 3496; *Eagle* 9 Par: 36; Yardage: 3507; Ratings: *Oak-Creek:* 72.9; *Oak-Eagle:* 73.1; *Creek-Eagle:* 73.0; Course Architects: Joe Lee (Oak-Creek), Art Hills (Eagle); Closed Monday.

Guest Policy: You must be a guest of a member or a member of a private country club outside the DFW metroplex. Phone for specifics.

——————WISE——————20

Bridgeport

BRIDGEPORT COUNTRY CLUB
A private club with one 9-hole course
Location: S.E. on FM 2123

Golf Data: Pro Shop Phone: (817) 683-9438; Club Pro: Lonnie Benham; Par: 35; Yardage: 3031; Open 7 days.

Guest Policy: Accepts daily fee play weekdays. Must play with member weekends.

Green Fees: $5 weekdays, $7.50 weekends and holidays; Carts: $6.31 per 9 holes.

Tee Time Procedure: 1st come, 1st served.

BAY GOLF & COUNTRY CLUB
A semi-private club with one 18-hole course
Location: At Lake Bridgeport

Golf Data: Pro Shop Phone: (817) 575-2225; Club Pro: Mac McCall; Par: 71; Yardage: 6569; Rating: 70.9; Open 7 days.

Guest Policy: 7:30-9:30 a.m. times blocked weekends and holidays for members; general play available all other times unless tournament scheduled.
NOTE: Resort facilities available, phone (817) 683-3020.

Green Fees: $10 weekdays, $14 weekends and holidays; Carts: $12.62 for 18 holes; AX, Visa and MC accepted.

Tee Time Procedure: 1st come, 1st served.

Decatur

DECATUR GOLF & COUNTRY CLUB
A private club with one 9-hole course
Location: N. on FM 730
Golf Data: Pro Shop Phone: (817) 627-3789; Club Manager: Johnny Coker; Par: 36; Yardage: 3143; Open 7 days.

Guest Policy: Accepts daily green fee play.
Green Fees: $6 weekdays, $8 weekends and holidays; Carts: $7 per 9 holes.
Tee Time Procedure: 1st come, 1st served.

5. How many times did Texan Ben Crenshaw finish second in the major championship before winning the 1984 Masters?

What Makes a Good Golfing Resort?

Many people won't take their vacation unless there are golf facilities close to their accommodations.

Others don't live for golf alone; they want more.

What makes a good golfing resort?

It depends on need. If you fall into the former category, you may be content with a good challenging golf course and little else. Mill Creek in Salado falls into this group. Designed by Robert Trent Jones, Mill Creek is an exciting Par 71, 6486-yard course, noted for its picturesque heart-shaped green at No. 3. These resorts that are principally known for their golfing activities are generally tied to hotels offering golf packages. Pecan Valley Golf Club in San Antonio is available through a package offered by The Menger Hotel. The TPC course at Las Colinas Sports Club can be played by guests of The Four Seasons or The Mandalay Hotels in Dallas. Tapatio Springs C.C. has 18 holes in Boerne.

If you fall into the latter category, you will want other amenities besides golf, such as boating, fishing, swimming, tennis, horseback riding, biking, dining, and entertainment.

Chuck Cook works with LPGA Pro Cindy Figg
at Lakeway Academy of Golf.

Cabanas overlook swimming pool and 18th green
at Waterwood Country Club.

Horseshoe Bay, about 50 miles west of Austin near Marble Falls, may
be the best of both worlds and also the best kept secret in Texas. Adver-
tising little, three golf courses designed by Robert Trent Jones are com-
plemented by boating, fishing, water sports, swimming, tennis,
horseback riding, two restaurants, and entertainment.

One of the Horseshoe golf layouts was rated as one of the top
6 inland resort courses by Dick Wilson in his book *America's Greatest
Golfing Resorts*. Accommodations include a motel as well as
condominiums/townhomes.

Another that offers both golf and amenities is Rancho Viejo just
north of Brownsville in south Texas. The resort is 22 miles from the Gulf
of Mexico so the beach and deep sea fishing are accessible, and 12
miles from Mexico, shoppers will be drawn across the border.

The two golf courses designed by Dennis Arp are challenging and
on site tennis, swimming pool, lake, boating, dining, dancing, and entertainment are available for the non-golfing hours.

Lakeway, 20 miles west of Austin, not only offers three excellent golf
courses, but it is the home of the Academy of Golf school, with sessions
nearly every week from March to November.

Leon Howard designed two of the courses—Live Oak and Yaupon—
and you can play either as a guest of the resort or of a Lakeway property.
The third course, The Hills of Lakeway, designed by Jack Nicklaus, can

only be played if you are a guest within the self-contained Hills development or are a participant in the Academy program.

Lakeway has the largest marina on the 65-mile long Lake Travis and also has a large tennis complex with 26 courts. Horseback riding over 26 miles of trails, swimming pools, dining, and entertainment are just some of the other family-time opportunities.

Others worth mentioning are Tanglewood at Lake Texoma, Waterwood C.C. at Lake Livingston, Rayburn Country Resort, and The Woodlands.

The map opposite lists the locations of those resorts or hotels with golf courses either adjacent or close to the accommodations.

6. When did the Ladies Professional Golf Association move to Texas and where is it located?

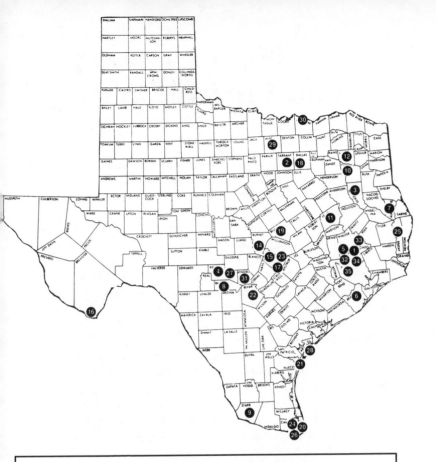

RESORTS AND COURSES WITH HOTEL AFFILIATIONS

1. April Sound
2. Bear Creek Golf Center
3. Birmingham Golf Club
4. Charles Schreiner Golf Course
5. Club Del Lago
6. Columbia Lakes
7. Fairway Farms Golf & Hunt Resort
8. Flying L. Ranch
9. Fort Ringgold Motor Inn
10. Garden Valley Resort
11. Hilltop Lakes Golf Club
12. Holly Lake Ranch
13. Horizon Resort & C. C.
14. Horseshoe Bay C. C.
15. Lago Vista
16. Lajitas G. C. & Hotel
17. Lakeway
18. Las Colinas Sports Club
19. Mill Creek C. C.
20. Outdoor Resorts South Padre Island
21. Padre Isles C. C.
22. Pecan Valley Golf Course
23. Point Venture
24. Rancho Viejo C. C.
25. Rayburn Country
26. River Bend C. C.
27. Riverhill C. C.
28. Rockport C. C.
29. Runaway Bay Golf & C. C.
30. Tanglewood at Lake Texoma
31. Tapatio Springs C. C.
32. Walden on Lake Conroe
33. Waterwood C. C.
34. Woodlands C. C.
35. World Houston Golf Club

3 in Texas in Top 75 Open for Public Play

Ranking golf courses for the average golfer in Texas is difficult. Private courses outnumber public ones, yet public players outnumber private ones. Many of the top golf courses in the state are not accessible to the majority of golfers.

Which are the best of the "everyone can play provided you get in line early enough and pay your green fees" public golf courses?

Golf Digest magazine attempts to answer that question each year in its "America's Best Public Golf Courses" feature and has done so since 1981. The rankings are decided by a panel of 242 members made up of golf administrators, leading public links players, members of the USGA men's and women's public links committees, and acknowledged experts on public course golf.

What makes a good public course? *Golf Digest* bases its evaluation on six standards and, to qualify for consideration, the course must be (1) publicly owned or (2) privately owned and operated on a daily fee basis primarily for nearby residents. Disqualified are (1) those attached to resort hotels or rental properties, (2) those built in hopes of attracting revenue from traveling golfers, and (3) courses operated by the military, colleges, or universities.

The six standards:

- **Shot values.** How fairly does it reward power, finesse, and accuracy?

- **Playability.** How playable is the course for golfers of all levels of ability?

- **Design balance.** How well do the holes vary in length and configuration?

- **Memorability.** How well do you remember each of the holes after you play the course?

- **Esthetics.** How would you rate the course on the beauty, enticement, and satisfaction derived?

- **Conditioning.** Is the course consistently maintained during the competitive season?

The rankings are decided, using a 1–10 point scoring system as values are assigned to each of the six standards.

Three Texas courses, two in the Dallas/Fort Worth area and one in Houston, scored high and are listed in *Golf Digest*'s "America's Top 75 Public Courses." They are Bear Creek East at DFW Airport, Bear Creek Masters in Houston, and Grapevine Municipal in Grapevine.

BEAR CREEK EAST

Golf Digest ranks the East course at Bear Creek in its top 25 public courses and justifiably so. This Par 72 course challenges all levels of golfer with its hilly, narrow fairways, meandering creek, small lakes, and fast bent grass greens. It measures up to the six criteria used to rank public courses by *Golf Digest*.

It is a true test of course management and one's shot making ability and, with the exception of July and August when the heat and amount of daily play affect the greens, the course is always in excellent shape.

The East plays as long as 6609 yards and as short as 5620. The player is rewarded for staying in the fairway and it might be best to leave your ego at home and use all the clubs in your bag to maintain position.

And who can forget the Texas winds which generally blow out of the south southwest during the spring and summer months. Expect to hit into the teeth of the wind four holes on the front 9 (including the No. 1 handicap hole) and the two most difficult holes of the back 9.

However, for those who wish to gamble there are rewards as well as double bogeys waiting. Three of the four Par 5's are reachable in two, and use of a driver or three-wood, when caution might dictate iron play, can leave you with a shorter second shot to the green on the Par 4's.

The four Par 3's are challenging with both short and long irons required. Three of the teeing areas are elevated and one requires a 150-yard shot over water.

PGA tour player Mark Brooks of Fort Worth holds the competitive course record, a 9-under par 63, shot during the 1984 Texas State Open.

The opening hole is Par 5, 528 yards with out-of-bounds left and two sand traps, one left and one right, in the driving area. Reachable in two with a strong, straight second shot (the fairway slopes to the green from 100 yards out), the fairway narrows to 25 yards at the 125-yard mark with trees lining both sides and a lake catching errant shots right. Some players will lay up on their second shot with an iron, leaving an approach of 150 yards to a green, bunkered front right and back left.

The most difficult hole, according to the handicap system, is the 416-yard Par 4 second hole which is bordered from tee to green by Bear Creek on the right. Two traps, 240 yards from the back tees, guard the right side of the fairway. A drive left of the traps creates a slight dogleg right as the slightly elevated green sits alongside Bear Creek and is bunkered front right and back left.

No. 4 at Bear Creek East

The first Par 3 on the east side is 175 yards, bordered by trees right and left. There is one sand trap along the right side of the green and shots over the green require lofted returns to a green that slopes back to front.

The double dogleg Par 5, 520-yard fourth is difficult to reach in two. Out-of-bounds left doesn't come into play on your drive. Still the "A" position is right center as trees line the left side of the fairway. A solitary tree guards the left corner approximately 150 yards from the two-tiered green. Beyond this tree, 75 yards from the green, is a sand trap, and the green is well-bunkered right and left.

No. 5 is the most photographed hole on the East course and places a premium on position. Only 359 yards, the hole doglegs sharply left and two trees at the end of the fairway, one right and one left, affect shot selection. The landing area from the tee is between 200 and 245 yards, leaving a shot of 130–150 over water to a green that slopes toward the water and is bunkered left and back right. Errant shots right fall off to the next tee leaving a blind approach to the green. The ideal tee position is right center and most players hit 2- to 4-irons off the tee.

Position is the most important consideration at the Par 4, 366-yard 6th hole. Trees guard the fairway right and left and a sand trap comes into play 215 yards from the tee on the left side. Sacrifice distance for accuracy and hit into the center of the fairway, leaving 150 to 170 yards to an elevated two-tiered green guarded front left, right and back with sand traps.

Hitting from an elevated tee, No. 7 doesn't seem 155 yards. Players hit between 7- to 9-irons depending upon wind velocity to a green guarded left by tree and bunker on this Par 3.

No. 8 is a lay-up hole with a 3- to 5-iron the most selected choice, leaving an approach of 175–200 yards over Bear Creek on this 400-yard Par 4 dogleg right. Errant approach shots can find bunkers back left and front right or a lake which runs along the right side and back of the green from 100 yards out.

Let it all hang out on the 402-yard, Par 4 9th hole as the driver is the order of the day. A lone sand trap, 190 yards from the tee, guards the left side of the fairway. Second shots are hit to a three-tiered green guarded back left and front right by sand traps.

The back 9 begins with a Par 5 hole that continues to dogleg to the right. Your 1st shot should be left center for two sand traps, from 200 to 255 from the tee, guard the right side of the fairway, but too far right off the tee forces a second shot over a row of trees. Out-of-bounds markers guard the left side of the fairway, but don't come into play on your tee shot. A good drive sets up an opportunity to reach this 510-yard hole in two, but trees on the left and a sand trap front right can grab an errant shot easily, turning a potential birdie into a bogey or worse.

No. 11 is a slight dogleg left, 365-yard Par 4. Trees and mounds come into play if you hit your tee shot too far left; there is relatively no trouble to the right. The green is guarded on the right side by a sand trap.

Position is important on the 344-yard Par 4 12th. There is a sand trap down the left side of the fairway 210 yards from the teeing area and beyond the trap is a hazard. Most players lay-up with a 3-wood or 2-to 4-iron depending on wind speed and direction, leaving an approach of between 120 and 150 yards to a green bunkered left.

No. 13 is a dogleg left whose club selection is determined by how much of the corner you wish to cut off. Most players hit a 3-wood or long iron over the trees on the left, leaving between 150 and 180 to a 3-tiered green. A shot from the tee too far left or too far right can catch trees, blocking your approach to the green, or worse, there is a lake which guards the right side of the fairway from approximately 150 yards. The green is bunkered left, back, and right.

Over a valley characterizes the 189-yard Par 3 14th guarded on the right by a sand trap the length of the green and beyond a hazard.

No. 15 is rated as the course's second most difficult hole. Par 4, 423 yards, there are trees and a sand trap right and two trees left that make accuracy a must if you are to set up a second shot on this dogleg right. A drive to the left center of the fairway will leave between 160–190 yards to a two-tiered green, guarded on the left by a large trap and to the right by a small bunker.

You can gamble or play safe on the 515-yard Par 5 16th. If you hit your driver straight, you can reach the green in two, setting up a possible eagle or a certain birdie. But if you hit right or left, you can be in trees or hazard, for a sure double bogey. Some players hit iron off the tee, then play their second shots to leave an approach between 140–160 to a green bunkered on the left and back right by sand.

No. 17 is a good Par 3, 175 yards over water. Shots hit left may very likely kick left under a willow tree or into the water. There is a trap short right and over the green left.

The finishing hole is narrow, guarded left and right by trees and hazard. Par 4, 383 yards, if your tee shot is in the fairway, you have between 150–175 yards to the green. A large trap catches errant approaches to the right.

Architect Ted Robinson has taken advantage of the natural terrain and habitat to create a truly challenging golf course.

Location: SW corner of DFW Airport off Airfield Drive
Green Fees: $25 weekdays, $31 weekends and holidays; Carts: $19 for 18 holes; AX, Visa and MC accepted.
Tee Time Procedures: Call 3 days in advance (214-453-0140).

BEAR CREEK MASTERS

Site of the All-American Intercollegiate Invitational Tournament in April, the Masters, one of three courses at Bear Creek Golf World in Houston, is ranked in the Top 50 public courses by *Golf Digest* magazine and the Par 4, 441-yard 18th hole is rated as one of the 50 best holes open to the public and as one of the "100 Greatest Holes in America" by *Golf* magazine.

Located in Addick's Reservoir on land owned by the Army Corps of Engineers and subleased from Harris County, the Masters Course was designed by Jay Riviere who made excellent use of the natural terrain, which includes tall pines and oak trees and a meandering Bear Creek.

The Masters plays as long as 7048 yards and as short as 5979, highlighted by narrow fairways and water on 16 of the 18 holes. Par is 72. From the back tees, the course rating is 74.2. Former University of Houston golfer Tray Tyner set the competitive course record in the 1984 Public Links Qualifying, a 62.

Fifty-three sand traps guard the Bermuda grass greens which are sloping and, in many instances, multi-tiered.

Concrete blocks located in the center of the fairway serve as yardage markers—Blue at 125 yards, Orange at 175, and White at 225—to help gauge distance.

Trees are a factor on nearly every hole with shots straying from the fairway forcing bogey or double bogey.

Two of the Par 5's are reachable in two and offer excellent opportunities for birdies. The Par 3's require short to medium irons with water a factor on each hole. The Par 4's provide the most challenge, requiring both length and accuracy to score well.

The first four holes feature out-of-bounds left. The first hole is a slight dogleg left 504-yard Par 5 that is reachable in two. A creek on the right side of the hole comes into play along with a clump of trees just right of the green. A large green, it is guarded by a sand trap front right and left.

The Par 4 2nd hole is straight-away, 408 yards to a 2-tiered green guarded left and right by traps. Too far right off the tee catches the lake which fronts No. 8 green.

No. 3 is 408 yards. There is a lone sand trap at the edge of the fairway 220 yards from the tee that can catch a pulled tee shot and there are trees right that can catch a push making the second shot difficult. A lake, left, beginning 100 yards from the green to the edge of the left sand trap also can come into play. Four bunkers surround this Par 4 green which slopes from back to front.

You must hit over a creek to a well-trapped green on this Par 3, 151-yard 4th hole. The green is deep and narrow, placing a premium on a well-hit approach.

The 5th hole doglegs slightly to the right approximately 320 yards from the tee. Because a creek runs along the right side of the fairway, hit your tee shot left to assure an open shot to the green on this 454-yard Par 4 hole. Two traps, one left and one right, guard the green.

The creek also comes into play on the Par 5, 557-yard 6th hole, in front of the tee and from tee to green along the right side. The rough slopes toward the creek which means hitting your tee shot left of center is a must. Trees also line both sides to the fairway, leading to a green bunkered with one trap left and two traps right.

No. 7 is 423 yards straight-away. Four traps, two in front and two in back, guard the green.

Two traps, one left and one right, guard the green on this 182-yard Par 3 8th hole which requires a shot of approximately 150 yards over water.

Though not selected by *Golf* magazine, No. 9 may be the most difficult hole on the Masters course. A Par 4, 464 yards, Bear Creek meanders in front of the tee and along the right side of the fairway. A large lake fronts a 12,000 square foot green guarded by four sand traps. Trees left and right frame this picturesque hole, with two irons or 4 woods the rule here on your second shot. This is the No. 1 handicap hole on the score-card.

A 420-yard, Par 4 starts the back 9. Two trees, right and left, mark Bear Creek approximately 190 yards from the teeing area and make for a narrow tee shot to a hole that doglegs slightly right. On the left, approximately 260 from the tee, is a lake and the right side of the fairway is lined with trees. The green is guarded front right and left by a sand trap.

No. 11 is a straight-away 431-yard Par 4. Your drive needs to be left center because the trees to the right can block your second shot to this two-tiered green. Sand traps right and left stretch the length of the green. Also, Bear Creek crosses the fairway approximately 90 yards from the green.

Bear Creek and a pond front the 184-yard Par 3 12th hole. Shots hit short will roll back into the pond. Five sand traps circle the green.

No. 13 is 412 yards with out-of-bounds right. A good tee shot will leave approximately 150–180 yards to a green guarded on four sides by sand. Too far left on your second shot can find a lake. The green itself is crowned in the center and slopes front and back.

The Par 5, 509-yard 14th hole is reachable in two. Out-of-bounds to the right stretches the length of the hole. A good drive sets up a 225–250 yard shot to a green bunkered left and right by sand and an opportunity for a birdie.

Behind #18, one of the 100 "Greatest Holes in America."

No. 15 is a dogleg right Par 5 with a lake on the right side from approximately 225 yards to green side. Four traps surround this L-shaped green. The hole plays 528 yards.

Water and five sand traps, U-shaped from front to back, guard the green at the Par, 392-yard 16th hole. The water starts from about 60 yards to the green and the fairway slants left at that point.

No. 17, 182 yards, is the best Par 3 on the course. Your tee shot must carry over water and two sand traps which leave a narrow opening to the green.

The finishing hole, No. 18, has been acclaimed as one of the "greatest 100 holes in America." 441 yards, the hole doglegs left around a lake approximately 220 yards from the tee. Second shots must carry another lake in front of the green and avoid trees right and left. Four sand traps guard this large green.

Location: I-10 to HWY 6, North to Bear Creek Golf World
Green Fees: $20 anytime; Carts: $16 for 18 holes
(single riders pay $13).
Tee Time Procedure: Weekends: Non-members call Friday;
Weekdays: Call 1 week in advance
(713-859-8188).

GRAPEVINE MUNICIPAL

Designed by Byron Nelson and Joe Finger, this Par 72 course ranks in *Golf Digest's* top 75 public courses. It is built in a hollow beneath Lake Grapevine Dam which borders the course to the north and a spillway for Lake Grapevine creates a river which comes into play on two holes on the back 9.

Grapevine Muny can play as long as 7022 yards from the blue tees and as short as 5913 from the reds. One of the holes, the 411-yard, Par 4 13th, has been rated by *Golf* magazine as one of the top 50 holes open for public play in the United States and features the tallest giant ash in Texas with a plaque on the tree commemorating the fact along the right side of the fairway.

The course is challenging as its 73.5 rating from the Blues will attest. Warren Aune of Dallas holds the competitive course record of 69.

The Par 5's are difficult to reach in two from the back tees, stretching from 544 to 574 yards. The Par 3's range from 150 to 230 yards, with the long No. 2 requiring a driver many days as it frequently plays into the wind.

There are seven dogleg lefts and five dogleg rights to test one's shot-making ability. Water, either lakes or rivers, come into play on nine holes.

View from Lake Grapevine Dam

The bermuda grass greens are large and hilly. If the course has a drawback, the greens tend to be grainy and bumpy.

Also, a word of caution dictates you keep the ball in the fairway. Shots astray can rest in or against the thick-bladed, weed-like grass which is prevalent and makes your next shot a challenge to keep on line.

No. 1 is a 558-yard Par 5 which doglegs slightly left near the green. There is a sand trap on the left and a tree on the right approximately 256 yards from the teeing area which can affect play. The green is guarded to the left by a small lake starting at 130 yards to the green and a sand trap borders right.

Length is the problem on the long Par 3 2nd hole. From the back tees, the hole plays 230 yards, generally into a wind. Even from the front tees or ladies tees, the hole plays 171 yards. One sand trap guards the right side of the green.

Keep your tee shot on right side of the fairway on the Par 4, 393-yard dogleg left to allow for an open shot to the 3rd hole. To the left means hitting over a tall oak tree and a ravine to reach this large green.

No. 4 is a 415-yard, Par 4 dogleg left guarded left by a ravine and a row of trees. Tee shots hit right mean your approach is over water and three small trees.

Playing safe or gambling with your tee shot can be the difference between a birdie or a double bogey on the 544-yard Par 5, sharp dogleg left 5th hole. Gambling means cutting the corner approximately 215 yards from the tee and requires going over or around a row of trees on the left, leaving a long iron to a well-guarded, by water and trap, hilly green. Playing safe means hitting to the right center of the fairway, then approaching the final 300 yards with two shots.

No. 6 doglegs slightly to the right with a lake stretching down the left side of the fairway approximately 230 yards, with four tall trees marking the turn of the dogleg. The two-tiered green on this 384-yard Par 4 is guarded by one sand trap on the left.

Another long iron shot is required to a hilly green on the Par 3, 198-yard 7th hole.

Water comes into play on the Par 4, 386-yard 8th hole which doglegs to the right. The green is guarded left, front, and right by two lakes. A drive hit right can catch one lake 250 yards from the tee.

No. 9 is a difficult front 9 finishing hole. 458 yards, the final 100 yards is uphill to a green surrounded by trees. A lone sand trap protects the left front of the green.

The back 9 begins with a challenging Par 5, 574-yard slight dogleg. Trees protect the corners of the fairway approximately 250 yards from the tee. Trees approximately 100 yards short of the green on the right discourage cutting too much of the dogleg on your second shot.

The Par 4 11th is 422 yards, doglegging to the left 150 yards from the green. A sand trap 250 yards from the tee can catch a drive at the corner. Another sand trap guards the left side of the green.

No. 12 is the most spectacular hole on the course, lying at the base of Lake Grapevine Dam which stretches upwards of 150 yards to its top along the right side of the fairway. Narrow with trees left, the 572-yard Par 5 has been playing as a 185-yard Par 3 while the Corps of Engineers work on the dam's embankment; however, work should be completed soon. There are trees left and right leaving a narrow opening to an elevated two-tiered green.

Position is important on the dogleg left 13th hole. A clump of trees at the left corner make it imperative to stay right to leave an open shot to a well-protected green. Too far right, however, blocks the approach to the green. A sand trap right and a river that curls around the green can catch errant shots.

No. 14 is 150 yards to an elevated green with the river stretching along the left side of the hole. This Par 3 green slopes from back to front.

No. 15 is a tantalizing 330-yard Par 4 with water and trees stretching the entire right side of the hole. There is plenty of room left to approach a green guarded front left and right by sand traps.

Shots hit right from the tee at 16 leave no chance to reach the 400-yard hole in two. There is one trap left and water right of the green on this Par 4 hole.

It's only 176 yards to the Par 3 17th, but the two-tiered sloping green makes two putts far from a certainty.

Another fine finishing hole completes the 18. Par 4, 421 yards, the 18th doglegs to the left. A mound runs along the right side of the fairway to approximately 190 from the green. A tee shot to the right center of the fairway leaves an approach to a green guarded in front (25 yards) right by trees with sand traps left and right.

Location: Off FM 2499 at the south end of Lake Grapevine on Fairway Drive

Green Fees: $7 weekdays, $9 weekends and holidays; Carts: $12.50 for 18 holes.

Tee Time Procedure: 3 days in advance at 7 a.m. in person or after noon by phone (817-481-0421).

7. The last of Walter Hagen's 5 PGA championships and the last of four in a row was won at this Texas golf course.

Central Corridor

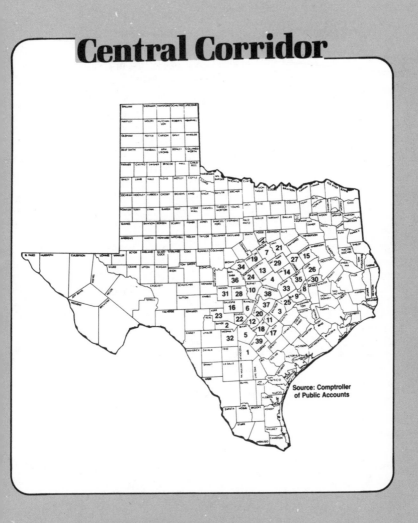

Source: Comptroller
of Public Accounts

More golf courses attached to military bases and more resorts are located within the Central Corridor than any other region.

Of the 115 courses open for public play, seven are on military bases and nine are resort golf centers.

Forty-three others are public golf courses, 18 are semi-private and 45 are labeled private.

While only two courses are under construction and plan to open later this year, over 10 are on the drawing board for future development.

CENTRAL CORRIDOR CITIES

8. Who was the last Texan to win the Masters tournament until Ben Crenshaw did it in 1984—Tom Kite, Charles Coody, or Byron Nelson?

Golf course weaves through housing development at Lakeway.

ATASCOSA 1

Pleasanton

PLEASANTON COUNTRY CLUB
A semi-private club with one 9-hole course
Location: HWY 281N, left at Bensdale, take 1st right after RR tracks
Golf Data: Pro Shop Phone: (512) 569-3486; Club Pro: Mike Yanity; Par: 36; Yardage: 3200; Rating: 70.5 (if 18 holes played); Closed Monday.
Green Fees: $6.30 weekdays, $12.10 weekends and holidays; Carts: $10.50 for 18 holes.
Tee Time Procedure: 1st come, 1st served.

BANDERA 2

Bandera

FLYING L RANCH
A resort club with one 18-hole course
Location: 1 mile S. on HWY 173
Golf Data: Pro Shop Phone: (512) 796-3001; Club Manager: John Junker; Par: 72; Yardage: 6787; Rating: 70.5; Course Architect: Jackson Brady; Open 7 days.
NOTE: For resort and golf information, phone (800) 292-5134 or write to Flying

L Ranch, HCR 1, Box 32, Bandera, TX 78003.
Green Fees: $6 weekdays, $10 weekends and holidays; Carts: $10.50 for 18 holes; AX, Visa and MC accepted.
Tee Time Procedure: Call anytime for weekends or weekdays play.

LAZY OAKS RANCH
A public club with one 18-hole course
Location: 2½ miles E. on HWY 16
Golf Data: Pro Shop Phone: (512) 796-3117; Club Manager: Mark Collier; Par: 72; Yardage: 6210; Open 7 days.
Green Fees: $5 weekdays, $7.50 weekends and holidays; Carts: $6 per 9 holes.
Tee Time Procedure: 1st come, 1st served.

BASTROP 3

Bastrop

LOST PINES GOLF CLUB
A public club with one 9-hole course
Location: Off HWY 21 at Bastrop State Park
Golf Data: Pro Shop Phone: (512) 321-2327; Club Pro: Rudy Balmares; Par: 36; Yardage: 3323; Rating: 71.5 (if 18 holes played); Course Architect: T. P. Haynie, Jr.; Open 7 days.

Green Fees: $5 weekdays, $6 weekends and holidays; Carts: $6.31 per 9 holes.
Tee Time Procedure: Weekends: Wednesday after 8 a.m. by phone or in person (Holidays: 3 days in advance); Weekdays: 1st come, 1st served.

PINE FOREST GOLF CLUB
A semi-private club with one 18-hole course
Location: 2½ miles E. off HWY 71
Golf Data: Pro Shop Phone: (512) 321-1181; Club Pro: Joe B. Priddy; Par: 72; Yardage: 6613; Rating: 71.3; Course Architect: Martin Dale; Closed Monday.
Green Fees: $10 weekdays, $15 weekends and holidays; Carts: $15 for 18 holes.
Tee Time Procedure: Weekends: Call Thursday after 8 a.m.; Weekdays: Call first, but generally no problem.

——— BELL ——— 4

Belton

LEON VALLEY GOLF COURSE
A public club with one 18-hole course
Location: E. on 24th Street
Golf Data: Pro Shop Phone: (817) 939-5271; Club Pro: Carlie Tice; Par: 72; Yardage: 6800; Rating: 70.3; Open 7 days.
Green Fees: $6 + tax weekdays, $8 + tax weekends and holidays; Carts: $12 + tax for 18 holes.
Tee Time Procedure: Weekends-Holidays: Thursday after 7 a.m. by phone or in person; Weekdays: 1st come, 1st served.

Fort Hood

ANDERSON GOLF COURSE
A semi-private club with one 18-hole course
Location: Take Rancier Road to East Gate
Golf Data: Pro Shop Phone: (817) 287-6921; Club Manager: Jerry Robertson; Par: 72; Yardage: 6703; Rating: 69.4; Closed Monday.
Green Fees: $5 weekdays, $6 weekends and holidays for general play; military fees are $4 weekdays, $5 weekends and holidays; Carts: $10 for 18 holes.

Tee Time Procedure: No tee times for general public. Handled 1st come, 1st served.

CLEARCREEK GOLF COURSE
A semi-private club with one 18-hole course
Location: Off Clearcreek on Batallion
Golf Data: Pro Shop Phone: (817) 287-4130; Club Manager: Wallace Bryant; Par: 72; Yardage: 6768; Rating: 72.0; Closed Tuesday.
Green Fees: $5 weekdays, $6 weekends and holidays for general play; military fees are $4 weekdays, $5 weekends and holidays; Carts: $10 for 18 holes.
Tee Time Procedure: Weekends-Holidays: No tee time for general play. 1st come, 1st served after 10 a.m.; Weekdays: 1st come, 1st served.

Killeen

CEDAR HILLS GOLF CLUB
A private club with one 9-hole course
Location: HWY 190W, exit 2410S to Cedar Knob, right 2½ miles to Fuller; right to Oakridge, right
Golf Data: Pro Shop Phone: (817) 698-4554; Club Pro: Myron T. Justin; Par: 36; Yardage: 3240; Rating: 68.8 (if 18 holes played); Closed Monday.
Guest Policy: You must play with a member or be a member of another private country club. Call in advance.

KILLEEN MUNICIPAL GOLF COURSE
A public club with one 18-hole course
Location: Take Bus. 190W, right at FM 2410
Golf Data: Pro Shop Phone: (817) 699-6034; Club Manager: Joe Cassell; Par: 72; Yardage: 6866; Rating: 72.9; Open 7 days.
Green Fees: $6 weekdays, $7.50 weekends and holidays; Carts: $12.62 for 18 holes; Visa and MC accepted.
Tee Time Procedure: 1st come, 1st served.

Salado

MILL CREEK GOLF & COUNTRY CLUB
A resort club with one 18-hole course
Location: I-35, exit 285W ½ mile
Golf Data: Pro Shop Phone: (817) 947-5698; Club Pro: Mike Cameron; Par:

71; Yardage: 6486; Rating: 71.5; Course Architect: Robert Trent Jones, Jr.; Closed Monday.

Guest Policy: You must be a guest of member, member of a U.S.G.A.-member private country club or a guest of the resort.

NOTE: For resort and golf package information, phone (817) 947-5141, or write Mill Creek, P.O. Box 67, Salado, TX 76571. Guest cards are also available through the Stagecoach Motor Inn (817) 947-5111.

Green Fees: $26 weekdays, $36 weekends and holidays; Carts: $15 for 18 holes; Visa and MC accepted.

Tee Time Procedure: Guests of the resort may make tee time arrangements anytime; motel guests may schedule play 48 hours in advance.

Temple

TEMPLE COUNTRY CLUB
A private club with one 18-hole course
Location: On W. Avenue D
Golf Data: Pro Shop Phone: (817) 778-2841; Club Pro: Greg Antune; Par: 70; Yardage: 5563; Rating: 66.3; Closed Monday.
Guest Policy: You must be a guest of a member or a member of another private country club.

TEMPLE JUNIOR COLLEGE GOLF COURSE
A public club with one 18-hole course
Location: Next to VA Hospital on S. 1st Street
Golf Data: Pro Shop Phone: (817) 778-9809; Club Pro: Paul Guillen; Par: 68 (two sets of tees); Yardage: 5526; Rating: 66.0; Open 7 days.
Green Fees: $3.65 weekdays, $4.70 weekends and holidays; Carts: $8.50 for 18 holes.
Tee Time Procedure: 1st come, 1st served.

WILDFLOWER COUNTRY CLUB
A private club with one 18-hole course
Location: Take FM 2305W, right at Kegley Road
NOTE: 18 holes designed by Leon Howard and developed by Country Clubs of America is due to open in Spring 1987.

San Antonio

Public Golf Courses

BRACKENRIDGE GOLF COURSE
A public club with one 18-hole course
Location: Off HWY 281 in Brackenridge Park at 2315 Avenue "B" (see #1 on locator map)
Golf Data: Pro Shop Phone: (512) 226-5602; Shop Manager: John F. Ervin; Par: 72; Yardage: 6185; Rating: 67.0; Open 7 days.
NOTE: This was first 18-hole public course in Texas.
Green Fees: $6.50 weekdays, $7 weekends and holidays; Carts: $12.68 for 18 holes.
Tee Time Procedure: Weekends-Holidays: Drawing Thursday at 6 p.m. in person; Weekdays: 1 week in advance in person.
NOTE: Must pay $2.50 non-refundable reservation fee for tee time.

OLMOS BASIN GOLF COURSE
A public club with one 18-hole course
Location: Off HWY 281 in Olmos Park (see #2 on locator map)
Golf Data: Pro Shop Phone: (512) 826-4041; Shop Manager: Jerry Hill; Par: 72; Yardage: 6894; Rating: 71.0; Open 7 days.
Green Fees: $6.50 weekdays, $7 weekends and holidays; Carts: $12.68 for 18 holes.
Tee Time Procedure: Weekends-Holidays: Drawing Thursday at 6 p.m. in person; Weekdays: 1 week in advance in person.
NOTE: Must pay $2.50 non-refundable reservation fee for tee time.

RIVERSIDE GOLF COURSE
A public club with 27 holes
Location: HWY 37S to Roosevelt Road, right to 203 McDonald Avenue (see #3 on locator map)
Golf Data: Pro Shop Phone: (512) 533-8371; Shop Manager: G. Boyd Humphries; Course Architect: LaVern Schmidt, *Regulation* 18 Par: 72; Yardage: 6723; Rating: 72.0; *Par 3* 9 Par: 27; Yardage: 920; Open 7 days.
Green Fees: $6.50 weekdays, $7 weekends and holidays for 18 holes; $3 weekdays, $3.50 weekends and holidays for

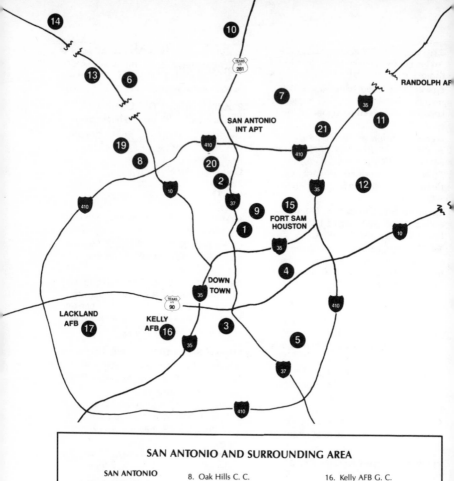

SAN ANTONIO AND SURROUNDING AREA

SAN ANTONIO
1. Brackenridge G. C.
2. Olmos Basin G. C.
3. Riverside G. C.
4. Willow Springs G. C.
5. Pecan Valley G. C.
6. The Dominion
7. Northern Hills C. C.

8. Oak Hills C. C.
9. San Antonio C. C.
10. Sonterra G. C.
11. Windcrest G. C.
12. Woodlake C. C.
13. Fair Oaks Ranch
14. Tapatio Springs C. C. & Resort
15. Fort Sam Houston G. C.

16. Kelly AFB G. C.
17. Lackland AFB G. C.
18. Randolph AFB G. C.
19. Carpenters Par 3
20. Joe Conrad's 19th Hole
21. Kurt Cox Par 3
22. Carmack Lake E. C.

Par 3; Carts: $7.75 for 9 holes, $12 for 18 holes.

Tee Time Procedure: Weekends-Holidays: Drawing Thursday at 6 p.m. in person; Weekdays: 1 week in advance in person.
NOTE: *Must pay $2.50 non-refundable reservation fee for tee time.*

WILLOW SPRINGS GOLF COURSE
A public club with one 18-hole course
Location: I-10, exit Houston Street, right to Coliseum (see #4 on locator map)

Golf Data: Pro Shop Phone: (512) 226-6721; Shop Manager: Ken Sealey; Par: 72; Yardage: 7085; Rating: 73.7; Open 7 days.

Green Fees: $6.50 weekdays, $7 weekends and holidays; Carts: $12.68 for 18 holes.

Tee Time Procedure: Weekends-Holidays: Drawing Thursday at 6 p.m. in person; Weekdays: 1 week in advance in person.
NOTE: *Must pay $2.50 non-refundable reservation fee for tee time.*

Semi-Private Golf Courses

PECAN VALLEY GOLF COURSE
A semi-private club with one 18-hole course
Location: I-37S, exit Southcross E. (see #5 on locator map)
Golf Data: Pro Shop Phone: (512) 333-9018; Club Pro: Tom Adams; Par: 72; Yardage: 7163; Rating: 73.9; Course Architect: Press Maxwell; Open 7 days.
NOTE: Site of 1968 PGA Championship, 3 Texas Opens.
Green Fees: $13 weekdays, $18 weekends and holidays; Carts: $15.15 for 18 holes; AX, Visa and MC accepted.
Tee Time Procedure: Weekends-Holidays: Thursday after 7 a.m. by phone or in person; Weekdays: 1 day in advance.

Private Golf Courses

THE DOMINION
A private club with one 18-hole course
Location: I-10, 12 miles W. of Loop, exit Camp Bullis Road (see #6 on locator map)
Golf Data: Pro Shop Phone: (512) 698-1146; Director of Golf: Buddy Cook; Par: 72; Yardage: 6927; Rating: 73.2; Course Architect: Bill Johnston; Closed Monday.
NOTE: Site of Dominion PGA Seniors Invitational.
Guest Policy: You must play with a member.

NORTHERN HILLS COUNTRY CLUB
A private club with one 18-hole course
Location: I-410, exit Perrin Beitel, N. to Thousand Oaks (see #7 on locator map)
Golf Data: Pro Shop Phone: (512) 655-8026; Club Pro: Barry Hansen; Par: 71; Yardage: 6503; Rating: 70.4; Course Architect: Joe Behlau; Closed Monday.
Guest Policy: You must play with a member or be a member of a reciprocating private country club. Phone for details.

OAK HILLS COUNTRY CLUB
A private club with one 18-hole course
Location: 5403 Fredericksburg Road, 1 mile outside loop 410 (see #8 on locator map)
Golf Data: Pro Shop Phone: (512) 349-6354; Club Pro: Warren Chancellor;

Par: 71; Yardage: 6850; Rating: 71.5; Course Architect: A. W. Tillinghast (Redesign: Jay Morrish 1984); Closed Monday.
NOTE: Site of 1987 $2,500,000 Nabisco Championship; 1986 Vantage Championship & 9 Texas Opens.
Guest Policy: You are welcome as a guest as long as prior arrangements have been made by your club professional or club manager. Times for unescorted guests are restricted. Please call for details.

SAN ANTONIO COUNTRY CLUB
A private club with one 18-hole course
Location: HWY 281N, exit Hildebrand E. 2 miles (see #9 on locator map)
Golf Data: Pro Shop Phone: (512) 824-8863; Club Pro: Charles Siver; Par: 72; Yardage: 6698; Rating: 70.2; Course Architect: Joe Finger (redesign); Open 7 days.
Guest Policy: You must play with a member or, as a member of another private country club, you play with approval of both clubs' managers. Phone for specifics.

THE CLUB AT SONTERRA
A private club with two 18-hole courses
Location: HWY 281N, exit FM 1604 (see #10 on locator map)
Golf Data: Pro Shop Phone: (512) 491-9900; Club Pro: Bob Putt; Sonterra *South* 18 Par: 72; Yardage: 6495; Rating: 70.1; Sonterra *North* 18 Par: 72; Yardage: 7070; Rating: 74.5; Course Architects: Bruce Devlin & Bob Von Hagge (both courses); Closed Monday.
Guest Policy: You must be a guest of a member or a member of another private country club. Phone in advance.

WINDCREST GOLF COURSE
A private club with one 9-hole course
Location: I-35, exit Walzem E. to Windcrest Development (see #11 on locator map)
Golf Data: Pro Shop Phone: (512) 655-1421; Club Manager: Richard Katz; Par: 34; Yardage: 2481; Rating: 61.9 (if 18 holes played); Closed Monday.
Guest Policy: You must be a guest of a member and that member should accompany guest of the club.

WOODLAKE COUNTRY CLUB
A private club with one 18-hole course
Location: I-35, exit Rittiman, E. 6 miles (see #12 on locator map)
Golf Data: Pro Shop Phone: (512) 661-6124; Club Pro: Rex Brinkman; Par: 72; Yardage: 7176; Rating: 72.0; Course Architect: Desmond Muirhead; Closed Monday.
NOTE: Site of 5 Texas Opens.
Guest Policy: You must be a member of another private country club. Have your pro phone in advance.

Boerne
FAIR OAKS RANCH
A private club with 27 holes
Location: I-10W 12 miles (from I-410 Loop), exit Fair Oaks Pkwy. (see #13 on locator map)
Golf Data: Pro Shop Phone: (512) 698-1682; Club Pro: Jim Deaton; *Live Oak* Par: 36; Yardage: 3398; *Spanish Oak* Par: 36; Yardage: 3486; *Blackjack Oak* Par: 36; Yardage: 3639; Ratings: Live Oak/Spanish Oak: 72.0; Live Oak/Blackjack Oak: 72.0; Spanish Oak/Blackjack Oak: 73.0; Closed Monday.
Guest Policy: You must play with a member or be a member of another private country club. Phone for specifics.

Military Golf Courses

FORT SAM HOUSTON GOLF COURSE
A private club with two 18-hole courses
Location: At Fort Sam Houston (see #15 on locator map)
Golf Data: Pro Shop Phone: (512) 222-9386; Pro/Mgr.: Johnny Mitchell; *La Loma* Par: 72; Yardage: 6740; Rating: 72.5; *Salada* Par: 72; Yardage: 6755; Rating: 71.0; Open 7 days.
Guest Policy: You must be military or a guest of the military.

KELLY AFB GOLF COURSE
A private club with one 18-hole course
Location: At Kelly AFB (see #16 on locator map)
Golf Data: Pro Shop Phone: (512) 925-7100; Club Manager: John Mochrie; Par: 72; Yardage: 6935; Rating: 73.0; Open 7 days.

Guest Policy: You must be a guest of the military.

LACKLAND AFB GOLF CLUB
A private club with one 18-hole course
Location: At Lackland AFB (see #17 on locator map)
Golf Data: Pro Shop Phone: (512) 671-3466; Club Pro: Wayne (Red) Davis; Par: 72; Yardage: 6822; Rating: 72.0; Open 7 days.
Guest Policy: You must be a guest of the military.

RANDOLPH AFB GOLF COURSE
A private club with one 18-hole course
Location: At Randolph AFB (see #18 on locator map)
Golf Data: Pro Shop Phone: (512) 652-4653; Club Manager: Ed Schieber; Par: 72; Yardage: 7172; Rating: 73.8; 9 holes closed Monday.
Guest Policy: You must be a guest of the military.

Par 3/Executive Golf Courses

San Antonio
CARPENTERS PAR 3
A public club with one 9-hole course
Location: I-10, exit Wurzbach Road S. (see #19 on locator map)
Golf Data: Pro Shop Phone: (512) 696-3143; Club Pro: Bob Estes; Par: 27; Yardage: 785; Open 7 days.
Green Fees: $2.50 per 9 holes; Visa and MC accepted; No carts available.
Tee Time Procedure: 1st come, 1st served.

JOE CONRAD'S 19TH HOLE
A public club with one 9-hole course
Location: HWY 281, exit Jackson Keller E. (see #20 on locator map)
Golf Data: Pro Shop Phone: (512) 344-2671; Club Pro: Joe Conrad; Par: 27; Yardage: 1000; Open 7 days.
Green Fees: $1.50 for 9, $2.50 for 18 holes; Visa and MC accepted; No carts available.
Tee Time Procedure: 1st come, 1st served.

KURT COX PAR 3
A public club with one 9-hole course
Location: I-35N, exit O'Connor Road W. (see #21 on locator map)

Golf Data: Pro Shop Phone: (512) 655-3131; Club Pro: Kurt Cox; Par: 27; Yardage: 911; Open 7 days.

Green Fees: $2.50 for 9, $4.50 for 18 holes; Visa and MC accepted; No carts available.

Tee Time Procedure: 1st come, 1st served.

Converse

CARMACK LAKE EXECUTIVE COURSE
A public club with one 18-hole course
Location: I-10E, exit FM 1518N (see #22 on locator map)
Golf Data: Pro Shop Phone: (512) 658-3806; Club Pro: Don Carmack; Par: 59; Yardage: 3200; Open Wed-Sun.

Green Fees: $4.50 anytime.

Tee Time Procedure: 1st come, 1st served.

——— BLANCO ——— 6

None

——— BOSQUE ——— 7

Meridian

BOSQUE VALLEY GOLF COURSE
A semi-private club with one 9-hole course
Location: 3 miles E. on Old Chilton HWY (FM 1991)
Golf Data: Pro Shop Phone: (817) 435-2692; Club Pro: Matt Child; Par: 36; Yardage: 3054; Closed Tuesday.

Green Fees: $5 weekdays, $10 weekends and holidays; Carts: $6 per 9 holes.

Tee Time Procedure: 1st come, 1st served.

——— BRAZOS ——— 8

Bryan

BRIARCREST COUNTRY CLUB
A private club with one 18-hole course
Location: On Briarcrest Drive, W. of HWY 6 Bypass
Golf Data: Pro Shop Phone: (409) 776-1490; Club Pro: Mike Higgins; Par: 72; Yardage: 6804; Rating: 70.1; Closed Monday.

Guest Policy: You must be a guest of a member or a member of another private country club. Phone in advance.

BRYAN GOLF COURSE
A public club with one 18-hole course
Location: Intersection of College & Villa Maria
Golf Data: Pro Shop Phone: (409) 823-0126; Club Pro: Jerry Honza; Par: 70; Yardage: 6217; Rating: 69.2; Open 7 days.

Green Fees: $7 weekdays, $8.50 weekends and holidays; Carts: $13 for 18 holes; Visa and MC accepted.

Tee Time Procedure: Call 1 week in advance.

College Station

TEXAS A&M UNIVERSITY GOLF COURSE
A public club with one 18-hole course
Location: A&M campus on Bizzell Street
Golf Data: Pro Shop Phone: (409) 845-1723; Club Pro: Andy Birmingham; Par: 70; Yardage: 6513; Rating: 70.2; Course Architect: Jackie Burke; Open 7 days.

Green Fees: $4.50 weekdays, $5 weekends and holidays for students; $5.50 weekdays, $6 weekends and holidays for staff; and $6 weekdays, $7 weekends and holidays for general play; Carts: $12.61 for 18 holes; Visa and MC accepted.

Tee Time Procedure: Call 1 week in advance.

——— BURLESON ——— 9

Caldwell

COPPERAS HOLLOW COUNTRY CLUB
A semi-private club with one 9-hole course
Location: On State HWY 36N
Golf Data: Pro Shop Phone: (409) 567-4422; Club Pro: Frank Bush; Par: 36; Yardage: 3190; Rating: 69.9 (if 18 holes played); Course Architect: John Johnson; Closed Monday.

Green Fees: $7 weekdays, $10 weekends and holidays; Carts: $6 + tax per 9 holes.

Tee Time Procedure: 1st come, 1st served.

Buchanan

HIGHLAND LAKES GOLF COURSE

A public club with one 9-hole course

Location: In Inks Lake State Park on Park Road 4

Golf Data: Pro Shop Phone: (512) 793-2859; Club Pro: Johnnie Tyson; Par: 36; Yardage: 2778; Open 7 days.

Green Fees: $5 weekdays, $6 weekends and holidays; Carts: $6.25 per 9 holes.

Tee Time Procedure: 1st come, 1st served.

Horseshoe Bay

HORSESHOE BAY COUNTRY CLUB RESORT

A resort club with three 18-hole courses

Location: From Marble Falls, HWY 281S over bridge, right on Ranch Road 2147; approximately five miles

Golf Data: Pro Shop Phone: (512) 598-2561 (Slick Rock) and (512) 598-6561 (Applerock-Ram Rock); Director of Golf: Brad Pullin; *Applerock* Par: 72; Yardage: 6999; Rating: 73.9; *Ram Rock* Par: 71; Yardage: 6946; Rating: 73.9; *Slick Rock* Par: 72; Yardage: 6839; Rating: 72.4; Course Architect: Robert Trent Jones; Open 7 days.

NOTE: *Ram Rock rated one of the six best inland resort courses by Dick Wilson in his book AMERICA'S GREATEST GOLFING RESORTS. Applerock rated best new resort golf course for 1986 by Golf Digest.*

Guest Policy: You must be a guest of a member or a guest of the resort.

NOTE: *For resort and golf package information, phone (800) 252-9363 in Texas or (800) 531-5105 if out-of-state, or write to Horseshoe Bay Country Club, P.O. Box 7766; Horseshoe Bay, TX 78654.*

Green Fees: $24 weekdays, $28 weekends and holidays; Carts: $15 for 18 holes; AX, Visa and MC accepted.

Tee Time Procedure: Call 1 week in advance.

Marble Falls

MEADOW LAKES COUNTRY CLUB

A semi-private club with one 18-hole course

Location: HWY 281S, right at Meadow Lake Drive (before bridge)

Golf Data: Pro Shop Phone: (512) 693-3300; Club Pro: William H. Tombs; Par: 72; Yardage: 6597; Rating: 70.5; Open 7 days.

Green Fees: $15 weekdays, $20 weekends and holidays; Carts: $15.62 for 18 holes.

Tee Time Procedure: Call anytime.

Lockhart

LOCKHART STATE RECREATION AREA

A public club with one 9-hole course

Location: Take 183S, W. on HWY 20

Golf Data: Pro Shop Phone: (512) 398-3479; Club Manager: Mike Masur; Par: 35; Yardage: 2989; Rating: 70.0 (if 18 holes played); Course Architect: Civilian Conservation Corp; Open 7 days.

Green Fees: $4 weekdays, $5 weekends and holidays; Carts: $8.85 for 18 holes.

Tee Time Procedure: 1st come, 1st served.

Luling

LULING PARK GOLF COURSE

A public club with one 9-hole course

Location: ½ mile W. on HWY 80

Golf Data: Pro Shop Phone: (512) 875-5114; Club Pro: Roy Abramite; Par: 70 (two sets of tees); Yardage: 5897; Rating: 68.0; Closed Monday.

Green Fees: $4 weekdays, $5 weekends and holidays; Carts: $10 for 18 holes.

Tee Time Procedure: 1st come, 1st served.

Canyon Lake at Startzville

WOODLANDS GOLF & COUNTRY CLUB

A public club with one 18-hole course

Location: Intersection of FM 3159 & FM 2673

Golf Data: Pro Shop Phone: (512) 899-3301; Club Manager: Robin Schultz; Par: 72; Yardage: 6407; Open 7 days.

Green Fees: $8 weekdays, $12 weekends and holidays; Carts: $12 for 18 holes; Visa and MC accepted.

Tee Time Procedure: Call anytime.

New Braunfels

LANDA PARK GOLF COURSE
A public club with one 18-hole course
Location: In Landa Park
Golf Data: Pro Shop Phone: (512) 625-3225; Club Pro: Bill Halbert; Par: 72; Yardage: 6103; Rating: 68.0; Open 7 days.
Green Fees: $4.50 weekdays, $6 weekends and holidays; Carts: $11 for 18 holes.
Tee Time Procedure: Weekends-Holidays: Drawing at 4 p.m. Thursday in person; Weekdays: 1st come, 1st served.

————— CORYELL ————— 13

Copperas Cove

COPPERAS COVE MUNICIPAL GOLF COURSE
A public club with one 9-hole course
Location: Avenue D to Wolf Road N., 2nd right after RR tracks, 1st left on Golf Course Road
Golf Data: Pro Shop Phone: (817) 547-2606; Club Pro: Walt Morgan; Par: 36; Yardage: 3097; Rating: 69.0 (if 18 holes played); Closed Monday.
Green Fees: $4.25 weekdays, $6.50 weekends and holidays; Carts: $10.50 for 18 holes + $1 key deposit.
Tee Time Procedure: 1st come, 1st served.

Gatesville

GATESVILLE COUNTRY CLUB
A private club with one 18-hole course
Location: On Strawsmill Road
Golf Data: Pro Shop Phone: (817) 865-6917; Club Pro: Larry Simons; Par: 72; Yardage: 6900; Rating: 71.6; Open 7 days.
Guest Policy: You must be a guest of a member or a member of another private country club.

————— FALLS ————— 14

Marlin

MARLIN COUNTRY CLUB
A private club with one 9-hole course
Location: N.W. of town near TV Tower
Golf Data: Pro Shop Phone: (817) 883-6101; Club Manager: Frank McKinley III; Par: 36; Yardage: 3050; Closed Monday.
Guest Policy: You must play with a member or be a member of another private club.

————— FREESTONE ————— 15

Teague

FREESTONE COUNTRY CLUB
A private club with one 9-hole course
Location: N.E. on HWY 84
Golf Data: Pro Shop Phone: (817) 739-3785; Club Pros: Joe Whitaker & Bill Newlin; Par: 36; Yardage: 3495; Closed Monday.
Guest Policy: You must be a guest of a member or a member of another private country club.

————— GILLESPIE ————— 16

Fredricksburg

LADY BIRD JOHNSON GOLF COURSE
A public club with one 9-hole course
Location: 4 miles S. on Hwy 16 in Lady Bird Johnson State Park
Golf Data: Pro Shop Phone: (512) 997-4010; Club Pro: Dennis Allen; Par: 36; Yardage: 3017; Rating: 69.4 (if 18 holes played); Closed Monday.
Green Fees: $6 weekdays, $7 weekends and holidays; Carts: $12 for 18 holes.
Tee Time Procedure: 1st come, 1st served.

————— GONZALES ————— 17

Gonzales

INDEPENDENCE GOLF CLUB
A public club with one 9-hole course
Location: 1/2 mile S. on HWY 183
Golf Data: Pro Shop Phone: (512) 672-9926; Club Manager: Butch Jackson; Par: 35; Yardage: 2760; Rating: 66.0 (if 18 holes played); Closed Monday.

Green Fees: $3 weekdays, $5 weekends and holidays; Carts: $6 + tax per 9 holes.
Tee Time Procedure: 1st come, 1st served.

——— GUADALUPE ——— 18

Cibolo

NORTHCLIFFE COUNTRY CLUB
A private club with one 18-hole course
Location: I-35 (N. from San Antonio), exit 178, stay on East Access Road
Golf Data: Pro Shop Phone: (512) 625-7351; Club Pro: John Clay; Par: 72; Yardage: 6532; Rating: 71.0; Course Architect: Joe Finger; Open Monday at noon.
Guest Policy: You must play with a member or be a member of another private country club. Phone for specifics.

Sequin

CHAPARREL COUNTRY CLUB
A private club with one 18-hole course
Location: 300 Chaparrel Road
Golf Data: Pro Shop Phone: (512) 379-6314; Club Pro: Roy C. Schneider; Par: 72; Yardage: 7008; Rating: 72.75; Closed Monday.
Guest Policy: You must be a member of another private country club or a guest of a member (once a month).

STARCKE PARK GOLF COURSE
A public club with one 18-hole course
Location: 1600 S. Guadalupe
Golf Data: Pro Shop Phone: (512) 379-4853; Club Pro: Biff Alexander; Par: 71; Yardage: 6769; Rating: 70.5; Open 7 days.
Green Fees: Sequin resident; $5 weekdays, $6 weekends and holidays; non-residents: $5.50 weekdays, $6.50 weekends and holidays; Carts: $11 for 18 holes.
Tee Time Procedure: 1st come, 1st served.

——— HAMILTON ——— 19

Hamilton

PERRY COUNTRY CLUB
A private club with one 9-hole course
Location: On Pottsville Road

Golf Data: Pro Shop Phone: (817) 386-3383; Club Manager: Eldor Wenzel; Par: 36; Yardage: 3110; Rating: 69.2 (if 18 holes played); Closed Monday.
Guest Policy: You must be a member of another private country club or a guest of a member. New residents of Hamilton County can play with member during first year.

Hico

BLUEBONNET COUNTRY CLUB
A private club with one 9-hole course
Location: E. of HWY 281
Golf Data: Pro Shop Phone: (817) 796-4122; Club Pro: Sam Maserang; Par: 36; Yardage: 3250; Open 7 days.
Guest Policy: You must play with a member or be a member of another private country club.

——— HAYS ——— 20

San Marcos

AQUARENA SPRINGS GOLF CLUB
A public club with one 9-hole course
Location: At Post Road & Bert Brown
Golf Data: Pro Shop Phone: (512) 392-2710; Club Pro: John Ferguson, Jr.; Par: 35; Yardage: 2850; Rating: 66.0 (if 18 holes played); Open 7 days.
Green Fees: $5.26 anytime; Carts: $13 for 18 holes; Visa and MC accepted.
Tee Time Procedure: 1st come, 1st served.

QUAIL CREEK COUNTRY CLUB
A semi-private club with one 18-hole course
Location: E. on HWY 21
Golf Data: Pro Shop Phone: (512) 353-1665; Club Pro: Steve Veriato; Par: 72; Yardage: 6481; Rating: 68.0; Closed Monday.
Green Fees: $10 weekdays, $15 weekends and holidays; Carts: $12 for 18 holes.
Tee Time Procedure: Call 48 hours in advance.

Wimberley

BROOKHOLLOW AT WOODCREEK
A semi-private club with one 18-hole course

Location: Take either HWY 12N or FM 2325 NW to entrance
Golf Data: Pro Shop Phone: (512) 847-9700; Club Pro: Larry Maciejewski; Par: 72; Yardage: 6398; Rating: 70.9; Open 7 days.
Green Fees: $20 weekdays, weekends and holidays for general play; Carts: $15 for 18 holes; AX, Visa and MC accepted.
Tee Time Procedure: Call anytime.

=========== HILL =========== 21

Hillsboro

HILLSBORO COUNTRY CLUB
A semi-private club with one 9-hole course
Location: I-35, take Old Brandon Road exit, turn W. at Gulf Station
Golf Data: Pro Shop Phone: (817) 582-8211; Club Pro: Jake Smith; Par: 72 (two sets of tees); Yardage: 5692; Rating: 70.2; Closed Monday until noon.
Green Fees: $5 weekdays, $7.50 weekends and holidays; Carts: $10 for 18 holes.
Tee Time Procedure: 1st come, 1st served.

Whitney

LAKE WHITNEY COUNTRY CLUB
A private club with one 18-hole course
Location: Take HWY 933N 1 mile, follow signs
Golf Data: Pro Shop Phone: (817) 694-2313; Club Manager: Jim Olenski; Par: 72; Yardage: 6311; Rating: 69.8; Closed Tuesday.
Guest Policy: You must be a guest of a member or a member of another private country club.

=========== KENDALL =========== 22

Boerne

TAPATIO SPRINGS COUNTRY CLUB
A resort club with 27 holes
Location: I-10W, exit Johns Road (see #14 on San Antonio locator map)
Golf Data: Pro Shop Phone: (512) 537-4197; Club Pro: Bill Keys; Par: 72; Yardage: 6543; Rating: 71.3; Course Architect: Bill Johnston; also executive 9 holes available; Open 7 days.

Guest Policy: You must be a guest of a member, a member of another private country club or a guest of the resort. Phone pro for specifics.
NOTE: For resort and golf package information, phone (512) 537-4611 or write to Tapatio Springs, P.O. Box 550, Boerne, TX 78006.
Green Fees: Guests of the hotel: $28 + tax Monday-Thursday (includes cart); $33 + tax Friday-Sunday & Holidays; Members of other clubs: $35 + tax Monday-Thursday, $45 + tax Friday-Sunday & holidays; AX, Visa & MC accepted.
Tee Time Procedure: Call 7 days in advance.

=========== KERR =========== 23

Kerrville

SCOTT SCHREINER GOLF COURSE
A public club with one 18-hole course
Location: N. on HWY 16 to #1 Country Club Drive
Golf Data: Pro Shop Phone: (512) 257-4982; Club Pro: Guy Cullins; Par: 72; Yardage: 6509; Rating: 70.47; Course Architect: R. D. Kaiser (back 9); Open 7 days.
Green Fees: $6 weekdays, $8 weekends and holidays; Carts: $12.62 for 18 holes.
Tee Time Procedure: Weekends: Friday after 7 a.m. by phone or in person; Weekdays: 1st come, 1st served.

RIVERHILL COUNTRY CLUB
A private club with one 18-hole course
Location: E. on Bandera HWY
Golf Data: Pro Shop Phone: (512) 896-8066; Club Pro: Bryan Hargrove; Par: 72; Yardage: 6902; Rating: 73.7; Course Architects: Joe Finger & Byron Nelson; Open 7 days.
Guest Policy: You must be a guest of a member or a member of another private country club. Phone for specifics.

=========== LAMPASAS =========== 24

Lampasas

HANCOCK PARK GOLF CLUB
A public club with one 9-hole course
Location: Hwy 281S to Hancock Park

Golf Data: Pro Shop Phone: (512) 556-3202; Club Manager: Al Langford; Par: 36; Yardage: 3029; Rating: 68.0 (if 18 holes played); Open 7 days.

Green Fees: $5 weekdays, $7.50 weekends and holidays; Carts: $11 for 18 holes.

Tee Time Procedure: 1st come, 1st served.

————— LEE ————— 25

Giddings

CUMMINS CREEK COUNTRY CLUB
A semi-private club with one 9-hole course
Location: 3 miles S. on Good Hope Road
Golf Data: Pro Shop Phone: (409) 542-3777; Club Pro: Oscar Green; Par: 36; Yardage: 3200; Rating: 69.3 (if 18 holes played); Closed Monday.

Green Fees: $6 weekdays, $8 weekends and holidays; Carts: $10 for 18 holes.

Tee Time Procedure: 1st come, 1st served.

————— LEON ————— 26

Hilltop Lakes

ROLLING HILLS GOLF COURSE
A resort club with one 18-hole course
Location: 9½ miles N. of Normangee on HWY 3
Golf Data: Pro Shop Phone: (409) 855-2222; Club Manager: George Myroup; Par: 72; Yardage: 6347; Rating: 70.2; Pro Shop closed Monday.

Guest Policy: You must be a guest of a member or a guest of the resort. Members of other private country clubs are welcome on a space available basis. Phone in advance.

NOTE: For resort information phone (409) 855-2222 or write to Hilltop Lakes Resort City, P.O. Box 42A, Hilltop Lakes, TX 77871.

Green Fees: $8 weekdays, $10 weekends and holidays; Carts: $12 for 18 holes; AX, Visa and MC accepted.

Tee Time Procedure: 1st come, 1st served.

————— LIMESTONE ————— 27

Mexia

OLDE OAKS GOLF & COUNTRY CLUB
A private club with one 9-hole course
Location: 2½ miles S.E. on HWY 39
Golf Data: Pro Shop Phone: (817) 562-2391; Club Pro: Terry Stephenson; Par: 72 (two sets of tees); Yardage: 6195; Rating: 68.3; Closed Monday.

Green Fees: $6 weekdays, $10 weekdays and holidays for 18 holes; Carts: $12 for 18 holes ($10 for single rider).

————— LLANO ————— 28

Blue Lake Estates

BLUE LAKE GOLF CLUB
A public club with one 9-hole course
Location: From HWY 71 & HWY 281, take HWY 71N, right at FM 2831
Golf Data: Pro Shop Phone: (512) 598-5524; Club Manager: Prentice Stewart; Par: 64 (two sets of tees); Yardage: 4793; Rating: 60.4; Course Architect: Joe Finger; Open 7 days.

Green Fees: $6 weekdays, $8 weekends and holidays; Carts: $12 + tax for 18 holes.

Tee Time Procedure: 1st come, 1st served.

Kingsland

PACKSADDLE COUNTRY CLUB
A public club with one 18-hole course
Location: Take Euel Moore Drive W.
Golf Data: Pro Shop Phone: (915) 388-3863; Club Pro: Ted Gross; Par: 72; Yardage: 7156; Rating: 71.6; Closed Monday.

Green Fees: $6 weekdays, $8 weekends and holidays; Carts: $11 for 18 holes.

Tee Time Procedure: 1st come, 1st served.

Llano

LLANO GOLF COURSE
A semi-private club with one 9-hole course
Location: 1½ miles W. on Ranch 152
Golf Data: Pro Shop Phone: (915) 247-5100; Club Pro: Buck Byers; Par: 72 (two sets of tees); Yardage: 6158; Rating: 69.0; Open 7 days.

Green Fees: $4 weekdays, $7 weekends and holidays; Carts: $12 for 18 holes.
Tee Time Procedure: 1st come, 1st served.

McLENNAN 29

Mart

BATTLE LAKE GOLF CLUB
A semi-private club with one 18-hole course
Location: On Battle Lake Road
Golf Data: Pro Shop Phone: (817) 876-2837; Club Pro: John Brewer; Par: 72; Yardage: 6515; Rating: 69.0; Course Architect: John Brewer; Closed Monday.
Green Fees: $5.25 weekdays, $7.50 weekends and holidays; Carts: $12 + tax for 18 holes.
Tee Time Procedure: 1st come, 1st served.

Moody

GREENBRIER GOLF & COUNTRY CLUB
A semi-private club with one 18-hole course
Location: 2 miles N. on HWY 371
Golf Data: Pro Shop Phone: (817) 853-2927; Club Manager: Walter Haynie; Par: 70; Yardage: 6457; Closed Monday.
Green Fees: $6.25 weekdays, $8.33 weekends and holidays; Carts: $13.54 for 18 holes.
Tee Time Procedure: 1st come, 1st served.

Waco

Public Golf Courses

COTTONWOOD CREEK GOLF CLUB
A public club with one 18-hole course
Location: 5200 Bagby Avenue
Golf Data: Pro Shop Phone: (817) 752-2474; Club Pro: Dale Morgan; Par: 72; Yardage: 7123; Rating: 73.3; Course Architect: Joe Finger; Open 7 days.
Green Fees: $7.50 weekdays, $9.50 weekends and holidays; Carts: $14 for 18 holes.
Tee Time Procedure: Call 1 week in advance.

JAMES CONNALLY GOLF COURSE
A public club with one 18-hole course
Location: 7900 Concord Road
Golf Data: Pro Shop Phone: (817) 799-6561; Club Pro: Jack Barger; Par: 72; Yardage: 6935; Rating: 72.8; Open 7 days.
Green Fees: $4.75 weekdays, $6.30 weekends and holidays; Carts: $6.33 per rider; Visa and MC accepted.
Tee Time Procedure: Weekends: Thursday after 7 a.m. by phone or in person; Weekdays: 1st come, 1st served.

SEAGOS PAR 3 GOLF COURSE
A public club with one 9-hole course
Location: HWY 6W, across Lake Waco, exit Speegleville, take access road 1 mile
Golf Data: Pro Shop Phone: (817) 848-4831; Club Manager: Rodney Hill; Par: 27; Yardage: 1057; Open 7 days.
Green Fees: $2.50 weekdays, $3 weekends-holidays; Carts: $2.50 per 9 holes.
Tee Time Procedure: 1st come, 1st served.

Private Country Clubs

LAKE OAKS COUNTRY CLUB
A private club with two 18-hole courses
Location: Near Waco Airport, N. of Lake
Golf Data: Pro Shop Phone: (817) 756-1888; Club Pro: Larry Salter; *Regulation* 18 Par: 72; Yardage: 6600; Rating: 70.4; *Executive* 18 Par: 54; Yardage: 2661; Course Architect: Warren Contrell; Closed Monday.
Guest Policy: You must be a guest of a member or a member of another private country club. Phone for specifics.

RIDGEWOOD COUNTRY CLUB
A private club with one 18-hole course
Location: I-35, exit HWY 6W, exit Lake Waco right, turn right on Fish Pond Road
Golf Data: Pro Shop Phone: (817) 772-0160; Club Pro: Gene Shields; Par: 70; Yardage: 6585; Rating: 71.2; Course Architect: Ralph Plummer; Closed Monday.
Guest Policy: You must play with a member or be a member of another private country club. Phone in advance.

WESTERN OAKS COUNTRY CLUB
A private club with one 18-hole course

Location: Take Bosque Blvd. to Western Oaks

Golf Data: Pro Shop Phone: (817) 772-8100; General Manager: Buddy Nieman; Par: 70; Yardage: 5658; Rating: 67.4; Closed Monday.

Guest Policy: Allow McLennan County residents green fee play twice a month; others should call to check course availability.

Green Fees: $10 anytime; Carts: $6 per person for 18 holes.

Tee Time Procedure: 1st come, 1st served.

MADISON 30

Madisonville

OAK RIDGE COUNTRY CLUB
A semi-private club with one 9-hole course

Location: 1 mile S. of HWY 21 on FM 1452

Golf Data: Pro Shop Phone: (409) 348-6264; Club Pro: Kenny Rucker; Par: 72 (two sets of tees); Yardage: 6817; Rating: 71.9; Closed Monday.

Green Fees: $8 weekdays, $10 weekends and holidays; Carts: $11.50 for 18 holes.

Tee Time Procedure: 1st come, 1st served.

MASON 31

Mason

COMMANCHE CREEK GOLF CLUB
A public club with one 9-hole course
Location: S. on HWY 87
NOTE: 9 holes designed locally is due to open in Spring 1987.

MEDINA 32

Devine

DEVINE GOLF COURSE
A public club with one 9-hole course
Location: 116 Malone Drive
Golf Data: Pro Shop Phone: (512) 663-9943; Club Pro: Kevin Yanity; Par:

36; Yardage: 3132; Rating: 69.1 (if 18 holes played); Open 7 days.

Green Fees: $6 weekdays, $8 weekends and holidays; Carts: $12 for 18 holes.

Tee Time Procedure: 1st come, 1st served.

Hondo

HONDO GOLF CLUB
A semi-private club with one 9-hole course

Location: W. side of town at old Air Base

Golf Data: Pro Shop Phone: (512) 426-8825; Club Pro: Bernie Yanity; Par: 72 (two sets of tees); Yardage: 5940; Rating: 68.4; Closed Monday.

Green Fees: $5.30 weekdays, $6.35 weekends and holidays; Carts: $11 for 18 holes.

Tee Time Procedure: 1st come, 1st served.

MILAM 33

Cameron

CAMERON COUNTRY CLUB
A private club with one 9-hole course
Location: 1 mile off HWY 77 on Old Marlow Road

Golf Data: Pro Shop Phone: (817) 697-2371; Club Manager: Ken Harrell; Par: 35; Yardage: 2915; Closed Monday.

Guest Policy: You must play with a member or be a member of another private country club.

Rockdale

ROCKDALE COUNTRY CLUB
A private club with one 9-hole course
Location: 5 miles S. on Alcoa Lake Road
Golf Data: Pro Shop Phone: (512) 446-4013; Club Pro: R. D. Kizer; Par: 36; Yardage: 3272; Rating: 69.0 (if 18 holes played); Course Architect: Leon Howard; Closed Monday.

Guest Policy: Non-county residents may pay green fees & play.

Green Fees: $8 weekdays, $12 weekends-holidays; Carts: $6 per 9 holes.

MILLS 34

None

Calvert

CALVERT COUNTRY CLUB
A private club with one 9-hole course
Location: Take FM 979W until fork, stay straight until next right fork
Golf Data: No Phone (For information, contact Gene Gibson: 409-364-2855); Par: 35; Yardage: 2700; Open 7 days.
Guest Policy: Out-of-county guests only.

Franklin

OAK GROVE COUNTRY CLUB
A private club with one 9-hole course
Location: 4 miles N. on HWY 46
Golf Data: No Phone. Club Secretary: Bob Kennedy (409-828-4125); Par: 35; Yardage: 2710; Open 7 days.
Guest Policy: Out-of-county guests only.

Hearne

HEARNE MUNICIPAL GOLF COURSE
A public club with one 9-hole course
Location: 405 Norwood Lane
Golf Data: Course Manager: Bob Henagen (409) 279-5666; Par: 37; Yardage: 3254; Open 7 days.
Green Fees: $3 weekdays; $5 weekends and holidays; No carts available.
Tee Time Procedure: 1st come, 1st served.

San Saba

SAN SABA MUNICIPAL GOLF COURSE
A semi-private club with one 9-hole course
Location: Take HWY 190E, turn left at green sign, go 1½ miles
Golf Data: Pro Shop Phone: (915) 372-3212; Club Pro: Larry McNeely; Par: 36; Yardage: 3392; Rating: 70.0 (if 18 holes played); Open 7 days.
NOTE: *Additional 9 holes to open in Spring 1987.*
Green Fees: $5 weekdays, $8 weekends and holidays; Carts: $12 for 18 holes.
Tee Time Procedure: 1st come, 1st served.

Austin

Public Golf Courses

BUTLER PARK PITCH & PUTT
A public club with one 9-hole course
Location: In Butler Park on W. Riverside Drive (see #1 on locator map)
Golf Data: Pro Shop Phone: (512) 477-9025; Club Pro: Winston Kinser; Par: 27; Yardage 805; Open 7 days.
Green Fees: $3.20 for 9, $2.65 for second 9; No carts available.
Tee Time Procedure: 1st come, 1st served.

HANCOCK PARK GOLF COURSE
A public club with one 9-hole course
Location: Off HWY 35, on E. 41st Street (see #2 on locator map)
Golf Data: Pro Shop Phone: (512) 453-0276; Club Pro: Lloyd Morrison; Par: 36; Yardage: 2828; Rating: 69.0 (if 18 holes played); Closed 4th Monday of month.
Green Fees: $6 for 9, $7.50 for 18 weekdays; $8 for 18 holes on weekends and holidays; Carts: $6 + tax per 9 holes + $1 key deposit.
Tee Time Procedure: Weekends-Holidays: Friday after 8 a.m. in person or by phone; Weekdays: 1 day in advance after 8 a.m. (reservations for foursomes and fivesomes only).

JIMMY CLAY MUNICIPAL GOLF COURSE
A public club with one 18-hole course
Location: From HWY 35, exit Stassney Lane E. (see #3 on locator map)
Golf Data: Pro Shop Phone: (512) 444-0999; Club Pro: Joe Balander; Par: 72; Yardage: 7135; Rating: 73.0; Course Architect: Joe Finger; Closed 3rd Monday of the month.
Green Fees: $7.50 weekdays, $8 weekends and holidays; Carts: $12.74 for 18 holes + $1 key deposit.
Tee Time Procedure: Weekends-Holidays: Friday at 7 a.m. in person or by phone; Weekdays: 1 day in advance after 7 a.m. (reservations for foursomes and fivesomes only).

LIONS MUNICIPAL GOLF COURSE
A public club with one 18-hole course

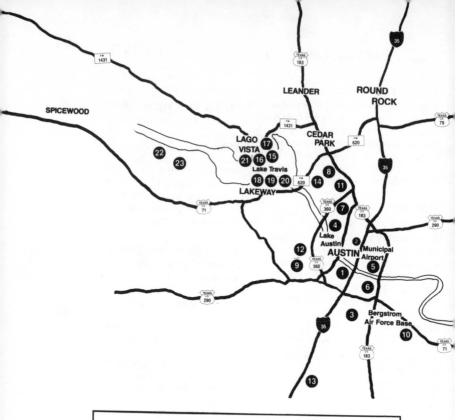

AUSTIN AND SURROUNDING AREA

AUSTIN

1. Butler Park Pitch & Putt
2. Hancock Park Golf Course
3. Jimmy Clay Municipal Golf Course
4. Lions Municipal Golf Course
5. Morris Williams Municipal Golf Course
6. Riverside Golf Club
7. Austin Country Club
8. Balcones Country Club
9. Barton Creek Country Club
10. Bergstrom AFB Golf Course
11. Great Hills Country Club

12. Lost Creek Country Club
13. Onion Creek Country Club
14. River Place Country Club
15. Lago Vista Country Club
16. Highland Lakes Country Club
17. Bar K Par 3
18. The Hills of Lakeway
19. Live Oak Golf Club
20. Yaupon Golf Club
21. Point Venture Golf Course
22. Hidden Hills on Lake Travis
23. Pedernales Country Club

Location: From HWY 1, take Enfield Road W. (see #4 on locator map)

Golf Data: Pro Shop Phone: (512) 477-6963; Club Pro: Lloyd Morrison; Par: 71; Yardage: 6001; Rating: 68.4; Closed 1st Monday of the month.

Green Fees: $7.50 weekdays, $8 weekends and holidays; Carts: $12.74 + $1 key deposit for 18 holes.

Tee Time Procedure: Weekends-Holidays: Friday at 7 a.m. in person or by phone;

Weekdays: 1 day in advance at 7 a.m. (foursome and fivesomes only).

MORRIS WILLIAMS MUNICIPAL GOLF COURSE

A public club with one 18-hole course

Location: From HWY 35, take Manor Road E. (see #5 on locator map)

Golf Data: Pro Shop Phone: (512) 926-1298; Club Pro: George Hannon; Par: 72; Yardage: 6538; Rating: 71.0;

Course Architect: Leon Howard; Closed 2nd Monday of month.

NOTE: Site of Harvey Penick (college) Tournament.

Green Fees: $7 weekdays, $7.50 weekends and holidays; Carts: $12.74 + $1 key deposit for 18 holes.

Tee Time Procedure: Weekends-Holidays: Friday at 7 a.m. in person or by phone; Weekdays: 1 day in advance after 7 a.m. (foursomes and fivesomes only).

RIVERSIDE GOLF CLUB
A public club with one 18-hole course

Location: From HWY 35, take Riverside Drive E. (see #6 on locator map)

Golf Data: Pro Shop Phone: (512) 389-1070; Club Pro: John Ott; Par: 74; Yardage: 6492; Rating: 70.4; Open 7 days.

Green Fees: $10 weekdays, $12 weekends and holidays; Carts: $15 for 18 holes; Visa and MC accepted.

Tee Time Procedure: 1 week in advance in person or by phone.

Private Country Clubs

AUSTIN COUNTRY CLUB
A private club with one 18-hole course

Location: Off HWY 360 on Long Champ Drive (see #7 on locator map)

Golf Data: Pro Shop Phone: (512) 328-0090; Club Pro: Tinsley Penick; Par: 72; Yardage: 6822; Rating: 74.3; Course Architect: Pete Dye; Closed Monday.

Guest Policy: You must play with a member.

BALCONES COUNTRY CLUB
A private club with two 18-hole courses

Location: Off HWY 183 N. on Balcones Club Drive (see #8 on locator map)

Golf Data: Pro Shop Phone: (512) 258-2775; Par: 71; Yardage: 6479; Rating: 68.4; *Spicewood* Pro Shop Phone: (512) 258-6763; Par: 72; Yardage: 6706; Rating: 71.0; Club Pro: Shayne Lockhart; One 18 closed on Monday & Wednesdays (alternate).

Guest Policy: You must be a guest of a member or a member of another private country club. Phone for specifics.

BARTON CREEK COUNTRY CLUB
A private club with one 18-hole course

Location: From Loop 360, take Lost Creek Blvd. W., left at fork, follow signs (see #9 on locator map)

Golf Data: Pro Shop Phone: (512) 328-2945; Club Pro: Brent Buckman; Par: 72; Yardage: 6917; Course Architect: Tom Fazio; Closed Monday.

Guest Policy: Will reciprocate if your head pro calls ahead.

BERGSTROM AFB GOLF COURSE
A private club with one 18-hole course

Location: Off HWY 71S at Bergstrom AFB (see #10 on locator map)

Golf Data: Pro Shop Phone: (512) 385-3161; Club Pro: Jack Bertrom; Par: 71; Yardage: 6427; Rating: 69.7; Open 7 days.

Guest Policy: You must be a guest of the military.

GREAT HILLS COUNTRY CLUB
A private club with one 18-hole course

Location: Off HWY 360 on Lost Horizon Drive (see #11 on locator map)

Golf Data: Pro Shop Phone: (512) 345-0505; Club Pro: Mark Coward; Par: 70; Yardage: 6461; Rating: 70.2; Course Architects: Don January & Billy Martindale; Closed Monday.

Guest Policy: You must play with a member or be a member of another private country club (your head pro must call to set tee time).

LOST CREEK COUNTRY CLUB
A private club with one 18-hole course

Location: Off HWY 360W on Lost Creek Blvd. (see #12 on locator map)

Golf Data: Pro Shop Phone: (512) 892-1205; Club Pro: John R. Price; Par: 72; Yardage: 6861; Rating: 72.5; Course Architects: Terry Deal & Dave Bennett; Closed Monday.

Guest Policy: You must be a guest of a member or a member of another private country club.

ONION CREEK COUNTRY CLUB
A private club with one 18-hole course

Location: 12 miles S. on HWY 35; exit #225A on Onion Creek PKWY E. (see #13 on locator map)

Golf Data: Pro Shop Phone: (512) 282-2162; Club Pro: Jack Gaudion; Par: 70; Yardage: 6367; Rating: 71.1; Course Architect: Jimmy Demaret; Closed Monday.

NOTE: Site of Liberty Mutual Legends of Golf PGA Seniors tournament, forerunner of modern PGA Seniors Tour.

Guest Policy: You must be a guest of a member or a member of another private country club.

RIVER PLACE COUNTRY CLUB
A private club with one 18-hole course
Location: From HWY 360, take FM 222 N to River Place Blvd. W. (see #14 on locator map)
Golf Data: Pro Shop Phone: (512) 346-1584; Director of Golf: Mancil Davis; Par: 71; Yardage: 6648; Course Architects: Jay Morrish & Tom Kite; Closed Monday.
Guest Policy: You must play with a member. Will also reciprocate with other U.S.G.A.-member clubs outside a 75 mile radius.

Lago Vista
LAGO VISTA COUNTRY CLUB
A semi-private club with 45 holes
Location: Take HWY 183N to HWY 1431, W. 15 miles to signs (see #15–16–17 on locator map)
Golf Data: Host Professional: Larry Gosewehr; *Lago Vista* Phone: (512) 267-1179; Par: 72; Yardage: 6611; Rating: 70.8; Closed Tuesday; *Highland Lakes* Phone: (512) 267-1685; Par: 72; Yardage: 6599; Rating: 72.1; Closed Monday; Course Architect: Robert Trent Jones (both courses); *Bar K* Par 3 Phone: (512) 267-1226; Par: 27; Yardage: 1165; Closed Monday.
Guest Policy: Out-of-town non-members may play anytime during the week and after noon on weekends and holidays.
NOTE: For resort and golf package information, phone (800) 252-3040 or write to World of Resorts Inn, 1900 American Drive, Lago Vista, TX 78645.
Green Fees: $20 weekdays, $26 weekends and holidays; Carts: $18 for 18 holes.
Tee Time Procedure: Weekends-Holidays: 3 days in advance for both Lago Vista and Highland Lakes, Bar K is 1st come, 1st served; Weekdays; 1st come, 1st served at all locations.

Lakeway Resort
THE HILLS OF LAKEWAY
A private club with one 18-hole course
Location: From Austin, take HWY 71W, right at HWY 620, left at World of Tennis Blvd., follow signs (see #18 on locator map)
Golf Data: Pro Shop Phone: (512) 261-7272; Director of Golf: Clayton Cole; Par: 72; Yardage: 6864; Rating: 73.1; Course Architect: Jack Nicklaus; Closed Monday.
Guest Policy: Members of out-of-town private country clubs may play as a guest of a member or as a guest of the club. Also, renters of property within The Hills may play as a guest of the club.
NOTE: For property rental information, phone (800) 525-3929 and ask for The Hills property rental desk or write to Lakeway Company, 1200 Lakeway Drive, #8, Austin, TX 78734.
Green Fees: $50 anytime; Carts: $20 for 18 holes.
Tee Time Procedure: Call 5 days in advance. Non-members may reserve times Tuesday-Thursday from 7:30 a.m. to 6:30 p.m.; Friday from 7:30 a.m. to 1 p.m., and weekends or holidays from 1 p.m. to 6:30 p.m.

LIVE OAK GOLF CLUB
A resort club with one 18-hole course
Location: From Austin, take HWY 71W, right at HWY 620, left at World of Tennis Blvd., right on Lakeway Drive (see #19 on locator map)
Golf Data: Pro Shop Phone: (512) 261-7349; Head Professional: Larry Bishop; Resident Pro: Darold Bauer; Par: 72; Yardage: 6643; Rating: 70.9; Closed 1st and 3rd Tuesday (every Tuesday in March + October).
Guest Policy: You must play with a member, be a member of another private country club or be a guest of the resort.
Green Fees: $25 weekdays, $30 weekends and holidays; Carts: $20 for 18 holes; AX, Visa and MC accepted.
Tee Time Procedure: Call 7 days in advance.

YAUPON GOLF CLUB
A resort club with one 18-hole course
Location: From Austin, take HWY 71W right at HWY 620, left at World of Tennis

Blvd., right at 2nd Street (see #20 on locator map)

Golf Data: Pro Shop Phone: (512) 261-7372; Head Professional: Larry Bishop; Club Pro: Matt Henderson; Par: 72; Yardage: 6595; Rating: 70.6; Course Architect: Leon Howard; Closed 1st and 3rd Monday (every Monday in March & October).

Guest Policy: You must be a guest of a member, a member of another private country club or a guest at the resort.

Green Fees: $25 weekdays, $30 weekends and holidays; Carts: $20 for 18 holes; AX, Visa and MC accepted.

Tee Time Procedure: Call 7 days in advance.

NOTE: Resort and Golf package information for Live Oak and Yaupon can be obtained by contacting Lakeway Inn, 101 Lakeway Drive, Austin, TX 78734 (800-Lakeway).

Leander

POINT VENTURE GOLF COURSE
A resort club with one 9-hole course
Location: Take HWY 183N to HWY 1431, W. 15 miles, follow signs (see #21 on locator map)

Golf Data: Pro Shop Phone: (512) 267-1151; Club Pro: Bob Nesmith; Par: 36; Yardage: 3100; Closed Tuesday.

Green Fees: $4 for 9, $6 for 18 holes weekdays, and $6 for 9, $10 for 18 holes weekends and holidays; Carts: $15 for 18 holes.

NOTE: Resort accomodations available through World of Resorts Inn, 1900 American Drive, Lago Vista, TX 78645 (800-252-3040), or through Point Venture, 350 Venture Blvd., Leander, TX 78645 (512-267-1151).

Tee Time Procedure: Call 3 days in advance.

Spicewood

HIDDEN HILLS ON LAKE TRAVIS
A private club with one 18-hole course
Location: From Austin, take HWY 71W, right at Haynie Flat Road and follow signs (see #22 on locator map)

Golf Data: Pro Shop Phone: (512) 693-4589; Director of Golf: Bucky Ayers;

Par: 71; Yardage: 6650; Course Architects: Arnold Palmer & Ed Seay; Closed Monday.

Guest Policy: You must be a property owner to be a member. Guest must be accompanied by a member. Phone for specifics.

PEDERNALES COUNTRY CLUB
A private club with one 9-hole course
Location: From Austin, take HWY 71W, right at FM 2322 (see #23 on locator map)

Golf Data: Pro Shop Phone: (512) 264-1489; Club Pro: Larry Trader; Par: 36; Yardage: 3350; Rating: 70.0 (if 18 holes played); Closed Monday.

Guest Policy: You must be a guest of a member or a member of another private country club. Phone in advance for specifics.

═══ WILLIAMSON ═══ 38

Georgetown

BERRY CREEK COUNTRY CLUB
A private club with one 18-hole course
Location: I-35, exit TX 195W, left at County 190

Golf Data: Pro Shop Phone: (512) 863-0568; Club Pro: Jack Haby; Par: 72; Yardage: 7003; Rating: 72.73; Course Architect: THK Developers; Closed Monday.

Guest Policy: You must be a guest of a member or a member of another private country club. Have your pro phone in advance to make arrangements.

GEORGETOWN COUNTRY CLUB
A private club with one 18-hole course
Location: I-35, exit Andice, W. to 2nd Street, left to Country Club Road

Golf Data: Pro Shop Phone: (512) 863-2893; Club Pro: Joe Behlau; Par: 70; Yardage: 5500; Rating: 65.0; Closed Monday.

Guest Policy: You must be accompanied by a member.

KURTH-LANDRUM GOLF COURSE
A public club with one 9-hole course
Location: I-35, take University exit, 2 miles E. on University, take last entrance to University.

Golf Data: Pro Shop Phone: (512) 863-1333; Club Manager: James Ellison; Par: 69 (two sets of tees); Yardage: 5600; Open 7 days.

Green Fees: $6.50 ($4.50 for 9 holes) weekdays, $9 ($5.50 for 9) weekends and holidays; Carts: $6 per 9 holes.

Tee Time Procedure: Weekends-Holidays: Friday at 8 a.m. by phone or in person; Weekdays; 1st come, 1st served.

Taylor

TAYLOR COUNTRY CLUB
A public club with one 9-hole course
Location: S. on Loop 79

Golf Data: Pro Shop Phone: (512) 352-8960; Club Manager: Philip Wheelis; Par: 68 (two sets of tees); Yardage: 5050; Rating: 64.0; Open 7 days.

Green Fees: $5 weekdays, $7 weekends and holidays; Carts: $6 per 9 holes.

Tee Time Procedure: 1st come, 1st served.

—————— **WILSON** —————— 39

None

9. This lady Hall of Famer from Texas was thought to be the first "glamour" girl of the LPGA.

Texas Golf Hall of Fame Honors Own

Four of the top 10 all-time winners on the PGA Tour and the top winner on the LPGA Tour are Texans.

They are honored along with 43 others in the Texas Golf Hall of Fame located at the Texas National Country Club in Willis.

From Ben Hogan, arguably the best golfer in the history of the game, to the modern era's Lee Trevino, who is fourth on the all-time money list with more than $3 million in earnings, Texas has a reputation as a breeding ground for fine golfers.

Hogan won 62 official events and ranks third on the all-time list. Byron Nelson is fifth with 54 wins, including a record-smashing 11 in a row in 1945. Lloyd Mangrum is eighth with 34 victories and Jimmy Demaret is 10th with 31 wins. On the LPGA-side, Monahans-born Kathy Whitworth has won 88 official tournaments, which ranks her as the all-time U.S. champ in all professional categories.

There are no hard and fast rules governing selection into the Hall of Fame, except that a member have definitive ties with the State of Texas.

Ben Hogan.

The "Babe," Babe Didrikson Zaharis, has been called the Greatest Woman Athlete.

Although the vast majority of the members were born in Texas, birthright is not a requirement. However, a reasonable time of residence—more than 15 years—is a requirement. Of the 48 members, 39 are still residents of Texas, five live out of state, and four are deceased.

Five categories—tour professional, retired/senior tour pro, club professional, men's amateur and woman golfer—are studied by the selection committee.

The induction ceremony is held annually at Texas National Country Club in the Fall, normally in October, depending upon the availability of the tour professional. The ceremony is held in conjunction with a Hall of Fame Pro-Am and the entire membership is invited back to play.

Former Texas National owner Russell Wiggins and Texas National professional Bob Payne originated the Hall in 1978.

Willis is located north of Houston off I-45 between Conroe and Huntsville. Take the Willis exit east to stop light, turn right and then left at FM 2432. The gate to the club is approximately two miles from Willis.

TEXAS GOLF HALL OF FAME
Inductions By Category

	Tour Professional	Retired/Senior Tour Pro	Club Professional
1978	Lee Trevino	Byron Nelson	Hardy Loudermilk
		Jimmy Demaret	
		Ben Hogan	
1979	Don January	Jack Burke	Harvey Penick
1980	Charles Coody	Ralph Guidahl	Dick Forester
1981	No inductee	Dave Marr	Henry Homberg
		Henry Ransom	
1982	Bill Rogers	Jay Herbert	Joe Black
1983	John Mahaffey	Jacky Cupit	Ramond Gafford
1984	Ben Crenshaw	Lloyd Mangrum	Ross Collins
1985	Tom Kite	Don Massengale	Art Hodde
1986	Miller Barber	Earl Stewart, Jr.	Robie Williams

	Men's Amateur	Woman Golfer	Special Category
1978	David "Spec" Goldman	Babe Didrikson Zaharias	
1979	Joe Conrad	Betty Jameson	
1980	Gus Moreland	Polly Riley	
1981	No inductee	Mary Ann Morrison	
1982	Billy Maxwell	Kathy Whitworth	Dave Williams
1983	Ed White	Betsy Rawls	Vic Cameron
1984	John Paul Cain	Sandra Haynie	
1985	Scott Verplant	Sandra Palmer	
1986	Marty Fleckman	Aniela Goldthwaite	Duke Bulter

Davis Thinks
Like "King"

When Mancil Davis gets to a Par 3 hole, his whole attitude changes. He actually thinks he is going to make a hole-in-one.

"No matter how bad I'm playing," Davis says, "when I get to a Par 3, I have a different mental attitude; I start thinking hole-in-one."

And he has a right to do just that. Dubbed by the press, the "King of Aces," the 32-year old holds the PGA world record for holes-in-one with 48 to date and was recently included in the World Golf Hall of Fame at Pinehurst, North Carolina. The odds of him succeeding are 300 to 1, according to the PGA.

The "King of Aces" started his world record trek at age 11 with No. 1 and has made at least one hole-in-one a year since 1966. That includes eight holes-in-one in one year (1967), three in five days (1967), and five on the same hole (#2, Odessa Country Club).

His longest hole-in-one is 379 yards and his shortest is 124 yards. He has made a hole-in-one with every club except putter, 9 iron, pitching wedge, and sand wedge. His average hole-in-one is 174 yards.

Mancil Davis has 47 holes-in-one!

What do you see when you look at this Par 3? Sand traps and water or the flag on the putting surface?

He has over 4 miles of holes-in-one. He said he's "flown 'em in, backed 'em in and bounced 'em in. I have down-right lucked 'em and I have also called 'em in."

He said once in Odessa he hit a shot 20–30 yards right of green with a 3 iron; it hit a tree, bounced left, hit a sprinkler head and went in the hole. In Abilene one day, he hit a 3-wood into the wind which sliced right into the hole.

Once at The Woodlands where he spent six years as Director of Golf, he told of giving a playing lesson. After everyone in the group had hit to the Par 3, they asked him how he planned to play the hole whose pin was tucked in the back left corner. He said, "I am going to hook a 3 iron, land it short, and run it up to the hole." And it went in.

How does he do it? Confidence! "I just feel I am going to make it. I aim at the hole. In my mind's eye, I eyeball the cup and bring it right up to the clubface."

Why not have the same feeling with each shot on the course? "I don't know," Davis said, "I am asked that a lot. I feel I make the same swing on every shot. When I get to Par 3s, I feel as if I go automatic."

"Mancil's uncanny," a fellow professional said. "He can shoot 80 and birdie all the Par 3s."

Davis has appeared on all three major television networks, ESPN, CNN, and has been featured in *People, Golf Digest, Golf, Sports Illustrated, Guinness Book of World Records* and *Ripley's Believe It or Not.*

He once caddied for Tom Weiskopf on the PGA Tour for 20 events during the 1968 season and tried competing professionally on the Canadian Tour in 1975. "I made more money caddying for Weiskopf than playing the tour," he said, explaining his other playing accomplishments.

He is now Director of Golf at River Place CC in Austin and also represents the National Hole-in-One Association of Dallas. For the latter, he is available for corporate, charity, member-guest or any special event golf tournament, spending a day at a designated Par 3 hole, and hitting a shot with each group competing in the event. Anyone who hits the ball closer to the hole than Davis receives a sleeve of balls imprinted with "I beat the King of Aces" and the first individual to score a hole-in-one receives $10,000 in cash. Further, any golfer scoring a hole-in-one on the day of the event is invited to the National Hole-in-One Association Golf Tournament at Woodlands CC near Houston for a chance at $100,000 for a hole-in-one on each of the four Par 3s.

PLAY PAR 3s BETTER

So you want to make a hole-in-one!

Mancil Davis thinks you can increase your chances. The "King of Aces" has four suggestions for better Par 3 play:

1. Visualize the positive.

If you saw the water and sand traps in the enclosed picture of a Par 3, then you have violated one of Davis' principal tenets. "You should only be concerned with the hole and seeing the shot fall into the hole. I plan the shot, take one practice swing, aim at the cup and, in my mind's eye, the cup comes right up to my clubface before I swing."

2. Know how far you hit your clubs.

So few people get the ball to the hole, Davis has found. "I am amazed that people don't know how far they hit the ball. The best players know which club will go 141 yards, 167, etc. You can find the answer to this question by hitting shots to the green from different distances during a practice round."

3. Aim at the hole.

Check your alignment before each shot on a Par 3. "I have found that a lot of people are afraid to aim at the hole. They are willing to accept less by aiming at the center of the green."

4. Don't use a tee; play your tee shot off the ground.

Davis feels you play the other 14 holes and never use a tee from the fairway, why use one on a Par 3. "The ball spins better coming off grass and is easier to control," he thinks. "When you tee it up, it looks different than it does the rest of the day."

He has been successful. According to the PGA, his chances of making a hole-in-one are 300 to 1. That compares to 3,000 to 1 for a PGA Tour professional and 30,000 to 1 for the average golfer.

10. What Texas golfer is Tom Watson's mentor?

LPGA Scores with Move to Texas

by Donna Pinnick
LPGA Staff Member

A chance to save $2 million which could be added to the newly created retirement program and a desire to fulfill other goals prompted the Ladies Professional Golf Association to move from New York to Sugar Land in the Houston area in 1982.

The move established an official headquarters where the LPGA could host a major championship, have a permanent site for its Hall of Fame, and conduct its qualifying schools, sponsor meetings and teaching division seminars.

When the move was considered, the LPGA, then under the direction of Ray Volpe, entertained bids from across the country. Sweetwater Country Club, a joint venture of Gerald Hines' Sugar Land Properties and Kindred and Company, a recreational management company, offered the needed ingredients, and new Commissioner John Laupenheimer orchestrated the move.

LPGA Headquarters and Hall-of-Fame.

Fountain entrance to Sweetwater Country Club clubhouse.

Noted golf course architect Roger Packard, receiving input from Betsy Rawls, Carol Mann, Judy Rankin, and Debbie Massey of the LPGA, designed four nine holes that challenge yet not discourage all levels of player. The championship 18 was designed with the outstanding woman golfer in mind.

Packard had to move 900,000 cubic yards of Texas flatlands, three times the normal amount, to carve nine holes on land that was once sugar and rice fields and three nines through pecan groves where Spanish moss frames the fairways.

An elaborate clubhouse, designed by Californian Charles Moore and valued at $14 million, includes four indoor and six outdoor tennis courts, eight racquetball courts, and a professionally staffed health club in addition to banquet and dining facilities.

The golf course and clubhouse were dedicated October 27, 1983. The legendary Patty Berg, one of the original founders, tearfully said, "Never in my wildest dream or ambitious hopes could I have envisioned all this as home for the Ladies Professional Golf Association 35 years ago when we got the LPGA started and were begging talented amateur players to turn professional."

With the inaugural of the Mazda Hall of Fame Championship at Sweetwater, the LPGA also dedicated its Hall of Fame building in July 1985. Designed by Jack Eby, senior design consultant to the Houston

Museum of Fine Arts, the 1800-square foot building is open to the public Monday-Friday from 9 to 5 with no admission fee. The Hall's main exhibits are 6- x 8-foot panels of rare photographs highlighting the 10 inductees careers and a 13-minute audio visual display captures each at the top of their games. Also on display are the six permanent trophies awarded each year to the LPGA's top players.

The LPGA has enjoyed phenomenal growth over the past 10 years. On the brink of bankruptcy in 1975, the LPGA prize money jumped from $1.2 million to $10 million in 1986. In 1985, over $3.3 million was donated to charity. Fifteen events were televised in 1986, compared to two in 1975.

FIVE TEXANS IN LPGA HALL

Enshrinement in the LPGA Hall of Fame may be the most difficult in all of sports to attain. And yet, of the 10 members, five have strong Texas ties. Two still live here; two don't, and one is deceased.

To become eligible for membership, a player must have been a member of the Association for 10 years and have won 30 official events including two Major championships, or 35 official events with one Major championship, or 40 official events.

The Hall itself was established in 1967 by the LPGA membership and moved to its present location at Sweetwater outside Houston in 1985. The original six inductees automatically qualified as members of the Women's Golf Hall of Fame. Since 1967 only four names have been added to the honor roll.

Of the first six, three were Texans. One was a Phi Beta Kappa at the University of Texas, one was perhaps the first "glamour" girl of the LPGA Tour, and one was the greatest woman athlete of all time.

Betsy Rawls grew up in Arlington, made a name for herself by winning back-to-back Texas State Amateur titles, and majored in mathematics and physics on her way to academic honors. She has won twice as many Major championships—8—among her 55 wins than any LPGA competitor, including four U.S. Opens. After retiring from active play, she became the LPGA Tournament Director before retiring again to live in the Philadelphia area. Her signature is on the 1951 LPGA articles of incorporation.

One of the original founders of the LPGA, Betty Jameson grew up in Texas winning the Texas Public Links Championship at age 13. The blonde who was thought to be the first glamour girl of the LPGA circuit won 10 events, including a U.S. Open, and left her mark by creating the Vare Trophy (named for Glenna Collette Vare) to honor the player with the lowest scoring average each year. She lives now in Florida.

Babe Didricksen Zaharias, the "Babe," was the greatest female athlete of all time. A museum in Beaumont honors her accomplishments which include participation in golf, track and field, tennis, baseball, swimming, softball, diving, skating, and bowling. It wasn't until after the 1932 Olympics where she won a silver and two gold medals in track and field that she took up golf, excelling first as an amateur, winning 17 consecutive amateur events, and then as pro, founding the LPGA, winning three U.S. Open tournaments among 31 wins. She died in 1956.

Other Texans since honored include Kathy Whitworth (1975) and Sandra Haynie (1977).

Born in Monahans, currently residing at the Trophy Club in Roanoke, Whitworth has won more professional golf tournaments, 88, than anyone, male or female. She became the first woman to earn $1 million in prize money, was the leading money winner eight times and has received more Vare Trophies (7) and Player-of-the-Year honors than anyone. In 1985, she teamed with Mickey Wright to become the first women's team to compete in the PGA-sanctioned Legends of Golf held in Austin.

Sandra Haynie has had two playing careers with the LPGA. She won 39 tournaments from 1961 to 1976 before injury and illness forced her to curtail her schedule. She suffers from arthritis. She returned to full action in 1981, winning one event, and then followed the next year with incredible earnings of $245,432 and a fourth Major. Born in Fort Worth, living now in Dallas, she has won 42 LPGA events, including two LPGA Championships, a U.S. Open, and the Peter Jackson Classic.

Both the "Babe" and Kathy Whitworth are enshrined in the World Golf Hall of Fame and are joined by Jameson, Haynie, and Rawls in the Texas Golf Hall of Fame. Whitworth is also enshrined in the Texas Sports Hall of Fame.

Patty Berg, Louise Suggs, and Mickey Wright were original inductees and Carol Mann (1977) and JoAnne Carner (1982) were admitted later.

11. Who has won more official professional tournaments—Sam Snead, Jack Nicklaus, or Kathy Whitworth?

The Plains

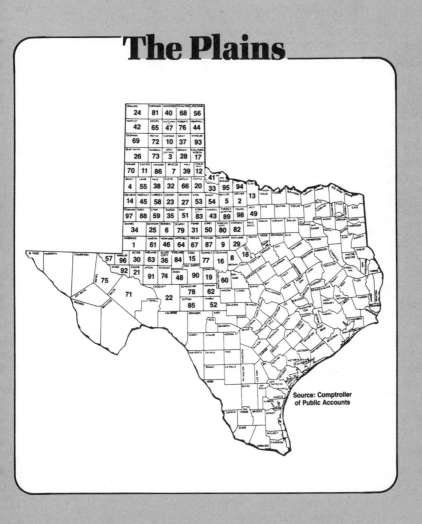

Source: Comptroller
of Public Accounts

Of the 144 golf courses in the area, 93 are either public or semi-private and open for general play.

There are also 44 private clubs and three courses attached to military installations within the region.

Two courses under construction are scheduled to open this year.

THE PLAINS CITIES

No. 18 hole with clubhouse in the background at Amarillo public course.

——— ANDREWS ——— 1

Andrews
ANDREWS COUNTRY CLUB
A public club with one 18-hole course
Location: Take Broadway to Mustang Drive, right to Golf Course Road
Golf Data: Pro Shop Phone: (915) 523-2461; Club Pro: Alan Pursley; Par: 71; Yardage: 6295; Rating: 69.2; Open 7 days.
Green Fees: $6 weekdays for in-county residents, $10 for non-county residents; $15 weekends and holidays for everyone; Carts: $13 for 18 holes.
Tee Time Procedure: Weekends-Holidays: Call Wednesday after 8 a.m.; Weekdays: 1st come, 1st served.

——— ARCHER ——— 2

Archer City
ARCHER CITY COUNTRY CLUB
A semi-private club with one 9-hole course
Location: 1005 S. Ash
Golf Data: Pro Shop Phone: (817) 574-4322; Pro Shop Manager: Billie Neill; Par: 35; Yardage: 2820; Open 7 days (pro shop closed Monday).

Green Fees: $4 weekdays, $5 weekends and holidays; Carts: Weekdays: $2.50 per rider per 9 holes, Weekends: $5 per 9 holes.
Tee Time Procedure: 1st come, 1st served.

——— ARMSTRONG ——— 3

None

——— BAILEY ——— 4

Muleshoe
MULESHOE GOLF & COUNTRY CLUB
A private club with one 9-hole course
Location: At Ithaca & Country Club Road
Golf Data: Pro Shop Phone: (806) 272-4250; Club Pro: Gearold Phipps; Par: 70 (two sets of tees); Yardage: 6054; Rating: 66.8; Open 7 days.
Guest Policy: Open for public play.
Green Fees: $6 weekdays, $12 weekends and holidays in summer; $3 weekdays, $6 weekends and holidays in winter (October-March); Carts: $6 for 18 holes.
Tee Time Procedure: Call anytime.

BAYLOR 5

Seymour

SEYMOUR GOLF & COUNTRY CLUB
A semi-private club with one 9-hole course

Location: 2 miles W. on Throckmorton HWY

Golf Data: Pro Shop Phone: (817) 888-2833; Club Manager: Richard Harvey; Par: 35; Yardage: 3002; Open 7 days.

Green Fees: $4 weekdays, $7 weekends and holidays; No carts available.

Tee Time Procedure: 1st come, 1st served.

BORDEN 6

None

BRISCOE 7

None

BROWN 8

Brownwood

BROWN COUNTY GOLF COURSE
A public club with one 9-hole course

Location: HWY 183N to Staley Drive, then right

Golf Data: Pro Shop Phone: (915) 643-2003; Club Pro: Debbie Adams; Par: 31; Yardage: 1757; Course Architect: Debbie Adams; Open 7 days.

Green Fees: $5 weekdays, $8 weekends and holidays; No carts available.

Tee Time Procedure: 1st come, 1st served.

BROWNWOOD COUNTRY CLUB
A private club with one 18-hole course

Location: 5 miles S. off HWY 377

Golf Data: Pro Shop Phone: (915) 646-1086; Club Pro: Eddie Flowers; Par: 72; Yardage: 6276; Rating: 68.0; Closed Monday.

Guest Policy: You must be a guest of a member.

FEATHER BAY RESORT
A resort club with one 18-hole course

Location: 5 miles N. at Lake Brownwood near junction of FM 2632 and FM 3021

NOTE: 18-hole course designed by Bill Johnson is scheduled to open Spring-Summer 1987.

CALLAHAN 9

Baird

SHADY OAKS GOLF CLUB
A semi-private club with one 9-hole course

Location: I-20W, exit Union Hill S., 1/2 mile, take first left

Golf Data: Pro Shop Phone: (915) 854-1757; Club Manager: Gary McDowell; Par: 36; Yardage: 3060; Open 7 days.

Green Fees: $7.50 weekdays, $10 weekends and holidays; Carts: $5.25 per 9 holes.

Tee Time Procedure: 1st come, 1st served.

CARSON 10

Panhandle

PANHANDLE COUNTRY CLUB
A semi-private club with one 9-hole course

Location: Take Broadway W., turn right at International Harvester

Golf Data: Pro Shop Phone: (806) 537-3300; Club Pro: David Mooring; Par: 71 (two sets of tees); Yardage: 6255; Closed Monday.

Green Fees: $5 weekdays, $10 weekends and holidays; Carts: $5 per 9 holes.

Tee Time Procedure: 1st come, 1st served.

CASTRO 11

Dimmitt

DIMMITT COUNTRY CLUB
A private club with one 9-hole course

Location: Take Hassel W.

Golf Data: Pro Shop Phone: (806) 647-4502; Club Manager: Cliff Cook; Par: 36; Yardage: 3400; Rating: 71.0 (if 18

holes played); Open 7 days.
Guest Policy: You must be a guest of a member or a member of another private country club.

CHILDRESS ___ 12

Childress
CHILDRESS COUNTRY CLUB
A private club with one 9-hole course
Location: N.W. on HWY 83
Golf Data: Pro Shop Phone: (817) 737-8552; Club Pro: Darrell Collins; Par: 35; Yardage: 2794; Rating: 67.0 (if 18 holes played); Open 7 days.
Guest Policy: You must be a guest of a member or a member of another private country club.

CLAY ___ 13

Henrietta
CLAY COUNTY GOLF COURSE & COUNTRY CLUB
A semi-private club with one 9-hole course
Location: E. on HWY 287 (Old Bowie HWY)
Golf Data: Pro Shop Phone: (817) 538-4339; Club Manager: Jerald Davis; Par: 72 (two sets of tees); Yardage: 6405; Closed Monday.
Green Fees: $5 weekdays, $6 weekends and holidays; Carts: $12 per person for 18 holes.
Tee Time Procedure: 1st come, 1st served.

COCHRAN ___ 14

Morton
MORTON COUNTRY CLUB
A private club with one 9-hole course
Location: Take FM 1780 E 6 miles
Golf Data: Pro Shop Phone: (806) 266-5941; Club President: Betty Greener; Par: 35; Yardage: 2867; Closed Monday.
Guest Policy: You must be a guest of a member or a member in good standing of another country club.

Green Fees: $5 weekdays, $8 weekends and holidays; Carts: $6 per 9 holes.
Tee Time Procedure: 1st come, 1st served.

COKE ___ 15

Bronte
SINGING WINDS GOLF COURSE
A public club with one 9-hole course
Location: HWY 277, turn at sign in center of town
Golf Data: Pro Shop Phone: (915) 473-7831; Club Manager: Benny Corley; Par: 36; Yardage: 3013; Open 7 days.
Green Fees: $3 weekdays, $4 weekends and holidays; No carts available.
Tee Time Procedure: 1st come, 1st served.

Robert Lee
MOUNTAIN CREEK GOLF CLUB
A public club with one 9-hole course
Location: In Coke County Park, 1 mile W. of HWY 208 & HWY 158
Golf Data: Pro Shop Phone: (915) 453-2317; Club Pro: Ray Roe; Par: 36; Yardage: 2855; Course Architect: Stanley Adams; Open 7 days.
Green Fees: $4.50 weekdays, $6.50 weekends and holidays; Carts: $10.50 for 18 holes.
Tee Time Procedure: 1st come, 1st served.

COLEMAN ___ 16

Coleman
COLEMAN COUNTRY CLUB
A semi-private club with one 9-hole course
Location: 4½ miles S. on San Angelo HWY
Golf Data: Pro Shop Phone: (915) 625-2922; Club Pro: Gary Henson; Par: 36; Yardage: 3070; Rating: 72.0 (if 18 holes played); Open 7 days.
Green Fees: $4.25 weekdays, $6.75 weekends and holidays for 18 holes; Carts: $12 for 18 holes.
Tee Time Procedure: 1st come, 1st served.

⸺ COLLINGSWORTH ⸺ 17

Wellington

WELLINGTON COUNTRY CLUB
A semi-private club with one 9-hole course
Location: Take HWY 203E 2½ miles, turn left at sign
Golf Data: Pro Shop Phone: (806) 447-5050; Club Pro: Danny West; Par: 36; Yardage: 3059; Rating: 69.0 (if 18 holes played); Closed Monday.
Green Fees: $5 weekdays, $7.50 weekends and holidays; Carts: $12 for 18 holes.
Tee Time Procedure: 1st come, 1st served.

⸺ COMMANCHE ⸺ 18

Commanche

P.A.R COUNTRY CLUB
A semi-private club with one 18-hole course
Location: At Lake Proctor
Golf Data: Pro Shop Phone: (817) 879-2296; Club Pro: Ken McCarty; Par: 72; Yardage: 6013; Rating: 67.8; Open 7 days.
Green Fees: $8 weekdays, $15 weekends and holidays; Carts: $12 for 18 holes.
Tee Time Procedure: 1st come, 1st served.

⸺ CONCHO ⸺ 19

None

⸺ COTTLE ⸺ 20

Paducah

PADUCAH GOLF CLUB
A private club with one 9-hole course
Location: 1 mile S. on FM 1038
Golf Data: No Phone; Secretary-Treasurer: John Weddle; Par: 36; Yardage: 3000; Open 7 days.
Guest Policy: You must be a guest of a member or a member of another private country club.

⸺ CRANE ⸺ 21

Crane

CRANE COUNTY COUNTRY CLUB
A semi-private club with one 9-hole course
Location: 2 miles N. on HWY 385
Golf Data: Pro Shop Phone: (915) 558-2651; Club Manager: Stan Allen; Par: 36; Yardage: 3137; Rating: 70.2 (if 18 holes played); Open 7 days.
Green Fees: $5 weekdays, $10 weekends and holidays; Carts: $6.25 per 9 holes.
Tee Time Procedure: 1st come, 1st served.

⸺ CROCKETT ⸺ 22

Ozona

OZONA COUNTRY CLUB
A private club with one 9-hole course
Location: N. on Barnhart HWY
Golf Data: Pro Shop Phone: (915) 392-2520; Club Manager: Larry Walker; Par: 71 (two sets of tees); Yardage: 6052; Closed Monday.
Guest Policy: You must be a guest of a member or a member of another private club.

⸺ CROSBY ⸺ 23

Lorenzo

LORENZO COUNTRY CLUB
A semi-private club with one 9-hole course
Location: Take Harrison Street E.
Golf Data: Pro Shop Phone: (806) 634-5787; Club Pro: Joe Smith; Par: 36; Yardage: 3467; Rating: 72.1 (if 18 holes played); Open 7 days.
Green Fees: $7 weekdays, $10 weekends and holidays; Carts: $6 per person for 18 holes.
Tee Time Procedure: 1st come, 1st served.

⸺ DALLAM ⸺ 24

None

Lamesa

LAMESA COUNTRY CLUB
A private club with one 9-hole course
Location: HWY 87S (Big Spring HWY)
Golf Data: Pro Shop Phone: (806) 872-7856; Club Manager: Jake Broyles; Par: 36; Yardage: 3301; Open 7 days.
Guest Policy: You must be a guest of a member or a member of another private country club.

PLAINS FAIRWAYS
A public club with one 9-hole course
Location: S. 1st & Avenue S.
Golf Data: Pro Shop Phone: (806) 872-8100; Club Pro: Ron Scott; Par: 35; Yardage: 2638; Open 7 days.
Green Fees: $5.30 weekdays, $8.40 weekends and holidays; Carts: $12 for 18 holes.
Tee Time Procedure: Call anytime.

Hereford

JOHN PITMAN GOLF COURSE
A public club with one 18-hole course
Location: On S. Main Street
Golf Data: Pro Shop Phone: (806) 364-2782; Club Pro: Mike Horton; Par: 71; Yardage: 6480; Rating: 67.5; Course Architect: Cal Garrett; Open 7 days.
Green Fees: $5 weekdays, $7.50 weekends and holidays; Carts: $12 for 18 holes.
Tee Time Procedure: Weekends-Holidays: Call Thursday after 7 a.m.; Weekdays: 1st come, 1st served.

Spur

SPUR GOLF CLUB
A public club with one 9-hole course
Location: In Swenson Park, N. of town
Golf Data: Pro Shop Phone: (806) 271-4355; Club President: Jerry Shobert; Par: 72 (two sets of tees); Yardage: 6278; Open 7 days.
Green Fees: $3 weekdays, $5 weekends and holidays; No carts available.

Tee Time Procedure: 1st come, 1st served.

Clarendon

CLARENDON COUNTRY CLUB
A semi-private club with one 18-hole course
Location: 5 miles N. on HWY 70
Golf Data: Pro Shop Phone: (806) 874-2166; Club Pro: Eddie Baker; Par: 71; Yardage: 6708; Rating: 72.0; Closed Tuesday.
Green Fees: $5 weekdays, $9 weekends and holidays; Carts: $12 for 18 holes.
Tee Time Procedure: 1st come, 1st served.

Cisco

LAKE CISCO COUNTRY CLUB
A semi-private club with one 9-hole course
Location: At Lake Cisco
Golf Data: Pro Shop Phone: (817) 442-2725; Club Manager: Bob Bennie; Par: 34; Yardage: 2596; Rating: 63.5 (if 18 holes played); Open 7 days.
Green Fees: $4 weekdays, $5 weekends and holidays; Carts: $10 for 18 holes.
Tee Time Procedure: 1st come, 1st served.

Eastland

LAKESIDE COUNTRY CLUB
A semi-private club with one 9-hole course
Location: 1 mile N.W. on FM 3101
Golf Data: Pro Shop Phone: (817) 629-2892; Club Pro: Ralph M. Cain; Par: 36; Yardage: 2952; Open 7 days.
Green Fees: $5 weekdays, $7 weekends and holidays; Carts: $10 for 18 holes.
Tee Time Procedure: 1st come, 1st served.

LONE CEDAR COUNTRY CLUB
A semi-private club with one 9-hole course
Location: Take FM 2214 to FM 570E to Lake Leon

Golf Data: Pro Shop Phone: (817) 647-3613; Club Pro: Jerry Doyle; Par: 36; Yardage: 3229; Rating: 69.7 (if 18 holes played); Closed Monday.

Green Fees: $7.29 weekdays, $10.41 weekends and holidays; Carts: $11.45 for 18 holes.

Tee Time Procedure: 1st come, 1st served.

Rising Star

LAKEWOOD RECREATION CENTER
A public club with one 9-hole course
Location: 4½ miles N. on HWY 36
Golf Data: Pro Shop Phone: (817) 643-7792; Club Managers: John & Lucille Roberts; Par: 36; Yardage: 3009; Closed Monday.

Green Fees: $5 weekdays, $7.50 weekends and holidays; Carts: $11 for 18 holes.

Tee Time Procedure: 1st come, 1st served.

————— ECTOR ————— 30

Odessa

ODESSA COUNTRY CLUB
A private club with one 18-hole course
Location: 8½ miles E. on HWY 80
Golf Data: Pro Shop Phone: (915) 563-1043; Club Pro: Jake Bechtold; Par: 72; Yardage: 6832; Rating: 70.3; Closed Monday.

Guest Policy: Out-of-town guests of members and out-of-town members of other private country clubs may play; in-town guests must play with a member.

SUNSET COUNTRY CLUB
A semi-private club with 27 holes
Location: 7 miles N. on Andrews HWY (HWY 385)
Golf Data: Pro Shop Phone: (915) 366-1061; Club Pro: Gidd Faircloth; 18 Par: 72; Yardage: 6912; Rating: 69.0; Par 3 Par: 27; Yardage: 1096; Open 7 days.

Green Fees: $8 weekdays, $13 weekends and holidays; Par 3: $4.25 anytime; Carts: $12.50 for 18 holes; Visa and MC accepted.

Tee Time Procedure: 1st come, 1st served for non-members.

————— FISHER ————— 31

Rotan

ROTAN GOLF COURSE
A public club with one 9-hole course
Location: 201 W. Snyder
NOTE: Closed for remodeling. Due to open in Summer 1987.

————— FLOYD ————— 32

Floydada

FLOYDADA COUNTRY CLUB
A semi-private club with one 9-hole course
Location: 2 miles S. on HWY 62
Golf Data: Pro Shop Phone: (806) 983-2769; Club Pro: Gene Mitchell; Par: 36; Yardage: 3101; Rating: 72.0 (if 18 holes played); Open 7 days.

Green Fees: $7.50 weekdays, $12 weekends and holidays; Carts: $6.25 per person for 18 holes; Visa, MC accepted.

Tee Time Procedure: 1st come, 1st served.

————— FOARD ————— 33

None

————— GAINES ————— 34

Seminole

GAINES COUNTY GOLF COURSE
A public club with one 9-hole course
Location: 8 miles N. on HWY 385
Golf Data: Pro Shop Phone: (915) 758-3808; Club Pro: Dale Newman; Par: 72 (two sets of tees); Yardage: 6511; Rating: 70.0; Course Architect: Warren Cantrell; Open 7 days.

Green Fees: $5 weekdays, $15 weekends and holidays; Carts: $10 for 18 holes.

Tee Time Procedure: 1st come, 1st served.

GARZA 35

Post

CAPROCK GOLF CLUB

A private club with one 9-hole course
Location: Take HWY 84W, right at County Road (2nd street), left 1 mile
Golf Data: Pro Shop Phone: (806) 495-3029; Club Pro: D. H. Bartlett; Par: 35; Yardage: 2750; Rating: 68.0 (if 18 holes played); Course Architects: D. H. Bartlett & Jimmie Bartlett; Open 7 days.
Guest Policy: Golf course is open for public play.
Green Fees: $4 weekdays, $5 weekends and holidays; Carts: $12 for 18 holes.

GLASSCOCK 36

None

GRAY 37

McLean

McLEAN LIONS GOLF ASSOCIATION

A semi-private club with one 9-hole course
Location: Take Old HWY 40 to Pampa HWY, N. ½ mile, left at first crossroads
Golf Data: No Phone; Course Manager: Casper Smith; Par: 36; Yardage: 2802; Open 7 days.
NOTE: Course has sand greens.
Green Fees: None.

Pampa

PAMCEL GOLF CLUB

A private club with one 9-hole course
Location: 5 miles S.W. on HWY 60
Golf Data: Celanese Corp Phone: (806) 665-1801, ext. 4342; Club Manager: W. A. (Bill) Smith; Par: 70 (two sets of tees); Yardage: 6021; Rating: 68.4; Open 7 days.
Guest Policy: You must play with a member.

PAMPA COUNTRY CLUB

A private club with one 18-hole course
Location: Hobart Street N., turn right at Harvester
Golf Data: Pro Shop Phone: (806) 665-8431; Club Pro: Mickey Piersall; Par:

71; Yardage: 6121; Rating: 68.85; Closed Monday.
Guest Policy: You must be a guest of a member or a member of another private country club.

HALE 38

Abernathy

ABERNATHY COUNTRY CLUB

A semi-private club with one 9-hole course
Location: 5 miles E. on FM 2060
Golf Data: Pro Shop Phone: (806) 328-5261; Club Pro: Don McDaniel; Par: 36; Yardage: 3244; Rating: 69.0 (if 18 holes played); Closed Monday.
Green Fees: $5 weekdays, $7 weekends and holidays; Carts: $6 per person for 18 holes.
Tee Time Procedure: 1st come, 1st served.

Hale Center

HILLSIDE ACRES COUNTRY CLUB

A semi-private club with one 9-hole course
Location: Take FM 1914W, turn left at Two Mile Road
Golf Data: Pro Shop Phone: (806) 839-2188; Club Owner: J. D. Black; Par: 36; Yardage: 3019; Open 7 days.
Green Fees: $4 weekdays, $5 weekends and holidays; Carts: $6 per person for 18 holes.
Tee Time Procedure: 1st come, 1st served.

Plainview

PLAINVIEW COUNTRY CLUB

A semi-private club with one 18-hole course
Location: 2900 block of W. 4th
Golf Data: Pro Shop Phone: (806) 296-6148; Club Pro: Jerry Dixon; Par: 71; Yardage: 6322; Rating: 69.0; Closed Monday.
Green Fees: $8 weekdays, $12.50 weekends and holidays; Carts: $14 for 18 holes ($10.50 for single rider).
Tee Time Procedure: Weekends: Call Thursday after 8 a.m.; Weekdays: 1st come, 1st served.

═══════ HALL ═══════ 39

Memphis

MEMPHIS COUNTRY CLUB
A private club with one 9-hole course
Location: 517 S. 10th Street
Golf Data: Pro Shop Phone: (806)
259-2169; Club Pro: Dick Atkins; Par:
34; Yardage: 2862; Rating: 66.5 (if 18
holes played); Open 7 days.
Guest Policy: You must be a guest of a
member or a member of another private
country club.

═══════ HANSFORD ═══════ 40

Spearman

HANSFORD GOLF CLUB
**A semi-private club with one 9-hole
course**
Location: Take HWY 15W, turn right at
FM 760
Golf Data: Pro Shop Phone: (806)
659-2233; Club Pro: Brian Noel; Par: 71
(two sets of tees); Yardage: 5600; Closed
Monday.
Green Fees: $5.26 weekdays, $7.89
weekends and holidays; Carts: $13.68 for
18 holes.
Tee Time Procedure: 1st come, 1st
served.

═══════ HARDEMAN ═══════ 41

Quanah

QUANAH COUNTRY CLUB
A private club with one 9-hole course
Location: 3 miles N.E. on FM 2640
Golf Data: Pro Shop Phone: (817)
663-2069; Club Pro: Mike Lamberton;
Par: 70 (two sets of tees); Yardage: 5841;
Rating: 68.8; Closed Monday.
Guest Policy: You must be a member of
another private country club or an out-of-
town guest of a member.

═══════ HARTLEY ═══════ 42

Dalhart

DALHART COUNTRY CLUB
A private club with one 9-hole course
Location: 2 miles W. on HWY 54

Golf Data: Pro Shop Phone: (806)
249-5596; Club Manager: Jean Ford; Par:
36; Yardage: 3280; Rating: 69.7 (if 18
holes played); Closed Monday.
Guest Policy: County residents must play
with a member. Non-county residents
may pay green fees and play.
Green Fees: $12 anytime. Carts: $12 for
18 holes.
Tee Time Procedure: Call anytime.

═══════ HASKELL ═══════ 43

Haskell

HASKELL COUNTY COUNTRY CLUB
**A semi-private club with one 9-hole
course**
Location: HWY 227N, turn right at
airport sign
Golf Data: Pro Shop Phone: (817)
864-3400; Club Pro: Jack Medford; Par:
36; Yardage: 2986; Rating: 68.0 (if 18
holes played); Open 7 days.
Green Fees: $5 for 18 holes anytime; No
carts available.
Tee Time Procedure: 1st come, 1st
served.

═══════ HEMPHILL ═══════ 44

Canadian

CITY OF CANADIAN GOLF CLUB
A public club with one 9-hole course
Location: 4 miles N. on HWY 83
Golf Data: Pro Shop Phone: (806)
323-5512; Club Pro: Bert Deselms; Par:
72 (two sets of tees); Yardage: 6253;
Rating: 68.9; Closed Monday.
Green Fees: $6 weekdays, $8 weekends
and holidays; Carts: $6 per 9 holes.
Tee Time Procedure: 1st come, 1st
served.

═══════ HOCKLEY ═══════ 45

Levelland

LEVELLAND COUNTRY CLUB
A private club with one 9-hole course
Location: Take Avenue H, S., left at
Country Club Lane
Golf Data: Pro Shop Phone: (806)
894-3288; Club Pro: Ronnie Rosson; Par:

71 (two sets of tees); Yardage: 6077;
Rating: 68.9; Closed Monday.
Guest Policy: You must be a member of
another private country club or a guest of
a member. Guests must play with a
member April thru September.

Sundown

SUNDOWN MUNICIPAL GOLF COURSE

A public club with one 9-hole course
Location: 3 blocks W. on Slaughter Street
Golf Data: Pro Shop Phone: (806)
229-6186; Club Pro: Joe Don Davis; Par:
70 (two sets of tees); Yardage: 6647;
Closed Monday until noon.
Green Fees: $7 weekdays, $10 weekends
and holidays; Carts: $6 per 9 holes.
Tee Time Procedure: 1st come, 1st
served.

———— HOWARD ——— 46

Big Spring

BIG SPRING COUNTRY CLUB

A private club with one 18-hole course
Location: From I-20, take HWY 87 4
miles S.
Golf Data: Pro Shop Phone: (915)
267-5354; Club Pro: Chuck Palmer; Par:
71; Yardage: 6920; Rating: 69.5; Closed
Monday.
Guest Policy: You must be a guest of a
member or a member of another private
country club.

COMMANCHE TRAIL GOLF CLUB

A public club with one 18-hole course
Location: Take HWY 87S to Commanche
Trail Park
Golf Data: Pro Shop Phone: (915)
263-7271; Club Pro: Al Patterson; Par:
71; Yardage: 6504; Rating: 70.8; Open 7
days.
Green Fees: $5 weekdays, $7 weekends
and holidays; Carts: $10 for 18 holes.
Tee Time Procedure: 1st come, 1st
served.

——— HUTCHINSON ═ 47

Borger

HUBER COUNTRY CLUB

**A semi-private club with one 18-hole
course**

Location: Take HWY 136S, turn left at
FM 1551, right at Broadmore
Golf Data: Pro Shop Phone: (806)
273-2231; Club Pro: W. R. "Andy"
Anderson; Par: 72; Yardage: 6229; Rating:
70.0; Open 7 days.
Green Fees: $6 weekdays, $10 weekends
and holidays; Carts: $13 for 18 holes.
Tee Time Procedure: Call Thursday for
weekends and holidays.

PHILLIPS COUNTRY CLUB

**A semi-private club with one 18-hole
course**
Location: Take HWY 207N, go W. at
traffic circle
Golf Data: Pro Shop Phone: (806)
274-6812; Club Pro: Danny Snider; Par:
72; Yardage: 6065; Rating: 68.1; Open 7
days.
Green Fees: $5.50 weekdays, $9.50
weekends and holidays; Carts: $7 per 9
holes.
Tee Time Procedure: 1st come, 1st
served.

————— IRION ——— 48

None

————— JACK ——— 49

Jacksboro

JACKSBORO GOLF CLUB

**A semi-private club with one 9-hole
course**
Location: From courthouse, take either
HWY 199 or 281, turn right at HWY 148
Golf Data: Pro Shop Phone: (817)
567-9416; Club Pro: James Gammon;
Par: 35; Yardage: 3143; Rating: 69.0 (if
18 holes played); Closed Monday.
Green Fees: $4 weekdays, $10 weekends
and holidays; Carts: $12 for 18 holes;
Visa and MC accepted.
Tee Time Procedure: 1st come, 1st
served.

————— JONES ——— 50

Anson

ANSON GOLF COURSE

A public club with one 9-hole course

Location: Next to City Park
Golf Data: Pro Shop Phone: (915) 823-9822; Club Manager: Donald Stalder; Par: 36; Yardage: 3000; Open 7 days.
Green Fees: $4 weekdays, $5 weekends and holidays; Carts: $10 for 18 holes.
Tee Time Procedure: 1st come, 1st served.

Hamlin

HAMLIN GOLF COURSE
A semi-private club with one 9-hole course
Location: HWY 83S, right at HWY 57W, right at Golf Course Road
Golf Data: No Phone; Club Manager: Dan Bogle; Par: 36; Yardage: 2950; Open 7 days.
Green Fees: $5 weekdays, $8 weekends and holidays; Carts: $12 for 18 holes.
Tee Time Procedure: 1st come, 1st served.

Stamford

STAMFORD GOLF & COUNTRY CLUB
A private club with one 9-hole course
Location: Take Hamilton Street E., stay straight when road curves right
Golf Data: Pro Shop Phone: (915) 773-5001; Club Pro: Don Mitchell; Par: 35; Yardage: 2878; Open 7 days.
Guest Policy: You must be a guest of a member. Non-county residents may also pay green fees and play.
Green Fees: $5 weekdays, $7.50 weekends and holidays; No carts available.
Tee Time Procedure: 1st come, 1st served.

―――――――― KENT ――――― 51

Jayton

KENT COUNTY GOLF COURSE
A semi-private club with one 9-hole course
Location: 2 miles W. of town
Golf Data: Pro Shop Phone: (806) 237-2206; Club Manager: Bunk Floyd; Par: 71 (two sets of tees); Yardage: 5451; Rating: 68.2; Open 7 days.

Green Fees: $3 weekdays, $5 weekends and holidays; No carts available.
Tee Time Procedure: 1st come, 1st served.

―――――――― KIMBLE ――――― 52

Junction

JUNCTION GOLF CLUB
A semi-private club with one 9-hole course
Location: Near race track at fairgrounds
Golf Data: Course Information: (915) 446-2968; Club Manager: Wil Wilson; Par: 35; Yardage: 2614; Open 7 days.
Green Fees: $5 weekdays, $7 weekends and holidays; Carts: $12 for 18 holes ($7.50 for 9).
Tee Time Procedure: 1st come, 1st served.

―――――――― KING ――――― 53

None

―――――――― KNOX ――――― 54

Knox City

KNOX CITY COUNTRY CLUB
A semi-private club with one 9-hole course
Location: Take HWY 6S
Golf Data: No Phone (for information, phone Doris at Chamber: (817) 658-3442); Course Manager: Dominges Garcia; Par: 35; Yardage: 3027; Open 7 days.
Green Fees: $5 anytime; No carts available.
Tee Time Procedure: 1st come, 1st served.

Munday

LAKE CREEK COUNTRY CLUB
A public club with one 9-hole course
Location: 2 miles E. on HWY 222
Golf Data: Club Secretary, Jeff Anderson: (817) 422-4041;Par: 35; Yardage: 2758; Open 7 days.

Green Fees: $3 weekdays, $4 weekends and holidays; No carts available.
Tee Time Procedure: 1st come, 1st served.

————— LAMB ————— 55

Littlefield

LITTLEFIELD COUNTRY CLUB
A semi-private club with one 9-hole course
Location: 3½ miles N. on HWY 385
Golf Data: Pro Shop Phone: (806) 385-3309; Club Pro: Mike Nix; Par: 36; Yardage: 3160; Rating: 69.7 (if 18 holes played); Closed Monday.
Green Fees: $5 weekdays, $10 weekends and holidays; Carts: $6 per 9 holes.
Tee Time Procedure: 1st come, 1st served.

Olton

OLTON COUNTRY CLUB
A semi-private club with one 9-hole course
Location: 2½ miles S. on HWY 168
Golf Data: Pro Shop Phone: (806) 285-2595; Club Pro: Harold W. Payne; Par: 72 (two sets of tees); Yardage: 6174; Rating: 71.6; Open 7 days.
Green Fees: $6 weekdays, $8 weekends and holidays; Carts: $10 for 18 holes.
Tee Time Procedure: 1st come, 1st served.

————— LIPSCOMB ————— 56

Booker

BOOKER COUNTRY CLUB
A semi-private club with one 9-hole course
Location: From HWY 15, left on Main Street, left at Santa Fe (1st street)
Golf Data: Pro Shop Phone: (806) 658-9663; Club Pro: Lewis Westfall; Par: 36; Yardage: 3140; Rating: 70.1 (if 18 holes played); Open 7 days.
Green Fees: $4.50 weekdays, $6 weekends and holidays; Carts: $10.51 for 18 holes.
Tee Time Procedure: 1st come, 1st served.

————— LOVING ————— 57

None

————— LUBBOCK ————— 58

Lubbock

Public Golf Courses

ELM GROVE GOLF COURSE
A public club with one 18-hole course
Location: 6800 W. 34th Street
Golf Data: Pro Shop Phone: (806) 799-7801; Club Pro: Terry Harvick; Par: 72; Yardage: 6650; Rating: 70.5; Open 7 days.
Green Fees: $5 weekdays, $6 weekends and holidays; Carts: $10 for 18 holes.
Tee Time Procedure: 1st come, 1st served.

MEADOWBROOK MUNICIPAL GOLF COURSE
A public club with two 18-hole courses
Location: At MacKenzie State Park
Golf Data: Pro Shop Phone: (806) 765-6679; Club Pro: Steve Shields; *Holes 1–18* Par: 71; Yardage: 6681; Rating: 71.65; *Holes 19–36* Par: 70; Yardage: 6214; Rating: 69.32; Open 7 days.
Green Fees: $5.50 weekdays, $7 weekends and holidays for all day play; Carts: $14 for 18 holes.
Tee Time Procedure: Weekends-Holidays: Thursday after 9 a.m. by phone or in person; Weekdays: 1st come, 1st served.

SHADOW HILLS GOLF CLUB
A public club with one 18-hole course
Location: 6002 3rd Street
Golf Data: Pro Shop Phone: (806) 793-9700; General Manager: Jerry Hughes; Par: 72; Yardage: 6657; Rating: 71.2; Open 7 days.
Green Fees: $6.50 weekdays, $8 weekends and holidays; Carts: $7 per person for 18 holes; Visa and MC accepted.
Tee Time Procedure: Weekends-Holidays: Call 1 week in advance. Walk-ons welcome.

TREASURE ISLAND GOLF CENTER
A public club with one 18-hole executive course
Location: 501 Frankford Avenue

Golf Data: Pro Shop Phone: (806) 795-9311; Club Owner: Mavis L. Miller; Par: 55; Yardage: 2400; Open 7 days.

Green Fees: $5.50 weekdays, $6.50 weekends and holidays; Carts: $8 for 18 holes; Visa and MC accepted.

Tee Time Procedure: 1st come, 1st served.

Private Golf Courses

HILLCREST COUNTRY CLUB
A private club with one 18-hole course
Location: N. University Avenue

Golf Data: Pro Shop Phone: (806) 765-5208; Club Pro: Richard Whittenbury; Par: 72; Yardage: 6842; Rating: 71.6; Closed Monday.

Guest Policy: You must be a guest of a member or a member of another private country club. Phone in advance.

LAKERIDGE COUNTRY CLUB
A private club with one 18-hole course
Location: 8802 Vicksberg

Golf Data: Pro Shop Phone: (806) 794-4444; Club Pro: Terry Dear; Par: 72; Yardage: 7906; Rating: 71.1; Course Architect: Billy Martindale; Closed Monday.

Guest Policy: You must be a guest of a member or a member of another private country club. In-town guests must play with a member. Phone for specifics.

LUBBOCK COUNTRY CLUB
A private club with one 18-hole course
Location: Take Amarillo HWY N., exit Yucca Lane left

Golf Data: Pro Shop Phone: (806) 763-1871; Club Pro: Mark Vinson; Par: 72; Yardage: 6907; Rating: 73.0; Closed Monday.

Guest Policy: You must be a guest of a member or a member of another private country club.

Military Golf Courses

GOLF COURSE AT REESE AIR FORCE BASE
A private club with one 9-hole course
Location: At Reese Air Force Base

Golf Data: Pro Shop Phone: (806) 885-3819; Club Pro: Dick Davis; Par: 72 (two sets of tees); Yardage: 6367; Rating: 71.0; Open 7 days.

Guest Policy: You must be a member of the military or a guest of the military.

Slaton

SLATON GOLF CLUB
A public club with one 9-hole course
Location: Take 9th Street 2 miles, right at Golf Course Road for 2 miles

Golf Data: Pro Shop Phone: (806) 828-3269; Club Pro: Mike Lewis; Par: 70 (two sets of tees); Yardage: 6107; Open 7 days.

Green Fees: $5 weekdays, $6 weekends and holidays; Carts: $3.50 per person for 9 holes.

Tee Time Procedure: 1st come, 1st served.

LYNN ====== 59

Tahoka

TAHOKA COUNTRY CLUB
A private club with one 9-hole course
Location: Take HWY 380W, located N. of hospital

Golf Data: Pro Shop Phone: (806) 998-5305; Course Manager: J. C. Elrod; Par: 36; Yardage: 3018; Open 7 days.

Guest Policy: Non-country residents may pay green fees.

Green Fees: $5 weekdays, $10 weekends and holidays; No carts available.

Tee Time Procedure: 1st come, 1st served.

McCULLOUGH == 60

Brady

BRADY MUNICIPAL GOLF COURSE
A public club with one 9-hole course
Location: 2 miles N. on HWY 87, turn right

Golf Data: Pro Shop Phone: (915) 597-6010; Club Manager: M. L. "Jack" Wootan; Par: 71 (two sets of tees); Yardage: 5835; Closed Monday.

Green Fees: $5.26 weekdays, $6.31 weekends and holidays; Carts: $13.04 for 18 holes.

Tee Time Procedure: 1st come, 1st served.

═══════ MARTIN ═══════ 61

Stanton

MARTIN COUNTY COUNTRY CLUB
A semi-private club with one 9-hole course
Location: ½ mile S. of old HWY 80 (see from highway)
Golf Data: Pro Shop Phone: (915) 756-2556; Club Manager: Ross Hay; Par: 35; Yardage: 3000; Rating: 67.0 (if 18 holes played); Open 7 days.
Green Fees: $6 Monday-Thursday, $10 Friday-Sunday and holidays for 18 holes; Carts: $11 for 18 holes.
Tee Time Procedure: 1st come, 1st served.

═══════ MENARD ═══════ 62

Menard

MISSION GOLF COURSE
A semi-private club with one 9-hole course
Location: 1 miles W. on El Dorado HWY (next to San Saba Mission)
Golf Data: Pro Shop Phone: (915) 396-4938; Club Manager: C. R. Brace; Par: 31; Yardage: 2067; Open 7 days.
Green Fees: $4 weekdays, $5 weekends and holidays; Carts: $10 for 18 holes (must call in advance to reserve cart).
Tee Time Procedure: 1st come, 1st served.

═══════ MIDLAND ═══════ 63

Midland

Public Golf Courses

HOGAN PARK MUNICIPAL GOLF COURSE
A public club with 27 holes
Location: 3600 N. Fairgrounds Blvd.
Golf Data: Pro Shop Phone: (915) 682-7891; Club Pro: Price Courter; *1st 18* Par: 70; Yardage: 6615; Rating: 68.5; *last 9* Par: 36; Yardage: 3410; Rating: 68.0 (if played twice); Open 7 days. (18 holes Mon.-Wed.)
Green Fees: $11 weekdays, $14.50 weekends and holidays; Carts: $12.50 for 18 holes.

Tee Time Procedure: Weekends-Holidays: Friday after 6 a.m. by phone or before 6 a.m. in person.

Private Golf Courses

GREEN TREE COUNTRY CLUB
A private club with 27 holes
Location: 4900 Greentree Blvd.
Golf Data: Pro Shop Phone: (915) 694-7726; Club Pro: Larry Bishop; *1st 18* Par: 71; Yardage: 6614; Rating: 68.8; *Last 9* Par: 36; Yardage: 3510; Closed Monday.
Guest Policy: You must play with a member or be a member of another private country club. Phone in advance for specifics.

MIDLAND COUNTRY CLUB
A private club with one 18-hole course
Location: Take Big Spring Street N. (turns into TX 349), turn left beyond loop
Golf Data: Pro Shop Phone: (915) 682-4378; Club Pro: George Clark; Par: 72; Yardage: 7354; Rating: 72.1; Course Architects: Kirby-Griffin; Closed Monday.
Guest Policy: You must be a guest of a member or a member of another private country club. Phone for specifics.

RANCHLAND HILLS COUNTRY CLUB
A private club with one 18-hole course
Location: 1600 E. Wadley
Golf Data: Pro Shop Phone: (915) 683-2041; Club Pro: Bob Pritchett; Par: 70; Yardage: 6568; Rating: 70.3; Course Architect: Ralph Plummer; Closed Monday.
Guest Policy: Members must accompany their guests. Will reciprocate with members of bonafide private country clubs. Phone for specifics and bring credentials.

Midland-Odessa

MISSION COUNTRY CLUB
A private club with one 18-hole course
Location: Between Midland-Odessa on HWY 191
Golf Data: Pro Shop Phone: (915) 561-8811; Club Pro: Doug Smith; Par: 72; Yardage: 7135; Rating: 72.5; Course Architects: Dick Nugent & Bob Killen; Closed Monday.
Guest Policy: You must play with a member or be a member of another private country club. Phone in advance.

MITCHELL 64

Colorado City

COLORADO COUNTRY CLUB
A semi-private club with one 9-hole course
Location: 4 miles E. on I-20, exit Country Club Drive, go N.
Golf Data: Pro Shop Phone: (915) 728-2528; Club Pro: Bob Hinn; Par: 71 (two sets of tees); Yardage: 5969; Closed Tuesday.
Green Fees: $6 weekdays, $10 weekends and holidays; Carts: $10 for 18 holes.
Tee Time Procedure: 1st come, 1st served.

MOORE 65

Dumas

NORTH PLAINS COUNTRY CLUB
A private club with one 9-hole course
Location: Take Maddox Avenue N. 4 miles
Golf Data: Pro Shop Phone: (806) 935-4910; Club Pro: Andy Anderson; Par: 72 (two sets of tees); Yardage: 6557; Rating: 71.0; Closed Monday.
Guest Policy: County residents must play with a member. Non-county residents who are members of other private country clubs may play.

MOTLEY 66

Roaring Springs

SPRINGS RANCH GOLF CLUB
A private club with one 9-hole course
Location: 2 miles S. on HWY 70
Golf Data: Pro Shop Phone: (806) 348-2671; Club Pro: Doug Terry; Par: 36; Yardage: 3050; Rating: 68.0 (if 18 holes played); Open 7 days.
Guest Policy: You must play with a member or be a member of another private country club.

NOLAN 67

Sweetwater

LAKE SWEETWATER MUNICIPAL GOLF COURSE
A public club with one 18-hole course

Location: I-20 E, exit FM 1856S
Golf Data: Pro Shop Phone: (915) 235-8816; Club Pro: James Patterson; Par: 71; Yardage: 6185; Open 7 days.
Green Fees: $6.50 weekdays, $7.50 weekends and holidays; Carts: $11.50 weekdays, $12.50 weekends and holidays for 18 holes.
Tee Time Procedure: 1st come, 1st served.

SWEETWATER COUNTRY CLUB
A semi-private club with one 18-hole course
Location: Take Broadway E. to Haley, left to Woodruff
Golf Data: Pro Shop Phone: (915) 235-8484; Club Pro: Leonard Perry; Par: 71; Yardage: 6100; Rating: 69.5; Course Architect: Norman Sapulvo; Open 7 days.
Green Fees: $10.50 weekdays, $12.50 weekends and holidays; Carts: $10.50 for 18 holes.
Tee Time Procedure: 1st come, 1st served (except weekends between 11 a.m.-1 p.m. which are reserved for members).

OCHILTREE 68

Perryton

PERRYTON MUNICIPAL GOLF COURSE
A public club with one 18-hole course
Location: 402 S.E. 24th Street
Golf Data: Pro Shop Phone: (806) 435-5381; Club Pro: James B. Smith; Par: 72; Yardage: 6450; Rating: 69.1; Closed Monday.
Green Fees: $5 weekdays, $6 weekends and holidays; Carts: $12 for 18 holes.
Tee Time Procedure: 1st come, 1st served.

OLDHAM 69

Vega

OLDHAM COUNTY COUNTRY CLUB
A semi-private club with one 9-hole course
Location: 5 miles S. on HWY 385
Golf Data: Pro Shop Phone: (806) 267-2595; Club Pro: Jim Basford; Par: 36; Yardage: 3150; Rating: 71.0 (if 18 holes played); Closed Monday.

Green Fees: $10.40 anytime; Carts: $12 for 18 holes.
Tee Time Procedure: 1st come, 1st served.

═══════ PARMER ═══════ 70

Farwell

FARWELL COUNTRY CLUB
A semi-private club with one 9-hole course
Location: Take HWY 60W., 1st left after 2nd RR tracks
Golf Data: Pro Shop Phone: (806) 481-9910; Course Manager: Mike Martin; Par: 72 (two sets of tees); Yardage: 6400; Rating: 68.3; Open 7 days.
Green Fees: $6.30 weekdays, $10.50 weekends and holidays; Carts: $6.30 per person for 18 holes.
Tee Time Procedure: 1st come, 1st served.

Friona

FRIONA COUNTRY CLUB
A private club with one 9-hole course
Location: 1505 W. 5th Street
Golf Data: Pro Shop Phone: (806) 247-3125; Club President; Tim Herring; Par: 36; Yardage: 2883; Closed Monday.
Guest Policy: Non-county residents may pay green fees.
Green Fees: $5 weekdays, $10 weekends and holidays; Carts: $6 per person for 18 holes.
Tee Time Procedure: 1st come, 1st served.

═══════ PECOS ═══════ 71

Fort Stockton

PECOS COUNTY MUNICIPAL GOLF COURSE
A public club with one 18-hole course
Location: 2 miles N.W. on HWY 285
Golf Data: Pro Shop Phone: (915) 336-7110; Club Manager: Bob Pounds; Par: 72; Yardage: 6598; Rating: 69.0; Closed Monday.

Green Fees: $7.81 weekdays, $13.02 weekends and holidays; Carts: $10.45 for 18 holes.
Tee Time Procedure: 1st come, 1st served.

Iraan

IRAAN GOLF CLUB
A public club with one 9-hole course
Location: Off HWY 349
Golf Data: Pro Shop Phone: (915) 639-8892; Club Manager: Ray Harber; Par: 36; Yardage: 3300; Rating: 69.0 (if 18 holes played); Open 7 days.
Green Fees: $3.50 weekdays, $5 weekends and holidays; No carts available.
Tee Time Procedure: 1st come, 1st served.

═══════ POTTER ═══════ 72

Amarillo

Public Golf Courses

AMARILLO PUBLIC GOLF COURSE
A public club with one 18-hole course
Location: I-40E, exit 80, HWY 228 N. to air base, right at Kimberly Street
Golf Data: Pro Shop Phone: (806) 335-1142; Club Pro: Alan Johnson; Par: 72; Yardage: 6853; Rating: 70.0; Open 7 days.
Green Fees: $4.50 weekdays, $6.50 weekends and holidays. A $2.50 Tuesday special is offered. Carts: $5 per 9 holes. Visa and MC accepted.
Tee Time Procedure: Weekends-Holidays: Thursday after 7 a.m. by phone or in person.

ROSS ROGERS MUNICIPAL GOLF COURSE
A public club with two 18-hole courses
Location: 722 N.E. 24th Street
Golf Data: Pro Shop Phone: (806) 378-3086; Club Pro: Sherwin Cox; *East* Par: 72; Yardage: 6912; Rating: 72.8; *West* Par: 72; Yardage: 6629; Rating: 71.4; Open 7 days.
Green Fees: $6 weekdays, $8 weekends and holidays; Carts: $13 for 18 holes.
Tee Time Procedure: Weekends-Holidays: Friday after 7 a.m. by phone or in person; Weekdays: 1st come, 1st served.

AMARILLO COUNTRY CLUB
A private club with one 18-hole course
Location: I-40W, exit Western, N. 2 miles, left at Bushland
Golf Data: Pro Shop Phone: (806) 355-5021; Club Pro: Troy Badgett; Par: 71; Yardage: 6581; Rating: 70.4; Course Architect: Jay Morrish (redesign in 1985); Closed Monday.
Guest Policy: You must be a guest of a member or a member of another private country club.

TASCOSA COUNTRY CLUB
A private club with one 18-hole course
Location: I-40W, exit Western, N. 4-5 miles
Golf Data: Pro Shop Phone: (806) 374-2351; Club Pro: Terry LeGate; Par: 72; Yardage: 6829; Rating: 70.0; Course Architect: Warren Cantrell; Closed Monday.
Guest Policy: You must be a current member of another private country club.

RANDALL 73

Amarillo

SOUTHWEST GOLF COURSE
A public club with one 18-hole course
Location: I-40W, exit Coulter Street S., right at Hollywood
Golf Data: Pro Shop Phone: (806) 355-7161; Club Pro: Guy D. Bailey; Par: 72; Yardage: 7018; Course Architect: Bobby Westfall; Open 7 days.
Green Fees: $5.25 weekdays, $7.50 weekends and holidays; Carts: $12.50 for 18 holes.
Tee Time Procedure: 1st come, 1st served.

Canyon

CANYON COUNTRY CLUB
A semi-private club with one 9-hole course
Location: Take HWY 60W, right at VFW Road, then 3 miles
Golf Data: Pro Shop Phone: (806) 499-3398; Club Pro: Greg Bachan; Par: 70; Yardage: 5879; Rating: 68.0; Closed Monday.

Green Fees: $8 weekdays, $14 weekends and holidays; Carts: $12.50 for 18 holes; Visa and MC accepted.
Tee Time Procedure: Call anytime.

HUNSLEY HILLS GOLF CLUB
A semi-private club with one 18-hole course
Location: I-40, exit Canyon EXPY, S. to Hunsley exit, W., left at Country Club Drive
Golf Data: Pro Shop Phone: (806) 655-1106; Club Pro: George MacKanos; Par: 71; Yardage: 6904; Rating: 69.9; Open 7 days.
Green Fees: $8 weekdays, $10 weekends and holidays; Carts: $12 for 18 holes; Visa and MC accepted.
Tee Time Procedure: Weekends-Holidays: Friday after 8 a.m. by phone or in person; Weekdays: 1st come, 1st served.

REAGAN 74

Big Lake

BIG LAKE GOLF ASSOCIATION
A semi-private club with one 9-hole course
Location: 1 mile E. on HWY 67
Golf Data: Pro Shop Phone: (915) 884-2633; Club VP: Wade Daugherty; Par: 72 (two sets of tees); Yardage: 6114; Closed Monday.
Green Fees: $7 weekdays, $10 weekends and holidays; No carts available.
Tee Time Procedure: 1st come, 1st served.

REEVES 75

Pecos

REEVES COUNTY GOLF COURSE
A public club with 11 holes
Location: 88 Starley Drive
Golf Data: Pro Shop Phone: (915) 447-2858; Club Manager: Royce Cassell; Par: 70; Yardage: 6212; Rating: 67.4 (if 18 holes played); Open 7 days.
Green Fees: $4 weekdays, $6 weekends and holidays; Carts: $14 for 18 holes ($10 for single rider).
Tee Time Procedure: 1st come, 1st served.

ROBERTS — 76

None

RUNNELS — 77

Ballinger

BALLINGER COUNTRY CLUB
A private club with one 9-hole course
Location: HWY 157N, left at Country Club Road
Golf Data: Pro Shop Phone: (915) 365-3214; Club Pro: Wayne Herrman; Par: 36; Yardage: 2902; Closed Monday.
Guest Policy: Non-county residents may pay green fees.
Green Fees: $10 anytime; No carts available.

Winters

WINTERS COUNTRY CLUB
A private club with one 9-hole course
Location: 5 miles S. on HWY 83
Golf Data: Pro Shop Phone: (915) 754-4679; Club Manager: Jim Beazley; Par: 34; Yardage: 2652; Open 7 days.
Guest Policy: You must be a guest of a member or a member of another private country club.

SCHLEICHER — 78

Eldorado

ELDORADO GOLF CLUB
A public club with one 9-hole course
Location: Take McCarder Avenue 7 blocks W. to County Airport
Golf Data: Pro Shop Phone: (915) 853-2036; Par: 32; Yardage: 2104; Open 7 days.
Green Fees: $5 anytime; No carts available.
Tee Time Procedure: 1st come, 1st served.

SCURRY — 79

Snyder

SNYDER COUNTRY CLUB
A private club with one 9-hole course
Location: N. on the old Lubbock HWY

Golf Data: Pro Shop Phone: (915) 573-7101; Club Pro: Rick Mammolite; Par: 71 (two sets of tees); Yardage: 6152; Closed Monday.
Guest Policy: You must play with a member.

WESTERN TEXAS COLLEGE GOLF COURSE
A semi-private club with one 9-hole course
Location: Take College Avenue S., left at "V" to Western State College campus
Golf Data: Pro Shop Phone: (915) 573-9291; Club Pro: Dave Foster; Par: 35; Yardage: 3000; Rating: 69.1 (if 18 holes played); Closed Monday.
Green Fees: $6 weekdays, $9 weekends and holidays; Carts: $10 for 18 holes.
Tee Time Procedure: 1st come, 1st served.

SHACKELFORD — 80

Albany

ALBANY GOLF COURSE
A public club with one 9-hole course
Location: Western edge of town
Golf Data: No Phone; Par: 35; Yardage: 3100; Open 7 days.
Green Fees: $5 anytime; No carts available.
Tee Time Procedure: 1st come, 1st served.

SHERMAN — 81

Stratford

STRATFORD COUNTRY CLUB
A private club with one 9-hole course
Location: 3 miles W. on HWY 54
Golf Data: Pro Shop Phone: (806) 396-2259; Club Manager: Dario Garza; Par: 36; Yardage: 3262; Open 7 days.
Guest Policy: You must be sponsored by a member. Non-county residents may pay green fees.
Green Fees: $5 weekdays, $10 weekends and holidays; Carts: $10 for 18 holes.
Tee Time Procedure: 1st come, 1st served.

———— STEPHENS ———— 82

Breckenridge

BRECKENRIDGE COUNTRY CLUB
A semi-private club with one 9-hole course
Location: 3 miles W. on HWY 180
Golf Data: Pro Shop Phone: (817) 559-3466; Club Pro: Paul Blackerby; Par: 72 (two sets of tees); Yardage: 6070; Open 7 days.
Green Fees: $5 weekdays, $7.50 weekends and holidays; Carts: $12 for 18 holes.
Tee Time Procedure: 1st come, 1st served.

———— STERLING ———— 83

Sterling

STERLING GOLF ASSOCIATION
A public club with one 6-hole course
Location: E. on HWY 87
Golf Data: No Phone; Club Manager: H.L. Bailey; Par: 19; Yardage: 825; Open 7 days.
Green Fees: None.
Tee Time Procedure: 1st come, 1st served.

———— STONEWALL ———— 84

Aspermont

ASPERMONT GOLF COURSE
A public club with one 9-hole course
Location: Take HWY 610 SW 1½ miles, turn left
Golf Data: No Phone; Par: 35; Yardage: 3000; Open 7 days.
Green Fees: $4 weekdays, $5 weekends and holidays; No carts available. (honor system).
Tee Time Procedure: 1st come, 1st served.

———— SUTTON ———— 85

Sonora

SONORA GOLF CLUB
A public club with one 9-hole course
Location: N. on HWY 277

Golf Data: Pro Shop Phone: (915) 387-3680; Club Pro: George Johnson; Par: 72 (two sets of tees); Yardage: 6050; Rating: 68.8; Open 7 days.
Green Fees: $10 weekdays, $15 weekends and holidays; Carts: $12 for 18 holes.
Tee Time Procedure: 1st come, 1st served.

———— SWISHER ———— 86

Tulia

TULE LAKE COUNTRY CLUB
A semi-private club with one 9-hole course
Location: 3½ miles E. on FM 1794
Golf Data: Pro Shop Phone: (806) 995-3400; Club Manager: Danny DeBoise; Par: 72 (two sets of tees); Yardage: 6300; Rating: 68.0; Open 7 days.
Green Fees: $6.25 weekdays, $10.41 weekends and holidays; Carts: $6.25 per rider for 18 holes.
Tee Time Procedure: 1st come, 1st served.

———— TAYLOR ———— 87

Abilene

Public Golf Courses

MAXWELL MUNICIPAL GOLF COURSE
A public club with one 18-hole course
Location: 1002 S. 32nd Street
Golf Data: Pro Shop Phone: (915) 692-2737; Club Pro: Randy Richardson; Par: 71; Yardage: 6190; Rating: 69.4; Open 7 days.
Green Fees: $6.25 weekdays, $7.30 weekends and holidays; Carts: $12.50 for 18 holes.
Tee Time Procedure: Call 7 days in advance.

Private Golf Courses

ABILENE COUNTRY CLUB
A private club with one 18-hole course
Location: 4039 S. Treadway
Golf Data: Pro Shop Phone: (915) 692-2583; Club Pro: Allen Botkin; Par: 71; Yardage: 6116; Rating: 67.5; Closed Monday.

Guest Policy: You must be a guest of a member or a member of another private country club.

FAIRWAY OAKS GOLF & RACQUET CLUB
A private club with one 18-hole course
Location: I-20, exit Treadway S., right at Antilley Road, right at Fairway Oaks Blvd.
Golf Data: Pro Shop Phone: (915) 698-4971; Club Pro: Charles Coody; Par: 72; Yardage: 7189; Rating: 72.6; Course Architects: Charles Coody & Ron Garl; Closed Monday.
NOTE: Site of PGA Southwest Golf Classic (September) and LaJet-Pelz Amateur Golf Classic (August).
Guest Policy: You must be a guest of a member during the week and play with the member on the weekend. Will reciprocate with members of other private country clubs outside a 75-mile radius of Abilene.

Military Golf Courses

DYESS AIR FORCE BASE GOLF COURSE
A private club with one 18-hole course
Location: At Dyes Air Force Base
Golf Data: Pro Shop Phone: (915) 696-4384; Club Pro: Alan Hardcastle; Par: 72; Yardage: 7005; Open 7 days.
Guest Policy: You play with a member of the military.

Merkel
COUNTRY CLUB OF MERKEL
A semi-private club with one 9-hole course
Location: I-20 W, exit HWY 126, N., 1 mile
Golf Data: Pro Shop Phone: (915) 928-5514; Club Owner: Michael Vah; Par: 36; Yardage: 3048; Open 7 days.
Green Fees: $5 weekdays, $7 weekends and holidays; Carts: $10 for 18 holes.
Tee Time Procedure: 1st come, 1st served.

————— TERRY ————— 88

Brownfield
BROWNFIELD COUNTRY CLUB
A private club with one 9-hole course

Location: 4 miles W. on HWY 380, then 2 miles S. on old Tahoka HWY
Golf Data: Pro Shop Phone: (806) 637-3656; Club Manager: Jerry Jolly; Par: 72 (two sets of tees); Yardage: 6503; Rating: 70.0; Closed Monday.
Guest Policy: The golf course is open for public play.
Green Fees: $6.25 weekdays, $10.41 weekends-holidays; Carts: $7.50 per person for 18 holes.

——— THROCKMORTON — 89

Throckmorton
THROCKMORTON COUNTRY CLUB
A semi-private club with one 9-hole course
Location: Take Haskell HWY W. to Lake Road, then S.
Golf Data: No Phone (for information, contact Greg Scarlett: (817) 849-3131); Par: 70 (two sets of tees); Yardage: 5365; Open 7 days.
Green Fees: $5 anytime for non-members; No carts available.
Tee Time Procedure: 1st come, 1st served.

——————— TOM GREEN ——— 90

San Angelo
Public Golf Courses

LAKESIDE GOLF COURSE
A public club with one 9-hole course
Location: Knickerbocker Road S., enter Mathis Field (airport)
Golf Data: Pro Shop Phone: (915) 949-2069; Club Pro: John Luna; Par: 36; Yardage: 3120; Open 7 days.
Green Fees: $3 anytime; Carts: $5 per 9 holes.
Tee Time Procedure: 1st come, 1st served.

RIVERSIDE GOLF CLUB
A public club with one 18-hole course
Location: Bryan Thruway N., left at W. 29th Street, take 1st street right
Golf Data: Pro Shop Phone: (915) 653-6130; Club Pro: Dick Barnes; Par: 72; Yardage: 5600; Rating: 70.0; Closed Monday until noon.

Green Fees: $5.50 weekdays, $6.50 weekends and holidays; Carts: $10 for 18 holes.
Tee Time Procedure: 1st come, 1st served.

SANTA FE PARK GOLF COURSE
A public club with one 9-hole course
Location: In Santa Fe Park on River Drive
Golf Data: Pro Shop Phone: (915) 657-4485; Club Pro: Mike Terrazas; Par: 34; Yardage: 2453; Open 7 days.
Green Fees: $4 weekdays, $5 weekends and holidays; No carts available.
Tee Time Procedure: 1st come, 1st served.

Private Golf Courses

BENTWOOD COUNTRY CLUB
A private club with one 18-hole course
Location: Knickerbocker Road S., 1 mile past Loop 306 on left
Golf Data: Pro Shop Phone: (915) 944-8575; Club Pro: Don Willingham; Par: 72; Yardage: 6993; Rating: 73.0; Course Architect: Billy Martindale; Closed Monday.
Guest Policy: You must play with a member or be a member of another private country club. Phone in advance for specifics.

SAN ANGELO COUNTRY CLUB
A private club with one 18-hole course
Location: HWY 87S, take Country Club Road exit, left
Golf Data: Pro Shop Phone: (915) 653-2373; Club Pro: Don Bryant; Par: 71; Yardage: 6687; Rating: 70.6; Closed Monday.
Guest Policy: You must be a guest of a member or a member of another private country club.

—————— UPTON —————— 91

McCamey
McCAMEY COUNTRY CLUB
A private club with one 9-hole course
Location: Take HWY 380 1½ miles, turn right
Golf Data: Pro Shop Phone: (915) 652-9904; Club Pro: Allen Coe; Par: 71

(two sets of tees); Yardage: 6142; Rating: 69.0; Closed Monday.
Guest Policy: Non-residents can play anytime. In-town residents can play twice a month.
Green Fees: $10 anytime; No carts available.
Tee Time Procedure: 1st come, 1st served.

Midkiff
MIDKIFF COUNTRY CLUB
A public club with 6 holes
Location: 4 miles E. on HWY 2401
Golf Data: No Phone; 1 Par 5, 2 Par 4s and 3 Par 3s; Open 7 days.
Green Fees: None.
Tee Time Procedure: 1st come, 1st served.

Rankin
RANKIN COUNTRY CLUB
A semi-private club with one 9-hole course
Location: HWY 67E, left at Truck Route (old motel)
Golf Data: Pro Shop Phone: (915) 693-2834; Club Manager: Ruphina Hopson; Par: 72 (two sets of tees); Yardage: 6347; Open 7 days.
Green Fees: $3 weekdays, $5 weekends and holidays; No carts available.
Tee Time Procedure: 1st come, 1st served.

—————— WARD —————— 92

Monahans
WARD COUNTY GOLF COURSE
A public club with one 9-hole course
Location: 2 miles N. on HWY 18
Golf Data: Pro Shop Phone: (915) 943-5044; Club Pro: Kenneth Wright; Par: 70 (two sets of tees); Yardage: 6093; Rating: 67.3; Open 7 days.
Green Fees: $3 weekdays, $4.50 weekends and holidays for in-county residents; all others pay $5 weekdays and $12.50 weekends and holidays; Carts: $10.40 for 18 holes.
Tee Time Procedure: 1st come, 1st served.

Shamrock

SHAMROCK COUNTRY CLUB
A public club with one 9-hole course
Location: N. on Main Street, right at sign
Golf Data: Pro Shop Phone: (806) 256-5151; Club Pro: Keith Atkins; Par: 72 (two sets of tees); Yardage: 6439; Rating: 67.3; Open 7 days.
Green Fees: $5 weekdays, $7.50 weekends and holidays; Carts: $12.50 for 18 holes.
Tee Time Procedure: 1st come, 1st served.

Burkburnett

RIVER CREEK PARK GOLF COURSE
A public club with one 18-hole course
Location: E. on FM 1177
Golf Data: Pro Shop Phone: (817) 855-3361; Club Pro: Tom Swiney; Par: 72; Yardage: 6700; Rating: 69.7; Open 7 days.
Green Fees: $5 weekdays, $6 weekends and holidays; Carts: $13 for 18 holes; Visa and MC accepted.
Tee Time Procedure: Call anytime.

Wichita Falls

LaVISTA GOLF & COUNTRY CLUB
A private club with one 18-hole course
Location: N.W. on HWY 287, exit Beverly Drive, left
Golf Data: Pro Shop Phone: (817) 855-0771; Club Pro: Jack Malone; Par: 70; Yardage: 6350; Rating: 68.7; Course Architect: Larry Flatt; Open 7 days.
Guest Policy: Guests may play by showing country club membership card, otherwise you must be a guest of a member.

SHEPPARD AIR FORCE BASE GOLF COURSE
A private club with one 18-hole course
Location: At Sheppard Air Force Base
Golf Data: Pro Shop Phone: (817) 851-6369; Club Pro: James W. Frazier; Par: 72; Yardage: 7048; Rating: 71.8; Open 7 days.

Guest Policy: A member of the military must accompany guest.

WEEKS PARK MUNICIPAL GOLF COURSE
A public club with one 18-hole course
Location: S. of Midwestern Pkwy on Lake Park Drive N.
Golf Data: Pro Shop Phone: (817) 767-6107; Club Pro: Larry Harper; Par: 71; Yardage: 6032; Course Architect: Golfscapes, Inc. (redesign); Open 7 days.
Green Fees: $6 weekdays, $8 weekends and holidays; Carts: $14 for 18 holes. Visa & MC accepted.
Tee Time Procedure: Call 7 days in advance.

WICHITA FALLS COUNTRY CLUB
A private club with one 18-hole course
Location: On Hamilton Road S.W. of city
Golf Data: Pro Shop Phone: (817) 767-1486; Club Pro: James H. "Dotta" Watson; Par: 72; Yardage: 6704; Rating: 72.3; Closed Monday.
Guest Policy: You are welcome as a guest as long as you have credentials proving your membership in another private country club located outside the community.

Vernon

HILLCREST COUNTRY CLUB
A private club with one 9-hole course
Location: W. on HWY 287
Golf Data: Pro Shop Phone: (817) 552-5406; Club Pro: Val Howard; Par: 71 (two sets of tees); Yardage: 6490; Rating: 69.0; Course Architect: Don Knaw; Open 7 days.
Guest Policy: You must be a guest of a member or a member of another U.S.G.A. member club.

Kermit

WINKLER COUNTY COUNTRY CLUB
A public club with one 9-hole course
Location: 7 miles W. on HWY 302

Golf Data: Pro Shop Phone: (915) 586-3994; Course Manager: Chris Koulovatous; Par: 72 (two sets of tees); Yardage: 6363; Rating: 69.0; Closed Monday.

Green Fees: County residents: $4 weekdays, $5 weekends and holidays; Non-county residents: $7.50 weekdays, $15 weekends and holidays; Carts: $12 for 18 holes.

Tee Time Procedure: 1st come, 1st served.

Denver City

YOAKUM COUNTY GOLF COURSE
A semi-private club with one 9-hole course

Location: 6 miles N. on HWY 214

Golf Data: Pro Shop Phone: (806) 592-2947; Club Pro: Wiley Osborne; Par: 36; Yardage: 3218; Rating: 69.0 (if 18 holes played); Course Architect: W. D. Cantrell; Open 7 days.

Green Fees: $5 weekdays, $7.50 weekends and holidays; Carts: $6 per 9 holes.

Tee Time Procedure: 1st come, 1st served.

Graham

GRAHAM COUNTRY CLUB
A semi-private club with one 9-hole course

Location: Elm Street N., left at HWY 380 Bypass, right at Fort Belknap, 2½ miles

Golf Data: Pro Shop Phone: (817) 549-7721; Club Pro: Lloyd Moody; Par: 36; Yardage: 3260; Rating: 71.1 (if 18 holes played); Closed Monday.

Green Fees: $10.41 weekdays, $15.62 weekends and holidays; Carts: $13 + tax for 18 holes.

Tee Time Procedure: 1st come, 1st served.

Olney

OLNEY COUNTRY CLUB
A semi-private club with one 9-hole course

Location: HWY 79SE, left at Country Club Road

Golf Data: Pro Shop Phone: (817) 564-2424; Par: 36; Yardage: 3200; Closed Tuesday.

Green Fees: $7.50 weekdays, $10 weekends and holidays; Carts: $6.25 per 9 holes.

Tee Time Procedure: 1st come, 1st served.

12. Who has coached more NCAA championship teams than any coach in any sport?

Stamp Out Slow Play

Five-and-a-half hour rounds of golf with long waits between hitting shots has driven many golfers to seek other sports, particularly during the long, hot Texas summers.

Slow play takes the fun and enjoyment out of the game.

The modern crusade against slow play was sounded over 20 years ago by *Golf Digest* in a cover story, "Slow Play: Crisis in American Golf," October 1965.

Editor-in-Chief William Davis pointed out "perhaps the most important measure for speeding up play would be for golfers to adopt an enlightened set of playing habits and a more responsible attitude toward self-regulation in the true spirit of the rules. Enforcing the spirit of the rules—Rule 37-7 reads: Players shall at all time play without undue delay—is everybody's job."

And, periodically, over the next 20 years, other have raised fears that slow play detracts from the game. In an April 1974 *Golf* Magazine essay, Ross Goodner placed some of the blame on televised golf. "The more golf is shown on television, the slower people play" as they emulate professional golfers' mannerisms.

Larry Box confers with marshall in front of pace awareness checkpoint at Bear Creek in Dallas.

However, the attempts to solve the problem of slow play, at best, have been sporadic and mostly frustrating. Courses are more crowded today and play moves slower than ever.

Recently, a new attempt at education was made by *Golf* Magazine, along with the USGA, PGA Tour, and PGA of America, who've picked up the charge. Tour golfers Lanny Watkins, Fuzzy Zoeller, and Craig Stadler have teamed for a series of posters against slow play called "Fast Friends" and these have been distributed to golf courses nationwide.

Making golfers aware of their slow pace is the first step in speeding up play, according to Larry Box, golf professional at Bear Creek Golf Course near Dallas/Fort Worth Airport.

Bear Creek, one of *Golf Digest* magazine's top 75 public golf courses, averages 320 golfers a day during the busy April-August time period, and the challenge of the two 18 hole golf courses lends itself to slow play with treelined, hilly fairways and tricky, bent grass greens.

From the moment you walk into Bear Creek's clubhouse, Box's staff encourages you to monitor your pace of play during the round with signs, such as

---

**Bear Creek and You
Will Overcome Slow Play
Monitor Your Pace—15 minutes Per Hole
Cooperate With Course Marshall Requests**

**The Group Behind You Appreciates Your
Efforts and Says Thanks for Making
Their Round More Enjoyable**

Scorecards also offer tips to speed up play, such as

S tay up with the group in front of you.
P ace—a hole should take 15 minutes to play.
E lect a player to monitor the group's pace.
E liminate honors—institute continuous play.
D o not waste time between shots.
U ndue delay—play without delays always.
P roceed to your ball and be ready to play.

Once on the course, "Pace Awareness Checkpoint" signs on holes 5 and 10 state, "You should be at this point in 1 hour (2½ hours)." Marshalls circle the course to monitor play.

Course Superintendent John Anderson has marked the cart paths and fairways with yardage discs, color coded for distance to the center of the green (Red: 100 yards; White: 150; Blue: 200; and Yellow: 250). This makes club selection easier. His staff has an on-going program to keep the areas off the fairway clear of trash and leaves, making it easier to find a stray golf shot.

Bear Creek Golf Course is not alone. Indian Creek Golf Course in Carrollton also has an on-going program, particularly on weekends, to speed up play. Golf Professional John Folwell begins golfers on No. 10 tee weekends and holidays (and sometimes on Friday) because there is less trouble on the back 9's first three holes than on the front 9's.

A very difficult course, with doglegs left and right and out-of-bounds on many holes, Indian Creek also has an on-going program to clear areas off the fairway to make it easier to find your ball.

However, no matter what the golf course does itself to help speed up play, it really depends on the individual golfer to keep the fun and enjoyment in the game by maintaining pace throughout the round.

The National Golf Foundation says there are many "little" things golfers can do to keep things moving:

- Try to play at a time when you have the best chance of playing fast, when the course is least crowded.
- Select playing companions who also like to concentrate on playing golf, not talking and eating/drinking.
- Arrange the match and bets in the locker room or pro shop, not after you get to the 1st tee.
- Have a game plan for how you want to play the course.
- Decide what club you want to use before you get to the ball.
- When in doubt about what club you will need, when leaving the golf cart or your bag, take two or three clubs.
- Get up and hit the ball without too much practice swinging.
- Watch the actions of other putts to learn about speed and break on that green.
- Mark a ball hit into trouble by mentally lining up on the spots ahead and behind you.
- Play the ball as it lies at all times; no winter rules.
- Walk briskly between shots.
- Carry a spare ball in case you need to hit a provisional.
- Take no "mulligans" to replay a shot or a putt.
- Know the rules and basic etiquette of the game.

- Mark your scores as you proceed to the next tee not on the green.
- When out of the hole and headed for a triple bogey or worse, pick up.
- Be conscious of the 5 minute rule when looking for a lost ball. Only the player should spend time looking while others hit.
- Repair ball marks and divots while waiting for other players, not while it's your turn.
- Be aware of routing from green to next tee and park cart or place clubs in that direction.
- When driving a golf cart, drop your playing partner off and go on to your ball.
- When you have a clear hole in front of you, wave the following group through and then try to keep up.

13. **The Southern Texas PGA created a Teacher of the Year Award and named it after this long time Austin professional.**

Precaution Necessary During Weather Extremes

Wide temperature variations from the northern part of Texas to the southern part and from the summer months to the winter months require special care on the part of golfers—or anyone who exercises. So says Dr. Bob Ward, conditioning coach of the Dallas Cowboys football team, whose concern gets the Cowboys ready for any type of climate.

"It's best to check the weather reports before playing or practicing to see if it is too hot or too cold," he said. Caution should be taken during the extremes. And he adds, "You can never drink too much water, whether it's hot or cold."

Since temperatures all over the state can reach into the 100s in the summer, heat is a factor in any area. Humidity is also a consideration reducing the loss of body heat. In fact, anytime the temperature is over 90 and the humidity is near 70, frequent breaks and increased liquid consumption are essential.

Light colored loose porous clothing (*not* polyester) promotes evaporation in hot weather, says Ward. Avoid wearing hats unless it is a visor with a brim since heat loss occurs through the head.

Drink plenty of water before, during, and after your round to avoid dehydration. A good sun screen liberally applied helps to prevent skin cancer.

If you begin to feel sick, dizzy, or faint, your pulse rate and breathing become faster or you have headaches or muscle cramps, you may be suffering heat exhaustion. Find a cool place, or if you're not near the clubhouse, wet a towel with cold water from one of the coolers on the course and wipe your face and neck to cool your body temperatures. Drink plenty of water.

Alcohol promotes dehydration and should be avoided while playing. There is also no need for salt tablets or other salt additives. "Replenish your salt through diet," Ward says. He suggests eating more fruits and vegetables during the summer months.

During the winter months, cold is a factor, particularly in the northern half of the state and the Panhandle in particular. Temperatures in the Panhandle can get as low as −10° during the winter and lows range from 0° to 20° in the north central region.

Wind also adds to the problem, lowering the effective temperature. Warm clothing is a must. Wind can lower a 30° temperature to 0° if it blows over 20 miles per hour. The following table is based on the more complicated "wind chill" indexes available from the National Weather Service:

Estimated Wind Speed MPH	Actual Temperature Reading						
	50	40	30	20	10	0	−10
	Equivalent Temperature						
Calm	50	40	30	20	10	0	−10
5	48	37	27	16	6	−5	−15
10	40	28	16	4	−9	−21	−33
15	36	22	9	−5	−18	−36	−45
20	32	18	4	−10	−25	−39	−53
25	30	16	0	−15	−29	−44	−59
30	28	13	−2	−18	−33	−48	−63
35	27	11	−4	−20	−35	−49	−67
40	26	10	−6	−21	−37	−53	−69

The danger zone magnifies itself at 25° below zero.

During prolonged periods of exposure to the cold, more body heat may be lost than can easily be replaced, reducing body temperature. A gradual physical and mental slowing down will take place, which may pass unnoticed. A person becomes increasingly clumsy, irritable, and speech may become slurred. Find shelter from the wind or get inside quickly. Drink warm liquids and cover the exposed parts with additional clothing.

Eat well during the cold months. The body needs more calories. Drink water freely before, during, and after exercise. Let thirst be your guide.

Use two or three layers of clothing rather than one heavy one. Protect the head, fingers, ears, etc.

Whether it's the summer or the winter, it will take you approximately nine days to become accustomed to the heat or cold. Gradually increase your daily exposure to acclimate yourself to the change of weather.

Even, after this acclimation period, care should be taken during the extremes.

14. Who is recognized by the Guinness Book of Records, Ripley's Believe It Or Not and the Professional Golf Association as holding the world record for hole-in-ones?

The Border

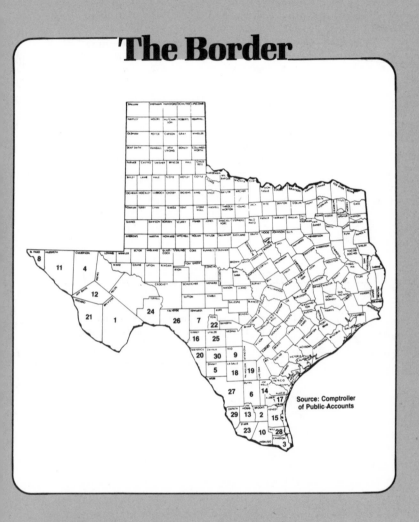

Source: Comptroller
of Public Accounts

There are 48 golf courses along the Border and two more are under construction.

Twenty-one are open for public play, nine are semi-private and 13 are private. One is attached to a military base and four are resorts.

THE BORDER CITIES

15. This Texan was a pioneer in TV Golf and co-hosted the Shell Wonderful World of Golf series.

El Paso Country Club

════ BREWSTER ════ 1

Alpine

ALPINE COUNTRY CLUB
A semi-private club with one 9-hole course
Location: On the Loop Road E. of town
Golf Data: Pro Shop Phone: (915) 837-2752; Club Pro: Robert Pettegrew; Par: 35; Yardage: 3500; Rating: 68.5 (if 18 holes played); Open 7 days.
Green Fees: $5 weekdays, $8 weekends and holidays; Carts: $6 per 9 holes.
Tee Time Procedure: 1st come, 1st served.

Lajitas

LAJITAS GOLF CLUB
A public club with one 9-hole course
Location: Near Big Bend National Park & Terlingua
Golf Data: Pro Shop Phone: (915) 424-3471; Club Pro: Terry Thomas; Par: 36; Yardage: 3300; Rating: 69.8 (when 18 holes played); Open 7 days.
Green Fees: $7 weekdays, $9 weekends and holidays; Carts: $5 per 9 holes.
Tee Time Procedure: 1st come, 1st served.

════ BROOKS ════ 2

Falfurrias

FALFURRIAS MUNICIPAL GOLF COURSE
A public club with one 9-hole course
Location: HWY 282N, E. on Travis Road
Golf Data: Pro Shop Phone: (512) 325-5348; Club Manager: Mike Salinas; Par: 71 (two sets of tees); Yardage: 6288; Course Architect: Bond Cosby; Open 7 days.
Green Fees: $3.50 weekdays, $4.50 weekends-holidays; Carts: $5 per 9 holes.

════ CAMERON ════ 3

Brownsville

BROWNSVILLE COUNTRY CLUB
A semi-private club with one 18-hole course
Location: 1800 W. San Marcelo Blvd., just off FM 802 (see #1 on Valley locator map)
Golf Data: Pro Shop Phone: (512) 541-2582; Club Pro: Jesse Lucio; Par: 70; Yardage: 5718; Rating: 68.0; Open 7 days.

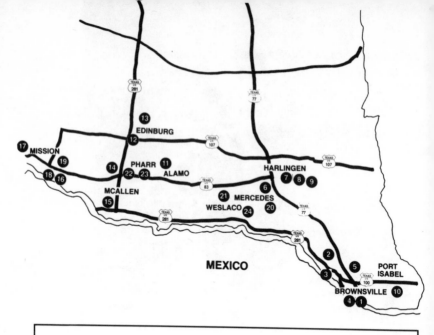

THE VALLEY

BROWNSVILLE
1. Brownsville C. C.
2. Rancho Viejo C. C.
3. River Bend Resort & C. C.
4. Riverview G. C.
5. Valley Inn & C. C.

HARLINGEN
6. Cottonwood C. C.
7. Tony Butler G. C.
8. Harlingen C. C.
9. Treasure Hills C. C.

PORT ISABEL
10. Outdoor Resorts G. C.

ALAMO
11. Alamo C. C.
12. Edinburg G. C.
13. Monte Christo C. C.

McALLEN
14. McAllen C. C.
15. Palm View G. C.

MISSION
16. Cimmaron C. C.
17. Martins C. C. Ranch
18. Meadow Creek C. C.
19. Shary Municipal G. C.

MERCEDES
20. Indian Hills C. C.
21. Llano Grande G. C.

PHARR
22. Plantation C. C.
23. Valley Golf Center

WESLACO
24. Village Executive G. C.

Green Fees: $6 anytime; Carts: $12 + tax for 18 holes; Visa and MC accepted.
Tee Time Procedure: Call 1 day in advance.

RANCHO VIEJO COUNTRY CLUB
A resort club with two 18-hole courses
Location: 12 miles N. on HWY 77 and 83 (see #2 on Valley locator map)
Golf Data: Pro Shop Phone: (512) 350-4000; Acting Club Pro: Art Guerra; *Angel* 18 Par: 70; Yardage: 6647; Rating: 72.0; *Diablo* 18 Par: 70; Yardage: 6899; Rating: 72.0; Course Architect: Dennis Arp (both 18s); Open 7 days.

Guest Policy: You must be a guest of a member, stay at the resort or be a member of another private country club.
NOTE: For information about the resort and its golf packages, phone 1-800-292-7263 (in Texas) or 1-800-531-7400 (out of State) or you can write to Rancho Viejo Resort & Country Club, P.O. Box 3918, Brownsville, TX 78520.
Green Fees: Guest of Resort: $20 anytime; Non-guest: $25; Carts: $18 for 18 holes.

Tee Time Procedure: Guest of Resort may make arrangements at time reservations accepted; Non-guests may call five days in advance.

RIVER BEND RESORT & COUNTRY CLUB

A semi-private club with one 9-hole course

Location: Take HWY 820W, right at Old Military PKWY (see #3 on Valley locator map)

Golf Data: Pro Shop Phone: (512) 548-0194; Club Pro: Manny Saldivar; Par: 36; Yardage: 3077; Open 7 days.

NOTE: For resort information, call (512) 548-0194, or write to River Bend Resort & C. C., Rte. 2, Box 649, Brownsville, TX 78520. RV accommodations also available.

Green Fees: Winter Rates: $4 weekdays, $6 weekends and holidays; Carts: $15 for 18 holes; Summer Rates (daylight savings time): $3 weekdays, $5.50 weekends and holidays; Carts: $10 for 18 holes.

Tee Time Procedure: Winter: Call 1 day in advance; Summer: 1st come, 1st served.

RIVERVIEW GOLF COURSE

A public club with one 18-hole course

Location: At EXPY end, turn right at International Bridge, left at Elizabeth Street (see #4 on Valley locator map)

Golf Data: Pro Shop Phone: (512) 542-9861; Club Pro: Joe Garcia; Par: 71; Yardage: 6020; Rating: 69.0; Open 7 days.

Green Fees: $5 anytime; Carts: $12 + tax for 18 holes. (Please note: Summer rates (daylight savings time): $4 anytime; Carts: $8 for 18 holes.)

Tee Time Procedure: Winter: Call 1 day in advance; Summer: 1st come, 1st served.

VALLEY INN & COUNTRY CLUB

A semi-private club with 27 holes

Location: N. on FM 802 (see #5 on locator map)

Golf Data: Pro Shop Phone: (512) 546-5331; Club Pro: Lyle McNeil; 18 Par: 70; Yardage: 6538; Rating: 70.0; Par 3 9 Par: 27; Yardage: 1052; Closed Monday during summer.

Green Fees: $10 weekdays, $15 weekends and holidays for 18; $4 weekdays, $5 weekends and holidays for Par 3; Carts: $14 for 18 holes; AX, Visa and MC accepted.

Tee Time Procedure: Call 1 week in advance.

Harlingen

Public Golf Courses

COTTONWOOD CREEK COUNTRY CLUB

A public club with one 9-hole Par 3 course

Location: Take HWY 83S, exit at Ed Carey Drive, turn S. (see #6 on Valley locator map)

Golf Data: Pro Shop Phone: (512) 428-7774; Club Manager: Lin Williams; Par: 54 (two sets of tees); Yardage: 2365; Open 7 days.

Green Fees: $2.50 for 9 holes; $4 for 18; No carts available.

Tee Time Procedure: 1st come, 1st served.

TONY BUTLER MUNICIPAL GOLF COURSE

A public club with 27 holes

Location: S. on HWY 83 (see #7 on Valley locator map)

Golf Data: Pro Shop Phone: (512) 423-9913; Club Pro: Rene Garza; 18 Par: 70; Yardage: 6209; Rating: 69.6; 9 Par: 35; Yardage: 2881; Rating: 29.6; Open 7 days.

Green Fees: $4.20 for 9 holes, $5.25 for 18 anytime; Carts: $12 for 18 holes.

Tee Time Procedure: Winter: Call 1 day in advance; Summer (daylight savings time): 1st come, 1st served.

Private Golf Courses

HARLINGEN COUNTRY CLUB

A private club with one 18-hole course

Location: On Stewart Place Road (see #8 on Valley locator map)

Golf Data: Pro Shop Phone: (512) 423-6046; Club Pro: Buddy Kalencki; Par: 72; Yardage: 6503; Rating: 69.4; Course Architect: Leon Howard; Open 7 days.

Guest Policy: Restricted to clubs who reciprocate with H.C.C. Restricted play from November to May. Phone pro first for starting times and availability of course.

TREASURE HILLS COUNTRY CLUB

A private club with one 18-hole course

Location: E. on Harrison Blvd. (see #9 on Valley locator map)

NOTE: 18-hole course designed by Richard Watson to open in Fall 1987.

Port Isabel

OUTDOOR RESORTS SOUTH PADRE ISLAND GOLF COURSE
A public club with one 18-hole Par 3 course
Location: HWY 100E, right at Garcia Street before Causeway (see #10 on Valley locator map)
Golf Data: Resort Phone: (512) 943-5921; Par: 54; Yardage: 1405; Open 7 days.
Green Fees: $4 anytime; No carts available.

CULBERSON 4

Van Horn

VAN HORN GOLF COURSE
A public club with one 9-hole course
Location: Old Hwy 80W, left (S.) at blinking light
Golf Data: Pro Shop Phone: (915) 283-2628; Club Manager: Refugio Corrales; Par: 37; Yardage: 3129; Closed Monday.
Green Fees: $4 weekdays, $5 weekends and holidays; Carts: $2.50 per 9 holes.
Tee Time Procedure: 1st come, 1st served.

DIMMITT 5

Carrizo Springs

CARRIZO SPRINGS MUNICIPAL GOLF COURSE
A public club with one 9-hole course
Location: N. of HWY 85 at Airport
Golf Data: Pro Shop Phone: (512) 876-2596; Club Pro: C. V. Speer, Jr.; Par: 72 (two sets of tees); Yardage: 7280; Rating: 70.6; Open 7 days.
Green Fees: $6 weekdays, $8 weekends and holidays; Carts: $6 per 9 holes.
Tee Time Procedure: 1st come, 1st served.

DUVAL 6

None

EDWARDS 7

Rocksprings

ROCKSPRINGS COUNTRY CLUB
A private club with one 9-hole course
Location: S. of HWY 55 at Joe Ball Ranch
Golf Data: Pro Shop Phone: (512) 683-4224; Club Manager: Joe Ball; Par: 36; Yardage: 2900; Open 7 days.
Guest Policy: You must play with a member.

EL PASO 8

El Paso

Public Golf Courses

ASCARATE GOLF COURSE
A public club with 27 holes
Location: From I-10, take Throwbridge exit S., right at Delta (see #1 on locator map)
Golf Data: Pro Shop Phone: (915) 772-7381; Club Pro: Steve Schoch; 18 Par: 71; Yardage: 6622; Rating: 70.0; 9 Par: 36; Yardage: 2677; Course Architects: Monroe, Light & Higgins, Inc.; Closed Monday.
Green Fees: $5.50 weekdays, $7 weekends and holidays for 18 holes; Short 9: $4 anytime; Carts: $11.55 for 18 holes, $6.31 for 9.
Tee Time Procedure: Call 3 days in advance.

CIELO VISTA MUNICIPAL GOLF COURSE
A public club with one 18-hole course
Location: 1510 Hawkins (see #2 on locator map)
Golf Data: Pro Shop Phone: (915) 591-4927; Club Pro: Mark Pelletier; Par: 72; Yardage: 6400; Rating: 68.0; Open 7 days.
Green Fees: $7 weekdays, $9 weekends and holidays; Carts: $13 for 18 holes.
Tee Time Procedure: Weekends-Holidays: Call after 7 a.m. Tuesday; Weekdays: 1st come, 1st served.

Private Golf Courses

CORONADO COUNTRY CLUB
A private club with one 18-hole course
Location: 1044 Broadmoor (see #3 on locator map)

Golf Data: Pro Shop Phone: (915) 584-1171; Club Pro: Danny Swain; Par: 70; Yardage: 6495; Rating: 70.6; Course Architect: Marvin Ferguson; Closed Monday.

Guest Policy: You must be a guest of a member or a member of another private country club.

EL PASO COUNTRY CLUB
A private club with one 18-hole course
Location: I-10, exit Mesa Road, S. to 400 Camino Real (see #4 on locator map)
Golf Data: Pro Shop Phone: (915) 584-0511; Club Pro: Bill Eschenbrenner; Par: 71; Yardage: 6793; Rating: 72.0; Course Architect: Ronald Freem (revision '84); Closed Monday.

Guest Policy: You must be a guest of a member or be a member of another private country club.

VISTA HILLS COUNTRY CLUB
A private club with one 18-hole course
Location: I-10, exit Lee Trevino, left 1 + miles, left at Trawood (see #5 on locator map)
Golf Data: Pro Shop Phone: (915) 592-6565; Club Pro: Terry Jennings; Par: 72; Yardage: 7186; Rating: 73.0; Course Architects: Bruce Devlin & Bob Von Hagge; Closed Monday.

Guest Policy: You must be a guest of a member or a member of another private country club.

Military Golf Courses

GEORGE V. UNDERWOOD GOLF COURSE
A private club with one 18-hole course
Location: N. of Fort Bliss at 3200 Coe Avenue (see #6 on locator map)
Golf Data: Pro Shop Phone: (915) 562-1273; Club Pro: Bobby Kaerwer; Par: 72; Yardage: 6406; Rating: 70.0; Course Architect: Val Despino; Closed Monday.

Guest Policy: You must play with a member, or out-of-town residents may play with a drivers license.

Green Fees: Civilian: $8 weekdays, $10 weekends and holidays; Carts: $10 for 18 holes ($5.50 for single rider).

Tee Time Procedure: Call anytime.

Horizon City
HORIZON RESORT & COUNTRY CLUB
A resort club with one 18-hole course
Location: 16000 Ashford (see #7 on locator map)
Golf Data: Pro Shop Phone: (915) 852-3150; Club Pro: Bill Peterson; Par: 71; Yardage: 6955; Rating: 71.5; Course Architect: Jack Hardin; Closed Monday.

Guest Policy: You must be a guest of a member or a member of another private country club. Guests of the resort may also play. Phone for specifics.

NOTE: *For resort and golf information, phone (915) 852-9141, or write to Horizon Resort, 16000 Ashford, Horizon City, TX 79927.*

Green Fees: $10.50 weekdays, $13 weekends and holidays; Carts: $6.25 per person.

Tee Time Procedure: Call 4 days in advance.

————— FRIO ————— 9

None

————— HILDAGO ————— 10
Alamo
ALAMO COUNTRY CLUB
A private club with one 9-hole course
Location: On Tower Road, 1 mile N. of HWY 83 (see #11 on Valley locator map)
Golf Data: Pro Shop Phone: (512) 787-5082; Club Pro: Gary Taylor; Par: 35; Yardage: 3535; Course Architect: Lonny Sumers; Closed Monday.

Guest Policy: You must be a guest of a member.

Edinburg
EDINBURG MUNICIPAL GOLF COURSE
A public club with one 9-hole course
Location: 300 W. Palm (see #12 on Valley locator map)
Golf Data: Pro Shop Phone: (512) 381-1244; Club Pro: Walter Shirah; Par: 35; Yardage: 3124; Rating: 68.5 (if 18 holes played); Open 7 days.

Green Fees: $3.68 anytime; Carts: $5.78 per 9 holes.

Tee Time Procedure: 1st come, 1st served.

MONTE CRISTO COUNTRY CLUB
A private club with one 18-hole course
Location: HWY 281N to Monte Cristo Road, then E. 2½ miles (see #13 on Valley locator map)
Golf Data: Pro Shop Phone: (512) 381-6621; Club Pro: John Aquillon, Jr.,; Par: 71; Yardage: 6204; Rating: 68.0; Open 7 days.
NOTE: For resort or golf course information, write to Monte Cristo Resort, Rt. 5, Box 985-D, Edinburg, TX. 78539 or phone (512) 381-6611.
Green Fees: $3.50 for 9, $5.50 for 18 holes; Carts: $6 for 9; $10 for 18 holes; AX, Visa & MC accepted.

McAllen

McALLEN COUNTRY CLUB
A private club with one 18-hole course
Location: Across from International Airport at 615 Wichita Road (see #14 on Valley locator map)
Golf Data: Pro Shop Phone: (512) 686-0923; Club Pro: Zack Padgett; Par: 71; Yardage: 6329; Rating: 68.4; Open noon Monday.
Guest Policy: You must be a guest of a member or a member of another private country club.

PALM VIEW GOLF COURSE
A public club with 27 holes
Location: 1+ mile S. of HWY 83 on S. Ware Road (see #15 on Valley locator map)
Golf Data: Pro Shop Phone: (512) 687-9591; Club Pro: Mimo Hernadez; *East* Par: 35; Yardage: 3008; *West* Par: 36; Yardage: 3288; *South* Par: 36; Yardage: 3285; Ratings: E&W: 68.0; E&S: 67.8; W&S: 69.1; Course Architects: Ralph Plummer (East & West), Michael Ingram (South); Open 7 days.
Green Fees: $4.20 for 9 holes, $5.25 for 18 anytime, additional 9s at $2; Carts: $6.35 for 9 holes, $12.55 for 18.
Tee Time Procedure: Winter: 1 day in advance; Summer (daylight savings time): 1st come, 1st served.

Mission

CIMARRON COUNTRY CLUB
A private club with one 18-hole course
Location: S. of HWY 83 at HWY 494 & Sharyland Road (see #16 on Valley locator map)
Golf Data: Pro Shop Phone: (512) 581-7408; Club Pro: Robert Singletary; Par: 72; Yardage: 6600; Rating: 72.4; Course Architect: Dave Bennett; Open Monday during winter months.
Guest Policy: You must be a guest of a member or a member of another private country club.

MARTINS COUNTRY CLUB RANCH
A public club with one 9-hole course
Location: 4½ miles W. on HWY 83 (see #17 on Valley locator map)
Golf Data: Pro Shop Phone: (512) 585-6330; Club Manager: Charlie Carter; Par: 35; Yardage: 3350; Course Architect: Charlie Carter; Closed Monday.
Green Fees: $5.25 for 18 holes anytime ($4 for 9); Carts: $6.25 per 9 holes.
Tee Time Procedure: Winter: Call 2 days in advance; Summer (daylight savings time): 1st come, 1st served.

MEADOW CREEK COUNTRY CLUB
A semi-private club with one 18-hole course
Location: 1 mile S. on Inspiration Road (see #18 on Valley locator map)
Golf Data: Pro Shop Phone: (512) 581-6267; Club Pro: Joan Gearhart; Par: 72; Yardage: 6900; Course Architect: Mike Ingram; Open 7 days.
Green Fees: $10 anytime; Carts: $7 per 9 holes (estimated). Visa & MC accepted.
Tee Time Procedure: 1st come, 1st served.

SHARY MUNICIPAL GOLF COURSE
A public club with one 18-hole course
Location: Off FM 495 at 2201 Mayberry (see #19 on Valley locator map)
Golf Data: Pro Shop Phone: (512) 581-6224; Club Pro: Chencho Ramirez; Par: 71; Yardage: 5740; Rating: 68.0; Open 7 days.
Green Fees: $5.25 for 18 anytime; Carts: $6.31 for 9 holes.
Tee Time Procedure: Winter: Call 1 day in advance; Summer (March-October): 1st come, 1st served.

Mercedes

INDIAN HILLS COUNTRY CLUB
A public club with one 18-hole course
Location: 3 miles on FM 491 (see #20 on Valley locator map)
NOTE: 18 holes designed by Lonny Summers is scheduled to open up in 1987.

LLANO GRANDE GOLF COURSE
A semi-private club with one 9-hole course
Location: 1+ mile S. of HWY 83 on Mile Two-W Road (see #21 on Valley locator map)
Golf Data: Pro Shop Phone: (512) 565-3351; Owner: Ted Freitag; Par: 36; Yardage: 3150; Rating: 69.3 (if 18 holes played); Closed Monday during summer.
Green Fees: $4.75 for 9, $7 for 18 holes anytime; Carts: $6 per 9 holes.
Tee Time Procedure: 1st come, 1st served.

Pharr

PLANTATION COUNTRY CLUB
A private club with one 18-hole course
Location: S. on HWY 281 at 2503 Palmer Drive (see #22 on Valley locator map)
Golf Data: Pro Shop Phone: (512) 781-6613; Club Pro: DeArmon Warden; Par: 72; Yardage: 6727; Rating: 71.48; Course Architect: Dave Bennett; Open 7 days.
Guest Policy: You must play with a member, though out-of-town guests may play once a month without member present. Club does reciprocate with other country clubs. Call for details.

VALLEY GOLF CENTER
A public club with one 9-hole Par 3 course
Location: On Ferguson Street (see #23 on Valley locator map)
Golf Data: Pro Shop Phone: (512) 787-9272; Club Manager: Bill Hayter; Par: 27; Yardage: 1075; Open 7 days.
Green Fees: $2.65 for 9 holes, $3.95 for 18 anytime; No carts available.
Tee Time Procedure: 1st come, 1st served.

Weslaco

VILLAGE EXECUTIVE GOLF COURSE
A public club with one 9-hole course (see #24 on Valley locator map)
Location: 2 miles S. on Bus. 83 (see #24 on Valley locator map)
Golf Data: Pro Shop Phone: (512) 969-3445; Club Manager: Robert Perez; Par: 31; Yardage: 1563; Open 7 days.
Green Fees: $3.75 for 9 holes, $5.50 for 18 anytime; No carts available.
Tee Time Procedure: 1st come, 1st served.

════ HUDSPETH ════ 11

None

════ JEFF DAVIS ════ 12

None

════ JIM HOGG ════ 13

None

════ JIM WELLS ════ 14

Alice

ALICE COUNTRY CLUB
A private club with one 9-hole course
Location: HWY 44 at Country Club Road
Golf Data: Pro Shop Phone: (512) 664-5702; Club Pro: Joe Demaret; Par: 72 (two sets of tees); Yardage: 6400; Rating: 70.2; Closed Monday.
Guest Policy: You must be a guest of a member or a member of another private country club.

ALICE MUNICIPAL GOLF COURSE
A public club with one 18-hole course
Location: Behind Anderson Park on N. Texas Blvd.
Golf Data: Pro Shop Phone: (512) 664-7033; Club Pro: Ricky Monsevais; Par: 70; Yardage: 5911; Rating: 69.3; Open 7 days.

Green Fees: $4 weekdays, $4.50 weekends and holidays; Carts: $5.25 per 9 holes; Visa and MC accepted.

Tee Time Procedure: Weekends: Call Wednesday after 7 a.m.; Weekdays: 1st come, 1st served.

KENEDY 15

None

KINNEY 16

Brackettville

FORT CLARK SPRINGS GOLF & COUNTRY CLUB
A semi-private club with one 18-hole course

Location: At Fort Clark Springs

Golf Data: Pro Shop Phone: (512) 563-9204; Club Pro: Bill Humrichouse; Par: 70; Yardage: 6124; Rating: 67.0; Closed Monday.

Green Fees: $8 weekdays, $10 weekends and holidays; Carts: $14 + tax for 18 holes.

Tee Time Procedure: 1st come, 1st served.

KLEBERG 17

Kingsville

BLUE LAKES NAVAL AIR STATION
A private club with one 9-hole course

Location: Off HWY 77 on FM 425

Golf Data: Pro Shop Phone: (512) 595-6167; Club Manager: Dewey E. Stewart; Par: 72 (two sets of tees); Yardage: 6477; Rating: 71.5; Open 7 days.

Guest Policy: You must be a member of the military or a guest of the military.

L. E. RAMEY GOLF CLUB
A public club with one 18-hole course

Location: 818 Elizabeth Street

Golf Data: Pro Shop Phone: (512) 592-1101; Club Pro: Carey Swanson; Par: 72; Yardage: 6955; Rating: 71.0; Open 7 days.

Green Fees: $5.50 weekdays, $6 weekends and holidays; Carts: $12 for 18 holes.

Tee Time Procedure: Call 1 week in advance.

LaSALLE 18

None

McMULLEN 19

None

MAVERICK 20

Eagle Pass

EAGLE PASS GOLF CLUB
A semi-private club with one 9-hole course

Location: In Fort Duncan Park

Golf Data: Pro Shop Phone: (512) 773-9761; Club Manager: Charles Ritchie; Par: 72 (two sets of tees); Yardage: 6425; Open 7 days.

Green Fees: $7 weekdays, $10 weekends and holidays; Carts: $10 for 18 holes.

Tee Time Procedure: 1st come, 1st served.

PRESIDIO 21

Marfa

MARFA MUNICIPAL GOLF COURSE
A public club with one 9-hole course

Location: FM 1112N, right at sign, then 3 miles

Golf Data: Pro Shop Phone: (915) 729-4043; Club Pro: Ernest Villarreal; Par: 72 (two sets of tees); Yardage: 6550; Rating: 69.8; Closed Monday.

Green Fees: $4 weekdays, $6 weekends and holidays; Carts: $6 per 9 holes.

Tee Time Procedure: 1st come, 1st served.

REAL 22

None

STARR 23

Rio Grande City

FORT RINGGOLD GOLF COURSE
A semi-private club with one 9-hole course

Location: Next to Best Western on HWY 83E
Golf Data: Pro Shop Phone: (512) 487-7904; Club Manager: Roel Villareal; Par: 35; Yardage: 2866; Course Architect: John Aquillon, Sr.; Open 7 days.
Green Fees: $5 weekdays and $5.50 weekends and holidays for 9 holes; $7.25 weekdays and $8.25 weekends and holidays for 18 holes; Carts: $14.50 for 18 holes ($7.25 for single rider); Visa and MC accepted.
Tee Time Procedure: 1st come, 1st served.

———— TERRELL ———— 24

None

———— UVALDE ———— 25

Uvalde
MEMORIAL PARK GOLF COURSE
A public club with one 9-hole course
Location: E. on Main, turn at Civic Center
Golf Data: Pro Shop Phone: (512) 278-6155; Club Pro: John Stone; Par: 71 (two sets of tees); Yardage: 6010; Rating: 67.5; Closed Monday.
Green Fees: $5 weekdays, $6 weekends and holidays; Carts: $6 per 9 holes.
Tee Time Procedure: 1st come, 1st served.

———— VAL VERDE ———— 26

Del Rio
SAN SELIPE COUNTRY CLUB
A semi-private club with one 9-hole course
Location: E. on HWY 90
Golf Data: Pro Shop Phone: (512) 775-3953; Club Pro: Phil Branch; Par: 71 (two sets of tees); Yardage: 6031; Rating: 68.5; Closed Monday.
Green Fees: $10 weekdays, $15 weekends and holidays; Carts: $12.65 for 18 holes.
Tee Time Procedure: 1st come, 1st served.
NOTE: The noon hour is reserved for members.

———— WEBB ———— 27

Laredo
CASA BLANCA GOLF COURSE
A public club with one 18-hole course
Location: HWY 59E to Casa Blanca Lake Road
Golf Data: Pro Shop Phone: (512) 727-9218; Club Pro: Carlos Guerra; Par: 72; Yardage: 6661; Closed Monday.
Green Fees: $6 weekdays, $8 weekends and holidays; Carts: $10 for 18 holes, Visa, MC accepted.
Tee Time Procedure: 1st come, 1st served.

LAREDO COUNTRY CLUB
A private club with one 18-hole course
Location: Exit HWY 35 at Delmar to Plantation subdivision, on McPherson Road
Golf Data: Pro Shop Phone: (512) 727-2900; Club Pro: Hal Winston; Par: 72; Yardage: 7125; Rating: 73.2; Course Architect: Joe Finger; Closed Monday.
Guest Policy: Reciprocate with list of private country clubs. Phone pro for specifics to see if you qualify.

———— WILLACY ———— 28

Raymondville
RAYMONDVILLE MUNICIPAL GOLF COURSE
A public club with one 9-hole course
Location: S. on Bus. 77 (142 S. 7th)
Golf Data: Pro Shop Phone: (512) 689-3314; Club Manager: Benny Serna; Par: 36; Yardage: 3310; Open 7 days.
Green Fees: $3 weekdays, $5 weekends and holidays for 18 holes; No carts available.
Tee Time Procedure: 1st come, 1st served.

———— ZAPATA ———— 29

None

———— ZAVALA ———— 30

None

Water Source Is Key to Golf Course Design

Water—the lack of or abundance of it—is the most crucial element in designing golf courses in Texas and is the common problem that ties together the diverse regions of the state.

So says Rick Robbins, chief of design and management for von Hagge and Devlin, Inc., a Houston-based golf course architectural firm which has designed courses in all sections of Texas and understands the problems each represents.

(NOTE: Of the 11 courses which have been designed by Hagge and Devlin, Inc. and are now open, five have been ranked in the top 10 in the Lone Star State, according to the Dallas Morning News. They are Sonterra C. C. near San Antonio, The Woodlands East TPC near in Houston, Gleneagles C. C. in Dallas, Crown Colony near Lufkin, and Walden at Lake Conroe.)

"The State of Texas is one of the most diverse regions of the country in natural land form. It has everything from seacoast to desert to mountains to eastern thicket forest.

"With that diversity the golf courses in a state like Texas will be quite different. The methods of dealing with their construction—why you build, where you build, and how you maintain and operate—will vary from region to region."

And the availability of water, along with natural conditions, dictates the form and substance, including the types of grass which can be grown for each golf course.

One of the first questions that must be answered before designing a course, according to Robbins, is "How are you going to get enough water for growing purposes on the golf course and continue to maintain it over a long period of time?"

For example in west Texas there are major water rights questions— who owns the water?—since most of the water has been allocated for years and years.

When designing a golf course in this region, you need to find the place where water has been allocated but is not being used so that you can buy the allotment for the golf course. The problem is further complicated during periods of drought because golf courses have low priority and are the first to be affected by cutback on supply.

New techniques in golf course irrigation to make better use of water as well as the use of effluent (or treated sewage) water help minimize the problem. Drought resistant grasses for fairways and greens are also used.

Along the seacoast, salt in the air and water creates a problem for golf course construction and maintenance. Unless there is good drainage, salt content can affect the growth of grasses.

At North Shore C. C. near Corpus Christi, Robbins said, the soil had a heavy clay content and didn't drain or perculate well. "We had to use a grass called Adolaide (also known as X-caliber) which was developed in South Africa and tested in Australia. It has proven to be quite tolerant to salt and is a good fairway grass.

"We can control the green's environment by creating good drainage which allows for washing or leeching salt from the greens. However, we can't afford to change the environment on 150–200 acres of golf course."

Lakes were created of water received from upsteam and used for irrigation purposes.

In the Houston area, where annual rainfall measures 56–60 inches and heavy rains are a norm, golf courses must be built with good drainage so that they will be open for play the maximum amount of time.

At Falcon Point near Katy, a residential golf course development, owners required the architects to store the equivalent of a 100-year flood within the 300 acre development. Thus, lakes were created taking into consideration which areas were not to flood at all, which can flood less frequently, and which areas can handle a flood while keeping the golf course open as much as possible.

The land itself was relatively flat and swales were created to direct the water into the holding lakes. Freeboards—the distance between the normal water level of the lake and the top of the lake adjacent to the fairway—were kept at 4½–5 feet instead of the normal 2½–3 feet to allow for the retention of heavy rainfall.

Of all the areas of the state, east Texas most resembles the rest of the south from North Carolina to Florida west with its rolling countryside, pine and oak forests, small intermittent streams and rivers, and silky soil and is most condusive to building a golf course.

Adequate rainfall keeps this area lush and green year round. However, the tall trees, high humidity, and lack of air circulation require use of bermuda grasses, rather than bent, to maintain the golf course.

Other problems designing Texas golf courses include the weather, topography of the land, types of soil, and amount of rock outcropping at the site.

In west Texas and on the high desert at El Paso, there are wide variations in temperature from season to season and, sometimes, from day-to-night. Choice of grasses used for the course must be able to withstand this variance and, generally, grasses designed for use in the mid section of the U.S. work well.

Rock outcroppings and lack of top soil are problems. At Possum Kingdom Lake, 75 miles west of Fort Worth, dynamite has been used to create trenches to lay irrigation piping and top soil has been trucked from other locations to create a foundation to grow grass.

At Sonterra just north of San Antonio, according to Robbins, the owner, Tom Turner, bought a ranch 17 miles south of town and transported between 450–500,000 cubic yards of topsoil to the site in order to create the quality course he wanted.

16. Ben Hogan came closer than any other golfer to winning golf's Grand Slam of major championships in 1953. He didn't play in the British Open. Why not?

East Texas

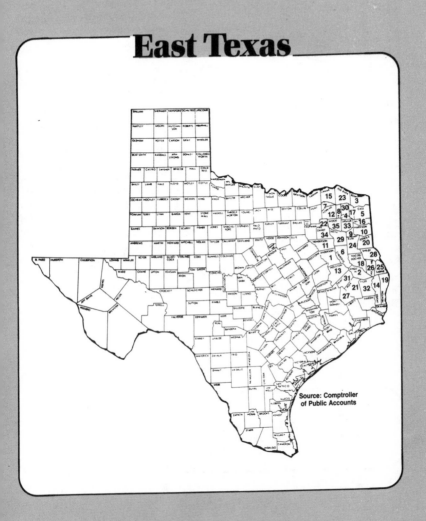

Source: Comptroller of Public Accounts

Fifty-nine courses, many through the piney woods of East Texas, include nine public facilities, 10 semi-private clubs and 34 private courses.

The area also has six golfing resorts.

Two courses are under construction and over five are in the planning stages.

EAST TEXAS CITIES

17. Lee Trevino, the "Merry Mex," has had a bad back since this event in the 1970s.

Approach shot to #13 at Waterwood near Lake Livingston.

ANDERSON 1

Frankston

PINE HILL LAKE & GOLF
A semi-private club with one 9-hole course
Location: 6 miles S. on HWY 155
Golf Data: Pro Shop Phone: (214) 876-2911; Club Manager: Miller Dial; Par: 36; Yardage: 3329; Course Architect: Bruce Littrell; Open 7 days.
Green Fees: $6.25 weekdays, $8.33 weekends and holidays; Carts: $12 for 18 holes.
Tee Time Procedure: 1st come, 1st served.

Palestine

MEADOWBROOK COUNTRY CLUB
A private club with one 9-hole course
Location: Off Link Street Road on Country Club Road
Golf Data: Pro Shop Phone: (214) 729-5954; Club Pro: Dale Smauder; Par: 36; Yardage: 3152; Closed Monday.
Guest Policy: You are welcome as a guest as long as you have credentials proving your membership in another private country club outside the community.

Allow non-county residents to pay green fee and play.
Green Fees: $8 weekdays; $15 weekends & holidays; Carts: $7 for 18 holes.

ANGELINA 2

Diboll

DIBOLL MUNICIPAL GOLF COURSE
A public club with one 9-hole course
Location: 401 Arrington Road
Golf Data: Pro Shop Phone: (409) 829-5086; Club Manager: Dewey Wolf; Par: 36; Yardage: 3356; Rating: 72.9 (if 18 holes played); Course Architect: Leon Howard; Closed Monday.
Green Fees: $8 weekdays, $9 weekends and holidays; Carts: $6.31 per 9 holes. AX, Visa and MC accepted.
Tee Time Procedure: Call anytime.

Lufkin

CROWN COLONY COUNTRY CLUB
A private club with one 18-hole course
Location: S. of Loop 287 on HWY 59
Golf Data: Pro Shop Phone: (409) 634-4927; Club Pro: Danny Silianoff; Par:

72; Yardage: 6842; Rating: 74.5; Course Architects: Bruce Devlin & Bob Von Hagge; Closed Monday.

Guest Policy: You must be a guest of a member or a member of another private country club.

LUFKIN COUNTRY CLUB
A private club with one 18-hole course
Location: Loop 287 at Sayers Road
Golf Data: Pro Shop Phone: (409) 639-3664; Club Manager: Dale Moore; Par: 72; Yardage: 6324; Rating: 69.65; Closed Tuesday.

Guest Policy: You must be a member of another private country club or a guest of a member.

BOWIE 3
Texarkana
NORTH RIDGE COUNTRY CLUB
A private club with one 18-hole course
Location: At 120 Bill Rogers Drive
Golf Data: Pro Shop Phone: (214) 792-9331; Club Pro: Joe Oldham; Par: 71; Yardage: 6503; Rating: 70.46; Closed Monday.

Guest Policy: You must be a member of another private country club or a guest of a member.

also, Texarkana, AR

SOUTH HAVEN GOLF CLUB
A public club with one 9-hole course
Location: Corner of Miller Avenue and Line Ferry Road
Golf Data: Pro Shop Phone: (501) 774-5771; Club Pro: Myron S. Miers; Par: 35; Yardage: 2690; Rating: 67.0 (if 18 holes played); Course Architect: John Reikmar; Open 7 days.

Green Fees: $5.20 weekdays, $7.30 weekends and holidays; Carts: $6.30 for 9 holes, $12.50 for 18.

Tee Time Procedure: 1st come, 1st served.

CAMP 4
Pittsburg
PRINCEDALE COUNTRY CLUB
A private club with one 18-hole course
Location: Off Daingerfield HWY

Golf Data: Pro Shop Phone: (214) 856-3737; Club Manager: Darcie Baggett; Par: 71; Yardage: 5451; Rating: 66.1; Open 7 days.

Guest Policy: You must be a guest of a member or a member of another private country club.

CASS 5
Atlanta
INDIAN HILLS COUNTRY CLUB
A private club with one 9-hole course
Location: Off HWY 59 on O'Farrell Road
Golf Data: Pro Shop Phone: (214) 796-4146; Club Pro: Joe Dawn; Par: 72 (two sets of tees); Yardage: 5695; Closed Monday.

Guest Policy: You must play with a member or be a member of another private country club.

CHEROKEE 6
Bullard
EMERALD BAY GOLF CLUB
A private club with one 18-hole course
Location: 6 miles W. on HWY 346
Golf Data: Pro Shop Phone: (214) 825-3444; Club Pro: Leon Smith; Par: 71; Yardage: 6683; Rating: 71.0; Closed Monday.

Guest Policy: You must play with a member.

PEACH TREE GOLF CLUB
A public club with one 9-hole course
Location: On FM 2493 between Flint and Bullard
Golf Data: Pro Shop Phone: (214) 894-7079; Club Manager: Dan Hurst; Par: 70 (two sets of tees); Yardage: 5236; Course Architects: Dr. C. R. Hurst & Buddy Bridges; Open 7 days.

Green Fees: $6.50 weekdays, $8.50 weekends and holidays; Carts: $12.50 for 18 holes.

Tee Time Procedure: 1st come, 1st served.

Jacksonville
CHEROKEE COUNTRY CLUB
A semi- private club with one 18-hole course

Location: 2 miles N. on HWY 79
Golf Data: Pro Shop Phone: (214) 586-2141; Club Pro: Wanda Hendrix; Par: 71; Yardage: 6061; Rating: 69.0; Open 7 days.
Green Fees: $10 weekdays, $15 weekends and holidays; Carts: $13 for 18 holes.
Tee Time Procedure: 1st come, 1st served.

Rusk

BIRMINGHAM GOLF CLUB
A resort club with one 9-hole course
Location: 1 mile S. of HWY 84 on HWY 69
Golf Data: Pro Shop Phone: (214) 683-2041; Club Pro: Milt Harris; Par: 72 (two sets of tees); Yardage: 6020; Open 7 days.
Green Fees: $7 weekdays, $10 weekends and holidays; Carts: $13 + tax for 18 holes; AX, Visa and MC accepted.
Tee Time Procedure: 1st come, 1st served.
NOTE: For information, phone (214) 683-2041 or write Birmingham Golf Club, P.O. Box 728, Rusk, TX 75785.

═══════ DELTA ═══════ 7

Cooper

DELTA COUNTRY CLUB
A private club with one 9-hole course
Location: E. on FM Road 1529 3½ miles to Old Country Club Road
Golf Data: Pro Shop Phone: (214) 395-4712; Club Pro: Benny Davis; Par: 70 (two sets of tees); Yardage: 6305; Rating: 67.0; Closed Monday.
Guest Policy: Non-county residents may pay green fees.
Green Fees: $6.50 weekdays, $8.50 weekends and holidays; Carts: $9.50 for 18 holes ($8 for single rider).
Tee Time Procedure: 1st come, 1st served.

═══════ FRANKLIN ═══════ 8

Scroggins

CYPRESS CREEK COUNTRY CLUB
A private club with one 9-hole course

Location: At Lake Cypress Springs
Golf Data: Pro Shop Phone: (214) 860-2155; Club Manager: Leslie M. West; Par: 36; Yardage: 3240; Closed Monday.
Guest Policy: You must be a guest of a member or a member of another private country club.

═══════ GREGG ═══════ 9

Kilgore

ROY H. LAIRD COUNTRY CLUB
A private club with one 9-hole course
Location: Off HWY 259 at 1306 Houston Street
Golf Data: Pro Shop Phone: (214) 984-3387; Club Pro: David Cline; Par: 36; Yardage: 3309; Closed Monday.
Guest Policy: You must be a guest of a member or a member of another private country club.

Longview

ALPINE GOLF CLUB
A public club with one 18-hole course
Location: On Old Jefferson Road
Golf Data: Pro Shop Phone: (214) 753-4515; Club Pro: Mike Williams; Par: 70; Yardage: 5995; Open 7 days.
Green Fees: $6 weekdays, $7.50 weekends and holidays; Carts: $12.48 for 18 holes ($8.32 for single rider).
Tee Time Procedure: Weekend: call anytime; Weekdays: 1st come, 1st served.

LONGVIEW COUNTRY CLUB
A semi-private club with one 18-hole course
Location: Harrison Road & HWY 42
Golf Data: Pro Shop Phone: (214) 759-9251; Club Pro: Buster Cupit; Par: 70; Yardage: 5895; Rating: 68.0; Course Architect: Bill Brewer; Open 7 days.
Green Fees: $6.25 weekdays, $7.80 weekends and holidays; Carts: $12 for 18 holes ($8 for single rider).
Tee Time Procedure: 1st come, 1st served.

OAK FOREST COUNTRY CLUB
A private club with one 18-hole course
Location: 601 Old Tomlinson PKWY
Golf Data: Pro Shop Phone: (214) 297-3448; Club Pro: Jim Terry; Par: 72;

Yardage: 6650; Rating: 71.5; Course Architects: Billy Martindale & Don January; Closed Monday.

Guest Policy: You must be a guest of a member or be a member of another private country club. Phone in advance.

PINE CREST COUNTRY CLUB
A private club with one 18-hole course
Location: I-20, exit Eastman Road, take HWY 149 N. 5 miles, turn right at Cotton Road
Golf Data: Pro Shop Phone: (214) 758-8000; Club Pro: Jack Goetz; Par: 70; Yardage: 6500; Rating: 70.2; Closed Monday.
Guest Policy: You must play with a member or a member of another private country club (depends upon availability of course).

——— HARRISON ——— 10
Marshall
CYPRESS VALLEY COUNTRY CLUB
A semi-private club with one 18-hole course
Location: I-20, exit 628, right on Frontage Road
Golf Data: Pro Shop Phone: (214) 938-4941; Club Pro: Clint Mace; Par: 71; Yardage: 6953; Rating: 72.8; Course Architect: Clint Mace; Open 7 days.
Green Fees: $5 weekdays, $8 weekends and holidays; Carts: $12.50 for 18 holes.
Tee Time Procedure: 1st come, 1st served.

MARSHALL LAKESIDE COUNTRY CLUB
A private club with one 9-hole course
Location: On Karmack HWY
Golf Data: Pro Shop Phone: (214) 938-6693; Club Pro: Bud Gibbs; Par: 36; Yardage: 3164; Closed Monday.
Guest Policy: You must be a guest of a member or a member of another private country club with credentials.

OAK LAWN COUNTRY CLUB
A private club with one 9-hole course
Location: HWY 80 E. to 300 Merrill
Golf Data: Pro Shop Phone: (214) 938-8522; Club Manager: Terry Morin; Par: 71 (two sets of tees); Yardage: 5947; Open 7 days (closed Monday during winter).

Guest Policy: You must be a guest of a member or a member of another private country club.

——— HENDERSON ——— 11
Athens
ATHENS COUNTRY CLUB
A private club with one 18-hole course
Location: Off Prairieville, on Park Avenue
Golf Data: Pro Shop Phone: (214) 677-3844; Club Pro: Ed Gatlin; Par: 71; Yardage: 5769; Rating: 66.8; Closed Monday.
Guest Policy: You must be a member of another private country club or a guest of a member (guest cannot live in Henderson County).

Payne Springs
THE PINNACLE CLUB
Location: Southeast side of Cedar Creek Lake near Payne Springs
NOTE: A 9-hole course designed by Don January is scheduled to open in Summer 1987 with a second 9 holes scheduled for Summer 1988.

——— HOPKINS ——— 12
Sulphur Springs
SULPHUR SPRINGS COUNTRY CLUB
A private club with one 18-hole course
Location: I-30E, exit at Best Western, follow Service Road to entrance
Golf Data: Pro Shop Phone: (214) 885-4861; Club Pro: J. C. Hunsucker; Par: 72; Yardage: 5998; Closed Monday.
Guest Policy: Pro or manager can approve guest to pay general fees. Phone for specifics.

——— HOUSTON ——— 13
Crockett
SPRING CREEK COUNTRY CLUB
A private club with one 9-hole course
Location: HWY 19N, left at FM 1260
Golf Data: Pro Shop Phone: (214) 544-7848; Club Pro: Pinky Hartline; Par: 35; Yardage: 2870; Closed Monday.
Guest Policy: You must play with a member or be a member of another private country club. Phone for specifics.

Jasper

JASPER COUNTRY CLUB
A private club with one 9-hole course
Location: 5 miles N. on HWY 96
Golf Data: Pro Shop Phone: (409) 384-8442; Club Manager: Belle Woodell; Par: 36; Yardage: 3207; Closed Monday.
Guest Policy: You must be a guest of a member or a member of a reciprocating club outside a 30-mile radius. Phone for specifics.

Sam Rayburn

RAYBURN COUNTRY
A public club with three 9-hole courses
Location: On FM 1007, 15 miles N. of Jasper
Golf Data: Pro Shop Phone: (409) 698-2444; Pro Shop Managers: Ray Minyard & James Northcutt; *Gold* 9 Par: 36; Yardage: 3371; Course Architect: Jay Riviere; *Blue* 9 Par: 36; Yardage: 3358; Course Architect: Robert Trent Jones; Gold/Blue Rating: 72.5; *Green* 9 Par: 36; Yardage: 3358; Course Architect: Bruce Devlin & Bob Von Hagge; Open 7 days.
NOTE: *Golf packages available: Phone (409) 698-2444 or write to Rayburn Country Resort & Country Club, P.O. Box 36, Sam Rayburn, TX 75951.*
Green Fees: $18 weekdays, $20 weekends and holidays; Carts: $18 for 18 holes (Winter Rates Available); AX, Visa and MC accepted.
Tee Time Procedure: Call anytime.

Paris

ELK HOLLOW GOLF CLUB
A public club with one 9-hole course
Location: From Loop 286, take Elk Hollow Drive E. 1 mile
Golf Data: Pro Shop Phone: (214) 785-6585; Club Pro: Pete Witter; Par: 36; Yardage: 3610; Rating: 70.0 (if 18 holes played); Open 7 days.
Green Fees: $5 weekdays, $6 weekends and holidays; Carts: $6 per 9 holes; MC accepted.
Tee Time Procedure: 1st come, 1st served.

PARIS GOLF & COUNTRY CLUB
A private club with one 18-hole course
Location: HWY 195 E. 3 miles
Golf Data: Pro Shop Phone: (214) 785-6512; Club Pro: Terry Ingram; Par: 70; Yardage: 6200; Rating: 68.0; Closed Monday.
Guest Policy: You must be a member of another private country club or a guest of a member. On weekends, you must play with a member.

Jefferson

RUSTY RAIL COUNTRY CLUB
A private club with one 9-hole course
Location: 7 miles N. on HWY 59
Golf Data: Pro Shop Phone: (214) 665-7245; Club Owner: John Reeves; Par: 71 (two sets of tees); Yardage: 6124; Course Architect: John Reeves; Open 7 days.
Green Fees: $6 weekdays, $10 weekends and holidays; Carts: $5 for 9 holes.
Tee Time Procedure: 1st come, 1st served.

Daingerfield

BEAVER BROOK COUNTRY CLUB
A private club with one 9-hole course
Location: 1 mile E. on HWY 11
Golf Data: Pro Shop Phone: (214) 645-2926; Club Manager: W. E. Stoddard; Par: 72 (two sets of tees); Yardage: 5653; Closed Monday.
Guest Policy: Guest must play with member.

Nacogdoches

PINEY WOODS COUNTRY CLUB
A private club with one 18-hole course
Location: Off HWY 259
Golf Data: Pro Shop Phone: (409) 569-6505; Club Pro: Richard Cook; Par: 72; Yardage: 6177; Rating: 68.3; Closed Monday.

Guest Policy: You must be a guest of a member or a member of another private country club.

WOODLAND HILLS GOLF COURSE
A semi-private club with one 18-hole course
Location: Off HWY 59 at 319 Woodland Hills Drive
Golf Data: Pro Shop Phone: (409) 564-2762; Club Pros: C. D. & Richard Thomas; Par: 72; Yardage: 6626; Course Architects: Billy Martindale & Don January; Open 7 days.
Green Fees: $6.25 weekdays, $8.50 weekends and holidays; Carts: $10.50 for 18 holes.
Tee Time Procedure: 1st come, 1st served.

NEWTON 19
None

PANOLA 20
Carthage
CARTHAGE COUNTRY CLUB
A private club with one 9-hole course
Location: 1 mile E. on HWY 79N
Golf Data: Pro Shop Phone: (214) 693-9062; Club Manager: Bob Larsen; Par: 72 (two sets of tees); Yardage: 6341; Rating: 68.0; Closed Monday.
Guest Policy: You must be a guest of a member or a member of another private country club. Phone for specifics.

POLK 21
Livingston
LIVINGSTON MUNICIPAL GOLF COURSE
A public club with one 9-hole course
Location: HWY 59 to Matthews Street
Golf Data: Pro Shop Phone: (409) 327-4901; Club Pro: Sonny Nash; Par: 70 (two sets of tees); Yardage: 6000; Rating: 68.0; Closed Monday.
Green Fees: $6 weekdays, $10 weekends and holidays; Carts: $6 per 9 holes.
Tee Time Procedure: 1st come, 1st served.

RAINS 22
None

RED RIVER 23
Clarksville
CLARKSVILLE COUNTRY CLUB
A private club with one 18-hole course
Location: 4 miles N. on HWY 37
Golf Data: Pro Shop Phone: (214) 437-3450; Club Manager: John Nichols; Par: 72; Yardage: 6087; Closed Monday.
Guest Policy: You must be a guest of a member.

RUSK 24
Henderson
HENDERSON COUNTRY CLUB
A semi-private club with one 9-hole course
Location: 1 mile E. of traffic circle on HWY 43
Golf Data: Pro Shop Phone: (214) 657-6443; Club Pro: Joey Brown; Par: 70 (two sets of tees); Yardage: 6400; Rating: 68.0; Closed Monday.
Green Fees: $6 weekdays, $12 weekends-holidays; Carts: $6 per 9 holes.
Tee Time Procedure: 1st come, 1st served.

Overton
OVERTON GOLF COURSE
A public club with one 9-hole course
Location: S. of FM 850 on Lakeshore Drive
Golf Data: Pro Shop Phone: (214) 834-6414; Club Manager: Gene Laughlin; Par: 70 (two sets of tees); Yardage: 5540; Open 7 days.
Green Fees: $5.25 weekdays, $8 weekends and holidays; Carts: $5.25 per 9 holes.
Tee Time Procedure: 1st come, 1st served.

SABINE 25
None

⟩ SAN AUGUSTINE ⟨ 26

San Augustine

FAIRWAY FARMS GOLF AND HUNT RESORT

A semi-private club with one 18-hole course

Location: 7½ miles E. on HWY 21

Golf Data: Pro Shop Phone: (409) 275-2334; Club Manager: Alan Evans; Par: 72; Yardage: 7573; Open 7 days.

NOTE: *For information on golf packages, phone (409) 275-2334 or write to Fairway Farm, Drawer T, San Augustine, TX 75972.*

Green Fees: $10.50 weekdays, $12.50 weekends and holidays; Carts: $12.50 for 18 holes.

Tee Time Procedure: 1st come, 1st served.

⟩ SAN JACINTO ⟨ 27

Cold Springs

CAPE ROYALE GOLF COURSE

A public club with one 18-hole course

Location: 5 miles S. of HWY 156 on FM 224

Golf Data: Pro Shop Phone: (409) 653-2388; Club Pro: Ron Phillips; Par: 70; Yardage: 6130; Rating: 67.9; Open 7 days.

Green Fees: $11 weekdays, $16 weekends and holidays; Carts: $14 for 18 holes.

Tee Time Procedure: 1st come, 1st served.

Huntsville

WATERWOOD NATIONAL RESORT & COUNTRY CLUB

A resort club with one 18-hole course

Location: 20 miles E. on HWY 190 at Lake Livingston

Golf Data: Pro Shop Phone: (409) 891-5211; Club Pro: Eddie Dey; Par: 71; Yardage: 6872; Rating: 75.2; Course Architect: Pete Dye; Open 7 days.

Green Fees: $20 weekdays, $25 weekends and holidays; Carts: $17 for 18 holes (NOTE: Reduced rates with golf packages available); AX, Visa and MC accepted.

Tee Time Procedure: Hotel guests can reserve time two months in advance. Non-hotel guests may reserve time one week in advance.

NOTE: *For information on resort, phone (409) 891-5211 or write Waterwood National Resort & Country Club, Waterwood Box 1, Huntsville, TX 77340.*

⟩ SHELBY ⟨ 28

Center

CENTER COUNTRY CLUB

A private club with one 9-hole course

Location: 6 miles N. on HWY 96

Golf Data: Pro Shop Phone: (409) 598-5513; Club Pro: Jo Ann Carlton; Par: 71 (two sets of tees); Yardage: 6438; Closed Monday.

Guest Policy: You must be a guest of a member or a member of another private country club. Phone for specifics.

⟩ SMITH ⟨ 29

Gladewater

GLADEWATER COUNTRY CLUB

A public club with one 9-hole course

Location: 2 miles S. on HWY 271

Golf Data: Pro Shop Phone: (214) 845-4566; Club Manager: Thomas Edmondson; Par: 36; Yardage: 2951; Open 7 days.

Green Fees: $5.22 weekdays, $7.82 weekends and holidays; Carts: $12.51 for 18 holes ($8.34 for single rider).

Lindale

GARDEN VALLEY SPORTS RESORT

A resort club with one 18-hole course

Location: I-20, exit 110 S., ½ mile, right on FM 1995

Golf Data: Pro Shop Phone: (214) 882-6107; Club Pro: Terry Brown; Par: 71; Yardage: 6589; Rating: 71.0; Open 7 days (Closed Tuesday during winter).

NOTE: *For resort information, call (214) 882-6107.*

Green Fees: $10 weekdays, $15 weekends and holidays; Carts: $12.50 for 18 holes; AX, Visa and MC accepted.

Tee Time Procedure: Weekends: Monday prior by phone or in person.

HIDE-A-WAY LAKE CLUB
A private club with one 18-hole course
Location: I-20, exit 552, go 5 miles W. on HWY 69
Golf Data: Pro Shop Phone: (214) 882-6531; Club Pro: Bob Diamond; Par: 71; Yardage: 6366; Rating: 69.7; Closed Monday.
Guest Policy: You must be a guest of a member.

Troup

HILLTOP COUNTRY CLUB
A private club with one 9-hole course
Location: E. on HWY 135
Golf Data: Pro Shop Phone: (214) 842-3516; Club Pro: Pete McCarty; Par: 69 (two sets of tees); Yardage: 5295; Closed Monday.
Guest Policy: Member must sign for guest.

Tyler

BELLWOOD GOLF CLUB
A semi-private club with one 18-hole course
Location: 1 mile W. of Loop on HWY 31, turn at sign on S. side of street
Golf Data: Pro Shop Phone: (214) 597-4871; Club Pro: Rodney Groom; Par: 70; Yardage: 6004; Rating: 68.3; Course Architect: Ty Stroud; Open 7 days.
Green Fees: $5 weekdays, $8 weekends and holidays; Carts: $5.50 for 18 holes; Visa and MC accepted.
Tee Time Procedure: 1st come, 1st served.

BRIARWOOD COUNTRY CLUB
A private club with one 18-hole course
Location: Loop 323W, right on Briarwood
Golf Data: Pro Shop Phone: (214) 593-7741; Club Pro: Alvin Odoms, Jr.; Par: 71; Yardage: 6527; Rating: 70.6; Course Architect: Lee Singletary; Closed Monday.
Guest Policy: You must be a member of another private country club with everything billed to your club.

HOLLYTREE COUNTRY CLUB
A private club with one 18-hole course
Location: HWY 69S, past HWY 323, turn right on Grande

Golf Data: Pro Shop Phone: (214) 581-7723; Club Pro: Bruce Furman; Par: 72; Yardage: 6700; Rating: 73.5; Course Architect: Bruce Devlin & Bob Von Hagge; Closed Monday.
Guest Policy: Do reciprocate with other private country clubs during week if pro phones in advance. Guest must reside outside 50-mile radius from course.

WILLOW BROOK COUNTRY CLUB
A private club with one 18-hole course
Location: From W. Loop 323, take HWY 64 or W. Irwin E.
Golf Data: Pro Shop Phone: (214) 592-8229; Club Pro: Jim Wise; Par: 71; Yardage: 6403; Rating: 71.1; Course Architect: Joe Finger; Closed Monday.
Guest Policy: You must be a guest of a member or a member of another private country club. Phone for specifics.

⎯⎯⎯⎯⎯ TITUS ⎯⎯⎯ 30

Mount Pleasant

MOUNT PLEASANT COUNTRY CLUB
A semi-private club with one 9-hole course
Location: HWY 271N, right on Greenhill
Golf Data: Pro Shop Phone: (214) 572-0751; Club Pro: Roy Stinson; Par: 36; Yardage: 3386; Rating: 71.0 (if 18 holes played); Closed Monday.
Green Fees: $10 + tax weekdays, $20 + tax weekends and holidays; Carts: $10 + tax weekdays, $15 + tax weekends and holidays.
Tee Time Procedure: 1st come, 1st served.

⎯⎯⎯⎯ TRINITY ⎯⎯⎯ 31

Trinity

WESTWOOD SHORES COUNTRY CLUB
A private club with one 18-hole course
Location: E. on FM 356
Golf Data: Pro Shop Phone: (409) 594-3502; Club Pro: Donny Baecker; Par: 72; Yardage: 6791; Rating: 71.6; Course Architects: Carlton Gibson & Bruce Belin; Closed Monday.
Guest Policy: You must be a guest of a member.

Woodville

DEER TRAIL COUNTRY CLUB
A semi-private club with one 9-hole course
Location: 2 miles W. on Livingston HWY
Golf Data: Pro Shop Phone: (409) 283-7985; Club Pros: Bob & Eric Carrington; Par: 72 (two sets of tees); Yardage: 6214; Closed Monday.
Guest Policy: Residents of Tyler County must be members. Non-county residents may pay green fees on a space available basis.
Tee Time Procedure: 1st come, 1st served.

═══════ UPSHUR ═══════ 33

Big Sandy

AMBASSADOR COLLEGE GOLF COURSE
A private club with one 9-hole course
Location: 2 miles E. on HWY 80
Golf Data: Pro Shop Phone: (214) 636-4311; Club Pro: Jim Kissee; Par: 69 (two sets of tees); Yardage: 5500; Open Sunday-Friday.
Guest Policy: Closed to public; contact PE Department.

Gilmer

GILMER COUNTRY CLUB
A private club with one 9-hole course
Location: 2 miles S. on HWY 155
Golf Data: Pro Shop Phone: (214) 734-4125; Club Pro: O. C. Duke; Par: 70 (two sets of tees); Yardage: 5967; Closed Monday.
Guest Policy: You must be a guest of a member.

PIN-OAK COUNTRY CLUB
A private club with one 18-hole course
Location: 8 miles S. on HWY 300
NOTE: 18 holes developed by Jim Lyles is scheduled to open in Spring 1987.

═══════ VAN ZANDT ═══════ 34

Canton

VAN ZANDT COUNTRY CLUB
A private club with one 18-hole course
Location: I-20, exit 19N, take Service Road ½ mile W.
Golf Data: Pro Shop Phone: (214) 567-2336; Club Pro: Coy Sevier; Par: 72; Yardage: 6760; Rating: 71.4; Open 7 days.
Guest Policy: Do accept daily green fee play on space available basis. Call in advance. Otherwise you must be a guest of a member or a member of another private country club.
Tee Time Procedure: Weekends-Holidays: Call anytime for times prior to 9:30 a.m. and after 2:30 p.m.; Weekdays: Made on space available basis.

═══════ WOOD ═══════ 35

Hawkins

HOLLY LAKE RANCH GOLF COURSE
A resort club with one 18-hole course
Location: I-20, exit HWY 14, N. 5 miles, turn right on FM 2869
Golf Data: Pro Shop Phone: (214) 769-2397; Club Pro: Jeff Davis; Par: 72; Yardage: 6705; Rating: 71.1; Closed Tuesday.
Green Fees: $14 weekdays, $20 weekends and holidays for general play; guest and property owners may pay $9 weekdays, and $12 weekends; Carts: $15.62 for 18 holes; Visa and MC accepted.
Tee Time Procedure: 2 days in advance of weekend or holiday in person or by phone.
NOTE: Resort information obtained by calling (214) 769-2138.

Mineola

MINEOLA COUNTRY CLUB
A private club with one 9-hole course
Location: HWY 80, W. to Country Club Drive
Golf Data: Pro Shop Phone: (214) 569-2472; Club Manager: Charles Brantley; Par: 71 (two sets of tees); Yardage: 6363; Rating: 71.4; Open 7 days.
Guest Policy: You must be a guest of a member or a member of an out-of-town private country club. Phone in advance.

McAlister's Two-Hole Ranch & Country Club

by Lew Johnson

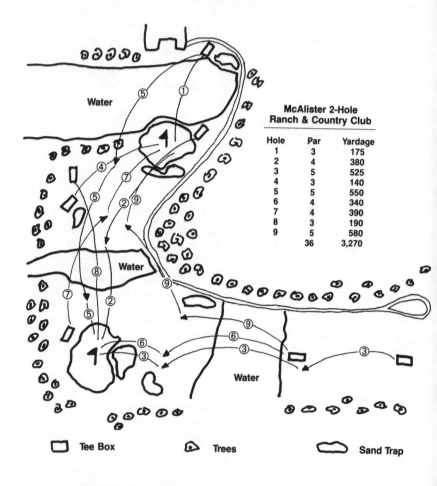

McAlister 2-Hole Ranch & Country Club		
Hole	Par	Yardage
1	3	175
2	4	380
3	5	525
4	3	140
5	5	550
6	4	340
7	4	390
8	3	190
9	5	580
	36	3,270

Tee Box   Trees   Sand Trap

Tucked away in southern Hopkins County up in northeast Texas, about seven miles from Sulphur Springs, is one of the most unusual golf courses in the great southwest.

It's unique for several reasons, not the least of which is that owner, designer, builder, and entrepreneur Mike McAlister launched the ambitious project quite by accident.

"I decided to build a golf green on the far side of the lake behind our house so I could get my friends over there to enjoy the beauty of our place from that vantage point," the 39-year-old Dallas business executive admitted sheepishly.

Two years and a lot of sore muslces, aching feet, and countless blisters later, McAlister and some of his closest golf cronies had built a nine-hole golf course.

Not just a golf course, mind you, but a first-class layout featuring three-quarters of a mile of concrete golf cart paths, a complete automatic irrigation watering system for the greens, fairways, and tee boxes, and plush 4500-square-foot greens built to United States Golf Association specifications.

Now, for the kicker.

The course has only two greens, plus an auxillary green for practice putting.

But the 2,790 yards of plush, rolling fairways are designed so ingeniously that you'd never guess you're playing into the same two greens on all nine holes—if you hadn't been tipped off before teeing off.

Eldridge Miles, former head golf professional at the prestigious Dallas Country Club and now the Director of Golf at the equally-elegant 36-hole Glen Eagles golf development in Dallas, offers unsolicited testimony to the links wrought by McAlister.

Miles, who has launched his own company in golf course design, construction, and management was shocked by the fact the course plays into only two greens.

"I didn't know I was playing the same two greens until we got about half way around the course. I was shocked. You have a completely different perception on every hole . . . they all play so differently," the noted golf pro explained.

"The true test of any course is to make a golfer use as many different clubs during the round as possible, and I guarantee you'll use just about every club in the bag playing Mike's course," Miles added emphatically.

"The layout reminds me more of North Carolina than East Texas," he added.

The course, which includes three par five holes, three par fours and a trio of par threes, is designed so imaginatively that 36 players can tour the course at the same time and maintain a smooth traffic flow.

Two beautiful lakes provide ample challenge for even the par shooters, and just as importantly, plenty of water for irrigation purposes.

Every hole plays across some water. Five sand traps, one of them about the size of West Texas, are situated strategically to short-circuit errant shots.

McAlister's Two-Hole Ranch & Country Club, as Mike affectionately tagged his little piece of Shangri-La, has been the residence of Judy and Mike, and their two children, 15-year-old Kip and 11-year-old Kate, for over three years now.

They purchased the 100-acre site over seven years ago, but maintained their home in Plano, a Dallas suburb, because of its proximity to McAlister's Lone Star Chemical Company in Dallas.

But once Judy got her spacious ranch-style home renovated, the McAlisters sold their Plano property and became full-fledged Hopkins County citizens.

"I have a great family. They enjoy living here so much that I don't mind commuting to Dallas," Mike said. "Judy and the kids helped a lot with the golf course project . . . Judy really got to be an expert at wheeling a tractor around."

The McAlister Ranch & Country Club includes four lakes spread around the wooded acres, all of them well stocked with Florida bass, catfish, and crappie, and a 'little' log cabin with three bed rooms, two baths, a huge fireplace, and central air and heat for overnight golfing guests who like to rough it.

"This isn't a bad way to spend a weekend. My toughest decision is whether to play golf with friends or go fishing—or both," Mike quips.

As much as he enjoys the layout now, McAlister says he probably wouldn't undertake the project again. "My friends thought I was crazy when I started this. I spent two years on a bulldozer, and let me stress that I got a lot of volunteer help from some very special friends.

"But there were days when we took one step forward and two steps back. We had bulldozers, a front end loader, tractor, two dump trucks, and a back hoe out here most of the time. When it got a little wet, this clay base gave us fits.

"At times, I thought we wouldn't make it, but it has been worth all the problems and disappointments," the weekend golf course builder allowed.

Among friends who helped with the project were Mike's long-time scramble tournament partner, Burl Gray, who has also moved to the Hopkins County area from Dallas; Gene Catalano, Bob Meador, Don Hudson, and one of Mike's business associates, brother Clint McAlister. "They moved a lot of dirt and came up with a lot of great ideas," he acknowledged gratefully.

Others who assisted with the project were Grady Foster of Dallas, who installed the underground sprinkling system; Jim Gossett, who is in the construction business in Sulphur Springs; Dallasites Michael Starnes, Kevin Howard, and Larry Benzine; and last (but not least) Warren Springer, the greenskeeper at Bent Tree Country Club in Dallas who has advised Mike on what fertilizers to use and when to use them, and many other technical aspects of grooming and maintaining a plush golf layout.

Benzine, of Plano, was McAlister's first greenskeeper, a position which is now held by Junior Horton, who quit a job with Rockwell Industries to oversee perhaps Texas' only family golf course. "Benzine helped us get our fairways, tee boxes, and greens moving along. Junior is doing an exceptional job as greenskeeper now," Mike said.

McAlister, a warm, outgoing person who treasures family and friends, admitted he was apprehensive about how his course would be accepted as the project neared completion.

But acclaim of his unique layout has come from PGA touring pros, weekend duffers, and celebrities in the sports and entertainment world.

Orville Moody, the 1969 United States Open champion and now a consistent money winner on the Seniors PGA Tour, holds the course record with a four-under par 36. Mike has shot the course in one-under par 35.

Longview native Jackie Cupit, former Canadian Open champion, says McAlister's two-green concoction is the most fascinating course he has ever played. Noted Dallas club professional Razz Allen says, simply, "you have to see it and play it to believe it."

Although McAlister says he's not going into the golf course construction business, he sees the day when such courses may be duplicated—and even franchised. "I think you could build a course on 12 acres if you had adequate water and suitable terrain and foliage," he speculated.

How much did his two-green layout cost? Mike was reluctant to reveal a solid figure, but he did admit that clearing the land and the actual construction work on the course would probably have run $500,000 if all the work had been contracted out.

His course isn't for sale. A Canadian industrialist with holdings in Dallas offered the McAlisters $1.7 million for their golf course and its considerable amenities.

"No, our place isn't for sale. I can't imagine having a better place to live and we've worked hard to get it. If it's ever sold, it will be Judy or the kids who sell it—not me," he vowed.

Seven years ago, the McAlisters rolled up their sleeves and etched themselves out a little spot of heaven in Hopkins County, USA.

"It can't get any better than this," Mike drawls, gazing out across his labor of love.

(Lew Johnson is sports editor of the Sulphur Springs News-Telegram.*)*

Texas Golf Trivia Answers

1. 1941, Colonial C. C. (Fort Worth), Craig Wood; 1952, Northwood C. C. (Dallas), Julius Boros; and 1969, Champions Golf Club (Houston), Orville Moody.

2. At the Texas National C. C. in Willis.

3. Babe Didricksen Zaharias.

4. At Onion Creek C. C. in Austin at the Legends of Golf tournament.

5. 5

6. 1981. Sweetwater C. C. in Sugar Land.

7. Cedar Crest C. C. (Dallas), 1927.

8. Charles Coody.

9. Betty Jameson.

10. Byron Nelson.

11. Kathy Whitworth.

12. University of Houston Golf Coach Dave Williams (16).

13. Harvey Penick.

14. Mancil Davis, "The King of Aces."

15. Jimmy Demaret.

16. The PGA was played at the same time as the British Open.

17. He was struck by lightning at the Western Open.

Texas Cities with Golf Courses